Buying a Business

Buying a Business

Business

(*For Very Little Cash*)

Joseph R. Mancuso

AND

Douglas D. Germann, Sr.

PRENTICE
HALL
PRESS

NEW YORK   LONDON   TORONTO   SYDNEY   TOKYO   SINGAPORE

This publication is designed to provide accurate and authoritative information in regard to the subject matter covered. It is sold with the understanding that the publisher and authors are not engaged in rendering legal, accounting, or other professional service. If legal advice or other expert assistance is required, the services of a competent professional person should be sought.

PRENTICE HALL PRESS
15 Columbus Circle
New York, NY 10023

PRENTICE HALL PRESS and colophons are registered trademarks
of Simon & Schuster Inc.

Library of Congress Cataloging-in-Publication Data

Mancuso, Joseph R.
Buying a business for very little cash / Joseph Mancuso and
Douglas D. Germann, Sr. — 1st ed.
p.   cm.
ISBN 0-13-109521-8 (pbk.)
1. Business enterprises—Purchasing.   I. Germann, Douglas D., Sr.
II. Title.
HD1393.25.M36   1990
658.1'6—dc20   89-23133
CIP

Designed by Irving Perkins Associates, Inc.
Manufactured in the United States of America

10   9   8   7   6   5   4   3   2   1

First Paperback Edition

To Karla and Linda

Acknowledgments

We wish to express our gratitude and sincere thanks to these people, without whose special efforts this work would not have been possible: Linda Germann, Elaine DeWitt, Jannell Gunn, Douglas Germann, Jr., Michael Germann, and Dayna Wagner. We extend our thanks to our many clients for teaching us the techniques we have shared in these pages.

Contents

Introduction

It doesn't take a million dollars in cash to buy a million-dollar business. Often, it doesn't take a million dollars cash to buy a ten-million-dollar or a one-hundred-million-dollar business. What it does take is hard work and a good plan. This book can help you with the latter, and it is up to you and your team to furnish the former.

Consider the following:

- Victor Kiam bought the Remington Company for 2 percent down.
- Margaret Haughery parlayed two cows into a good-size milk delivery business, and with the milk business she bought a troubled bakery from owners who had not been able to pay her milk bill. The bakery in turn was built up to the extent that she became known as "The Bread Woman of New Orleans." From her earnings, she donated more than $600,000 to charity—not a mean accomplishment for a widow in the 1800s!
- Allen Neuharth built up the Gannett papers (publishers of *USA Today*) by acquiring printing companies and newspapers around the country.
- Peter M. purchased a series of $1 million to $3 million manufacturing concerns in different industries in a little over three years, giving himself and his family a comfortable living for years to come. One of these acquisitions put more than $100,000 *cash* in his pocket.
- J. B. Fuqua built Fuqua Industries, a $4 billion conglomerate, from a dead start to a Fortune 500 firm, in less than four years.

Many of these acquisitions, if not all, were accomplished with little or no cash out of the buyer's pocket.

WHY DO PEOPLE SELL BUSINESSES?

Nobody keeps statistics on this matter, but our experience (and those of other experts whom we've consulted for this book) indicates these are the top reasons:

1. **Boredom.** This is a major factor in most business sales, even if it is not a stated reason: The old zing is missing; I don't seem to have that bounce in my step; maybe I'd

like something new and exciting; I don't like my customers anymore. When it comes time to publish a reason, it gets translated as "other business interests" or "retirement." We all know people in their eighties younger than those in their fifties: Age alone is simply not a good reason to sell a business.

2. **Death or ill health.** Interestingly, it's less often the death of the owner as it is the death of someone close to the owner: "What will become of my business if it happens to me?"

3. **Divorce.** Divorce is more often an excuse to get out of a business, when the real reason is boredom, again. If there were any real enthusiasm for the business, the owner would likely find a way around the perceived "financial necessity."

4. **Partnership squabbles.** When a business is starting, everybody is pulling in the same direction. But when it is making money, Bob wants to go lie on the beach, and Delores wants to plow the profits back into the business. If it's a serious enough dispute, the business suffers, and both realize the business may be better off in a new owner's hands.

5. **Help, it hurts.** In other words, I've got a problem (poor sales, incompetent administration, maybe even bankruptcy) and I don't know how to solve it, so I've lost interest (boredom, again), and don't want to try anymore.

6. **Retirement.** See Boredom.

7. **The need for liquidity.** The owner approaches the later years of his or her life and decides traveling, family, and hobbies are better ways to spend those years. But all the wealth is tied up in the business. Again, the business has become boring. Alternatively, the business has incessant cash needs from which the owner would like to be freed.

WHO WAS THIS BOOK WRITTEN FOR?

• The middle-level manager who feels the entrepreneurial urge, but wants to reduce the risk inherent in start-ups.

• The senior manager who knows how to run a company, but wants a chance to discover what he or she can do.

• The "encore entrepreneur" who has gotten out of a previous business, and is looking for new frontiers to conquer.

• The owner of a mid-market ($500,000 to $50 million) business who wants to expand by purchasing another, either a competitor or one in a completely different field.

WHY THIS BOOK IS DIFFERENT

1. **It is based on experience and is therefore practical.** It is based on Joe's experiences buying and selling a half-dozen companies himself or as a member of an acquisition team. It is based on Doug's experience as an attorney in dozens of business acquisitions, and what his clients have taught him about the process.

2. **It explains why as well as how.** Thus, you don't need to memorize a series of steps or tactics for your negotiations or clauses for your documents. There is both a science and an art to the business acquisition process. We have given you plenty of checklists and forms for the science side, and enough of the color, texture, and taste of the art side for you to be able to successfully put together your own acquisition.

3. **You will find uncommon information in these pages.** There are books written every year about buying companies. Most are written in an elementary fashion, assuming the reader has never seen the inside of a business. On the other hand, there are texts for corporate growth departments of Fortune 100 companies that assume the reader already knows who the players are, or where to go for help, and deal too much with the legal pitfalls or finer points of putting together mezzanine financing and junk bond deals. There is little written for those in between: the sophisticated business executive who needs to find and put together a deal in a reasonable period of time, without repeating kindergarten or attending a full-blown law school course.

4. **The system works.** Many books in the field are based on one deal or consist of a summary of what the author has looked up elsewhere. Instead, this book is based on real life experiences, on many deals that resulted in the successful purchase of a business (and even on some that were not successful). The system here works in the real world.

5. **You are provided with time- and effort-saving tools.** From the list of ninety-odd financing sources to the deal flow concept, from the IRS business valuation rulings to the exercises in financial statement and financing source analysis in the appendixes, from the many sources of agencies, companies, and books to the checklist of due diligence steps, you are given tools to build your own acquisition.

6. **We tell you how to profit from the information.** For instance, not only do we tell you when to use attorneys, CPAs, business brokers, and bankers but we tell you how to manage them and get the best service without letting them take over your deal.

In the late 1960s, V. and G., having just sold a profitable single restaurant operation, bought a small restaurant chain in a Midwestern city. Four months later, both restaurants were closed, and V. and G. were out of pocket cash equal to 42 percent of the purchase price!

What went wrong? The seller, it turned out, was keeping two sets of books! When a seller sets out to actively defraud a buyer, it is difficult to uncover the truth. In this case, using some of the techniques we discuss in the following pages, V. and G. would have known to visit the restaurants at various times to check volume. (Visits would have revealed that on most nights the restaurants paid out more in wages than they took in.) They would have been alerted to engage store personnel in "small talk" about the health of the business. (One of the employees knew about the second set of books.)

But most important, V. and G. would have known to watch out for their own attitudes. To get too anxious to do a deal can be your financial downfall. Nobody ever lost money on a deal they didn't do.

There is an old adage among real estate pros that says you make your money when you buy a building, not when you sell it. The same holds true of business deals. We want to show you not just how to buy but how to buy *well*.

MYTHS THIS BOOK WILL SHATTER

1. **You can buy a business with no cash out of pocket.** True, there are situations in which the buyer has come to the closing with no cash. There have been instances in which the financing was more than 100 percent of the price. We even detail a few in this book. But those deals are unusual. Often, the buyer probably had to first pay out thousands of dollars in accounting, legal, and other professional fees, even if she was reimbursed shortly after closing.

The no-cash promise is just too great. The deals with the easiest seller financing are, many times, an attempt by an owner to unload a headache. We take you the step beyond, showing you how to investigate your potential acquisition, and how to target the best ones in advance, so you avoid acquiring someone's problem child.

2. **A cookbook approach is possible for buying a business.** You can't just follow a recipe when you're buying a business. Each side has its management team. Many of the persons on the team have husbands or wives. Each team has an attorney, a CPA, and one or more bankers involved. Each actor in that troupe will constantly draw upon individual hopes, fears, dreams, bad experiences, and good experiences. How can you predict how they will interact? Add to that a constantly changing business, economic, sociological, financial, and legal fabric, and you begin to realize why it is impossible to have a prearranged script for acquiring a business. It is essential to learn the art of the process and then mold and fit and chop and chisel and hammer and knead and fit and push and shove until the entire deal fits your particular people and situation.

3. **Buying a business is like buying real estate.** Most of the time, only a few

people are involved in a real estate transaction. There is only one thing about which to negotiate. While it might be possible to buy real estate with little or no money down, the truth of the matter is very few real estate deals are done that way. Too many rules have to be bent or broken to make it happen. But in business, nobody expects the buyer to have a million dollars cash on hand in order to buy a million-dollar business. It just would not be good business to keep that much cash lying idle. So it is indeed common for businesses, particularly in the middle market, to be purchased without a great deal of cash out of the buyer's pockets at closing. That is not to say the financing comes entirely from the seller. Indeed, sellers typically get 45 percent to 55 percent of the price in cash at closing.

4. **Buying a business is the road to instant wealth and early retirement.** Frequently, it is just the opposite. Drive down Main Street in middle America at 7 A.M. and see who is shoveling the walks or washing the windows: the owner. Drive down the same street at 10 at night, and see who is burning the lights to get something done: the owner. There are certainly softer jobs where you can be paid a top-rate salary and still go home in the evenings and on weekends, "leaving the office at the office." As for instant wealth, guess who doesn't get a salary the first three years, and then doesn't take a check when cash is short for payroll?

We don't want to paint a bleak picture of business ownership today. Business ownership definitely has its rewards. There are people who do experience "instant" wealth and "early" retirement. It's just that business is like every other pursuit: It has as many ups and downs, as many good days and bad days as any other pursuit. But for avid business persons, despite all its ups, downs, highs, and lows, business is still the best possible life.

WHAT'S YOUR GOAL?

Picture yourself having *everything* you seek:

A job
A calling
Freedom
Family security
Fame
Recognition
Acceptance

Money
Creating jobs for others
Building a better community and country
Sex (well, *almost* everything)

It is possible to realize these things when you acquire an established business. This book will show you how to make these dreams come true. But remember, it still takes hard work.

WHAT DO YOU DO NEXT?

1. **Skim this book.** Get an overview.
2. **Pick what fits.** Remember, buying a business is an art. Not everything will apply to your acquisition.
3. **Do it!** Even if your goal is not to build a better community or a better world, if you build a better business you can't help but make our world a better place. So go out and do it. We're counting on you!

I

Finding the Deal

1

Where to Go to Start the Deal Flow

Where ask is have, where seek is find, where knock is open wide.
—CHRISTOPHER SMART, *SONG TO DAVID*

THERE IS A definite art to the business acquisition process. It consists of doing those extra things that keep you one step ahead of the competition, that make the difference between a deal and no deal, that turn an ordinary deal into an extraordinary deal.

The art of the business acquisition process begins with techniques to find a large number of business deals and to find them *before* they come on the market, get listed with a broker or in a newspaper, and attract potential competitors onto the scene to outbid you. These techniques collectively come under the rubric, "the deal flow."

The deal flow is a system for creating a stream of potential business acquisitions moving across your desk, to broaden your range of opportunities, to increase the number and quality of the deals, and to make optimum use of your time. A deal flow is an ongoing parade of businesses marching across your desk in a quantity that allows you to select the few that meet your criteria. Most people who attempt to buy businesses and fail do so because they only look at one business and have to say "yes" or "no": They have few other choices, no comparisons. In short, the idea is not to *find* yourself in the right place at the right time, but to *put* yourself there.

The purpose of a deal flow is to generate many high-quality leads, which accomplishes three things for the business buyer. First, more choices mean a higher probability of finding a deal that matches your criteria. Second, practice improves your analysis skills, since each deal in your deal flow teaches you new questions to ask and more information to seek on all deals you are investigating. Third, each not-quite-right deal helps you refine your criteria.

A strong positive deal flow also has the side benefit of reducing your "buyer remorse." Most people, when making major purchases (automobile, home, etc.), typically experience regret: "Maybe I shouldn't have bought that one." "I really did like the other one better after all." "I spent too much money." It happens to all of us. But if we have done a good job of studying the market and our needs, and particularly if we looked at a lot of "candidates," we are likely to have fewer pangs of buyer remorse.

There are, however, dangers of a strong positive deal flow, dangers for which you must be prepared. You can become very good at analyzing deals and finding reasons to say "no." Obviously, the more you say "no," the more deals you get to see. If you say "yes," you have to do a thorough investigation, and that takes more time and effort. The danger is that you overanalyze facts and figures, turn down too many deals, and never take the step of acquiring a business. That danger, in turn, translates into fewer and lower-quality leads: Referrers will lose interest in you; finders will feel they are wasting their time.

You can go into information overload and get bogged down in the sheer number of deals. Here we can help. We'll show you a system of ever-finer sieves you can use to quickly sort good deals from bad deals.

We have helped dozens of people buy businesses, and typically the ones who come up with the best deals and the best terms have regularly applied strong positive deal flow techniques. In short, the deal flow is a key to getting good deals on favorable terms. If you have only limited funds (have you ever met anyone with *un*limited funds?), put them into developing a strong positive deal flow, rather than into the back end of the acquisition process when the closing takes place. With the right deal, you stand a good chance of needing less cash to close.

Below we'll reveal numerous sources of a strong positive deal flow. Chapter 2 will show you how to contact your sources and make the best use of them: in short, how to get your deals flowing. However, it would be a mistake to use this list as is: No list can be comprehensive. The artistic element must be brought into play: Use your imagination to make your own list of every person who might give you a lead to *your* targeted business. Then methodically work your list in the way described in the next chapter.

YOUR OWN COMPANY

Insider buyouts are becoming commonplace. Look first at your own division, plant, or group. Look for clues to management discontent or headaches. Is it a close match with the rest of the company, or is it in an "alien" industry? Does it regularly miss profitability targets? Is it saddled with unneeded controls or costs from outside? Is it simply a small tree in a large forest, unable to get the room it needs to grow? Ask the same questions about other divisions.

How do you find out if management will consider a buyout? Remember, insider buyouts are in the normal range of business transactions currently, and you can expect to be taken seriously. You need to approach the question giving due regard to both formal and informal corporate hierarchies and procedures. Find someone in the organization whom you think might be favorably disposed to the idea of an insider buyout, who would be willing to act as your champion or sponsor at headquarters. Then approach that person in an offhand fashion, such as by a request to "run an idea past you." Present the question in a nonthreatening way, perhaps as one of a series of choices: Sell off some assets; scale down operations; sell to outsiders; sell to insiders; hire more specialized managers. Many of the best deals come from this category. Don't overlook it!

BUSINESS BROKERS

Business brokers can be a good source of leads, or a poor source. It all depends on how you use them.

There are three levels of intermediaries in business deals. "Business Opportunity Brokers" are what most people mean when they speak of business brokers. These are people who work on deals priced generally up to $1 million. They can be located via yellow pages ads under "Business Brokers" or similar entries, and through newspaper ads. "Business Intermediaries" put together deals in the range of $1 million to $20 million. Intermediaries can be found in the telephone listings under "Business Brokers" as well, but their entries are apt to be a little more understated: no red type, no bold print, and their names often sound more like law firms ("Smith and Jones") than trade names ("Businesses Unlimited"). Ask your banker, lawyer, and accountant for the best introductions. "Investment Bankers" work in the rarified atmosphere of deals above $20 million. Investment bankers are best approached through lawyers specializing in securities law, and through stock brokers. (There is no magic to these amounts—some Business Opportunity Brokers work on larger deals, and a Business Intermediary may occasionally put together a $500,000 deal.)

The first group of leads you produce through a business opportunity broker, especially those business opportunity brokers who work in the under one-million-dollar market, will be mediocre. Why?

Businesses, especially those priced below the magic million-dollar mark, usually do not reach a broker until the owner has exhausted all the "normal" (and confidential) means of selling the business on his or her own. For instance, he might call his attorney or accountant, he might mention it to his employees and suppliers, or he might even discuss the matter with friends—all before he ever thinks of calling a business broker.

You are not after the normally stale leads on the business opportunity broker's printed flyers or lists. You are after the leads she develops with you in mind, or the ones about which she calls you to say, "George, from our office, has an appointment at 2 P.M. tomorrow to list a business that fits your criteria perfectly, and I wanted you to be the first person to look at it!" Therefore, it will pay you to visit all of the good business opportunity brokers early on. They'll do more than increase your deal flow, if you take the time to give them your criteria up front and keep in frequent contact with them.

The business opportunity brokerage industry is in its infancy, and there are few industry standards. There are many excellent, top-notch, first-rate business opportunity brokers, and they operate their brokerages with the highest standards of ethics and business efficiency. But there are a number of the other kind. For instance, beware of the business opportunity broker who wants to charge you an up-front fee to review your financials or list you with his company as a buyer. Almost all business opportunity brokers work for the seller, and to charge both buyer and seller a fee or commission would be unusual, and probably unethical. Evaluate these people very carefully.

Many of the best go-betweens have gravitated toward the business intermediary level, leaving the businesses priced below a million dollars to be handled by the business opportunity brokers. But the good go-betweens are out there, and if your target market is below this range, you'll just have to search more diligently. They exist, and you can find them. The best way to find one is from a referral. Doug even ran across one who still gives away his time by counseling people with little or no capital but lots of knowledge and determination!

Check out any broker or business intermediary you want to work with before you deal with him or her. Get references from both buyers and sellers who have dealt with the broker or business intermediary. Yes, and actually call or visit these references. Call real estate brokers and ask them if they can recommend a business broker or business intermediary and then mention the name of the one you are investigating. Call bankers and do the same. Call the Better Business Bureau or the Chamber of Commerce and see if they can give you a reading. Call the court clerk's office and see if that intermediary has been involved in many lawsuits. Once you are satisfied, then begin dealing in earnest with the go-between.

How to Use a Broker

If you buy a business through a business opportunity broker, be aware that you should not normally use the broker as the negotiator for the entire deal. Business deals are not like real estate, where the discovery of the deal is 90 percent, and communication between the parties is 10 percent. In the purchase of a business, with so many different aspects requiring open discussions (employees, suppliers, promissory notes, outside lenders, stockholders, and so forth), much information has to be traded accurately, and in a spirit of candor. If you are constantly going through third parties, the transfer of information is slowed and distorted.

For the same reason, attorneys and accountants shouldn't be allowed to do the entire deal, either. The two principals have to be working together. If it is a corporate deal, the two sets of teams have to negotiate the deal. So if you have a broker involved, thank him for putting the parties together, encourage him to pick up additional information not easily found, assure him about the commission, and gently ease him out of the mainstream of the negotiating process.

Obviously, the broker needs to be kept informed of how the transaction is progressing, but he should not be allowed to run interference between the parties. There will be times that you will need him to act as arbitrator/conciliator in some ticklish spot, so don't cut the broker out entirely, but as a rule of thumb, do most of the negotiations yourself.

PRINTERS

Printers? Yes, printers. Printers are a marvelous source of information about businesses for sale. What one line of business has customers in every other line of business? What one business owner knows when your business is going strong or drastically falling off? And what one business owner gets to read the major business news before the public? The printer, of course. Printers can be a higher-quality business acquisitions lead source than lawyers and accountants. Lawyers and accountants can give you many leads, but printers, who don't get called on as frequently, will give you leads to businesses that few, if any, other people know are for sale. They are bound by fewer confidentiality restrictions, and can give you more insight into the prospects of the business. In short, you'll probably have a higher "hit ratio" with leads from printers.

If you will take the time to get to know a few printers, and ask them the right questions, you will find they can be a direct route to finding good businesses for sale.

Wouldn't a direct mail campaign to printers or advertising in the printer magazines be a fitting way to create some of your deal flow?

NEWSPAPER ADS

Just as owners of smaller businesses wait until the last minute to list with a broker, so too they will not start the process with an ad in the newspaper. Therefore, unless you are dealing with someone who has absolutely no advisors or friends (and do you want to buy such a business?), by the time an ad reaches the newspaper, it is likely that a number of people have already rejected it. That may say something, but it may also be an opportunity, since the business could be so highly specialized that only someone like you would understand it and see the real opportunities. Be your own judge.

You should respond to newspaper ads and get as much information as you can. One of the reasons you investigate the newspaper ads is to gather data on the range of deals available. You might even put a deal together through a newspaper ad, but it is not likely.

Do not expect an answer to your response. Many advertisers are just testing the salability of a business they are not yet ready to sell. Or they may want to see who is interested, and will screen carefully anyone to whom they send information. Many letters are just ignored. However, once in a while you will find a little gem in the paper, so don't ignore the ads.

WALL STREET JOURNAL

The Thursday morning edition contains the greatest concentration of businesses for sale. While newspaper ads generally are not the best source of businesses for sale, the *Journal* attracts a couple that are worth special attention: the large businesses and the seller in a hurry. The reasons that militate against your own local paper do not apply to this national newspaper. Although you might think the *Journal* is too expensive for all but the most highly priced companies, the *Journal* actually consists of less costly regional editions. For example, the smallest is Texas and it is about 10 percent of the listings the *Journal* publishes nationally. You'll have to procure more than one of the regional editions of the *Journal* to get 100 percent of the opportunities.

You might also want to look into the "Businesses for Sale" columns of *Venture* and

Inc. magazines. Since these magazines are monthlies, you are not apt to find many in a hurry to sell. You will find more franchise offerings here.

NEWSPAPER BACK ISSUES

If newspapers generally only list yesterday's businesses for sale, why would you want to look into back issues? One of the insider tricks in the business acquisition business is based on the infrequently considered fact that a major acquisition is often followed by a divestiture of unwanted divisions. Many "management LBOs" happen this way. The smaller division operating within a larger parent may not have gotten the attention it needed, or might have been stifled by corporate policy. When a new owner comes along, the small unprofitable division may be sold to raise cash for the corporate till. And it's not just unprofitable divisions that are divested. Doug once had a client who bought a business for about $1.5 million, which was paid for 100 percent out of cash flow within two years! The divesting company simply wanted to be rid of a company in a different industry that was taking an inordinate amount of management time and talent for what (to them) was a small return.

Therefore, if you read the back issues of business and local periodicals, you will find news of who bought whom several months ago. For instance, in Doug's community a few months ago, a conglomerate headquartered miles away bought a lumber and hardware retailer, also based miles off. Within months, a local management team bought the local retail department store operation, which didn't fit either parent, but had been owned by the lumber company.

There is a wonderful little directory you can find at your local library called *Who Owns Whom: The Directory of Corporate Affiliations,* published by National Register Publishing Co., Inc. Check through the list of subsidiaries to find those in your target area.

Divestiture deals can be some of the sweetest deals around. Management is often so glad to get rid of a headache that it is willing to take back some of the financing (paper) at favorable terms. The amount of financing the seller takes back might be comparatively high, since the sales price of the small division might be inconsequential compared to the seller's annual budget.

In addition, think what the divestiture can mean in the realm of local politics. There is almost hysteria about local businesses being gobbled up by distant corporate "raiders." Couple that with a potential loss of jobs to the local economy if the company consolidates the local plant, sells it off to another distant corporation, or just closes the doors in order to "cut costs." If you have seen any of these happen in your own local area, you know what we mean. Many localities are only too quick to grant loans, tax abatements, free land in the municipal industrial park, and other incentives to the business (and its new owner) to stay in town. See our comments in Chapter 10 on finding the way to finance your deal.

The management guru Peter F. Drucker, in his book *Innovation and Entrepeneur-ship* (New York, Harper and Row, 1985), gives another reason back issues of news-papers may be a fertile source of deals. He suggests that hyper-growth companies usually experience an equally hyper need for cash in their early years. Thus, headlines two or three years old often presage financial difficulties today. Look for headlines in your fields of interest.

BANKERS

Bankers generally don't enter the picture until the deal has been negotiated and somebody wants financing. However, you will find certain bankers exceptionally knowledgeable about businesses for sale. Bankers are quite often in the inner circle of advisors for small businesses and will know when a business is for sale, sometimes before the other professional advisors do.

You should work with commercial loan officers (be sure to get at least to the level of a vice-president or the head of a department), branch managers, executive vice-presidents, and presidents. In larger banks, you may not be able to get in touch with the president or an executive vice-president, but why not look around your area for all the banks that have only one or two branches?

You have to check out thoroughly whatever leads you are given. Bankers will tell you about profitable businesses for sale, and about the ones facing foreclosure, but they won't tell you which is which. You have to find that out for yourself. By the way, a business that is in trouble is not necessarily a bad deal, as we will discuss later.

ATTORNEYS

Attorneys are also in the inner circle of advisors for most businesses. You should seek out attorneys who practice heavily in the business and corporate law areas. You can pick out some of these people from their telephone book ads. Others can be found by calling divorce or real estate attorneys (or anyone who doesn't practice business law) and asking for referrals. Check with bankers and small business owners for refer-rals, too.

ACCOUNTANTS

The outside accountant is on the innermost of the inner circle of advisors for most small businesses. The accountant works on the books twelve months a year, or at least quarterly, helps with the tax return, and sees her client many times during the year to talk about business. The accountant therefore knows which businesses are for sale. The accountant is a must and should be contacted early and often. The accountants who advise small businesses can be located in much the same way as attorneys, through bankers and business attorneys. Business (especially its professional advisors) is one big fraternity.

SUPPLIERS

Let's say you are in a highly competitive business. Your customers are other businesses. The owner of one of your larger customers is getting ready to retire. He will either sell to an outsider, or just liquidate and go out of business.

What's your stake? If your customer goes out of business, you have just lost a chunk of your profits. If your customer sells out to someone who is used to dealing with your competitor, you lose again. So what will you do? You will try to stay on top of your industry and make sure you know when your customers are for sale. You may even be willing to loan some of your hard-earned money to help someone buy your customer's business, just to keep the account. Besides, you know whose sales are doing what; you know how old your customers' owners are; you know who is getting fed up with the business and who is getting ready to retire. If you keep your ear to the ground, you are an excellent source of information about businesses for sale.

SALES PEOPLE AND MANUFACTURERS' REPRESENTATIVES

When a pharmacist was looking for a drugstore to buy, the ethical drug salesman who supplied his boss's store gave him leads to about a half-dozen drugstores for sale, one of which he eventually bought.

Just as the supplier does not want to lose his customers, neither does the supplier's commissioned salesperson or manufacturer's rep. And since the salesperson or rep is in the customers' stores or plants daily, weekly, or monthly, the salesperson has a finger on the pulse of the marketplace. Therefore, a professional salesperson is probably one of the best "underground" sources of information about businesses for sale.

Often, in fact, salespeople and manufacturers' representatives know so much about how well or how poorly a business is doing, or about the health and enthusiasm of the owner, they may know *before the owner does* when a business is for sale.

INSURANCE AGENTS

Everyone groans when a new insurance agent calls. Insurance agents generally have a poor public image. But talk to many small business owners about their own insurance agents, and you will discover the insurance agent is often a trusted advisor. The insurance agent is perhaps advising about health insurance, pensions, disability insurance, fire coverages, and other year-to-year needs of the business. The life insurance agent, as opposed to the property and casualty agent, may also be advising on pensions, buy-sell agreements among co-owners, and a multitude of ways for the business owner to get money out of his corporation for personal needs. As such, insurance agents may have an inside track on when a business is for sale. Since they see so many businesses, they have exposure to a wide marketplace. They make their living by knowing their clients well. They can be an excellent source of information for you.

FIRST LIST

The First National Bank of Maryland publishes an excellent quarterly listing of about nine hundred businesses for sale. The address is:

First List
First National Bank of Maryland
25 S. Charles Street, 15th Floor
Baltimore, MD 21201
(301) 244–7943.

SBA LIQUIDATION OFFICERS

When a Small Business Administration guaranteed or direct loan "turns sour" it is turned over to the liquidation officer. It is the job of the liquidation officer to do whatever can be done to recoup the losses. Many, if not most, businesses on the bad loan list are for sale. All you need to do to identify these businesses is to contact both the liquidation officer in your local area (see the list of SBA offices in Appendix C) and

Liquidation Officer
Small Business Administration
1441 L Street NW
Washington, DC 20416
(800) 424–5201.

Visit the liquidation officer in person. Taking time to show up personally effectively demonstrates your commitment, much more so than a phone call. Send a follow-up note after the meeting. None of this paper is thrown away. Remember, bureaucrats eat, sleep, and drink paper. And you don't want to be forgotten.

Be sure to visit the SBA's Management Assistance Officers (MAOs) in your area. These are the counselors to troubled businesses. The liaison officers in the smaller SBA regional offices also perform these duties and should be visited. We told you creating a deal flow was a lot of work. In contacting any of these officials be aware that they consider their work with their clients to be confidential. Therefore, ask indirectly. For instance, ask if they have any clients who are seeking buyers, or who might be seeking buyers sometime soon. Don't ask for names; instead, ask them to give your name to companies they think might be interested in selling. Then keep checking back at the SBA.

EXECUTIVE SECRETARIES OF TRADE ASSOCIATIONS

Trade associations in just about every industry are headed by a president and vice-president elected from among the membership. Many of the trade associations also have a position called executive secretary. This person is the top paid executive in the association—the person who runs the day-to-day operations.

The executive secretary is the person the president calls on to find out "what is usually done in a situation like this" or which committee handles what. He is also called by the members directly for all types of help. The executive secretary is paid to help the members and to know what's up. Therefore, the executive secretary is a natural person for members to contact when they want to sell their business. He is also the person who sees most business-for-sale ads *before* they appear in the organization's publications.

The *Directory of Directories* and *Encyclopedia of Associations*, both published by Gale Research, Detroit, Michigan, and available at your library, contain listings of most of the major trade associations in the country. Look in your target industries, and you will probably find two or three dozen associations in or near your field, many of which have state-by-state chapters or affiliates. And each one of those has an executive director or executive secretary who will often be happy to talk with you, since you might be able to solve a problem for one of his members.

Another innovative way to use a trade association is to attend its meetings and conferences. You might even extend this technique to include associations in the industries that supply your target industry. Your goal is to meet and rub elbows with as many people as possible during the conference, passing along the word that you have a management team that specializes in turnarounds and buying businesses. You could also run an advertisement in the trade show newspapers. Few people are doing this, so it gives you an opportunity to find some of the better businesses for sale before the masses find them. It's usually the more socially outgoing people who attend conventions and continuing education seminars and they are excellent sources of acquisition information.

CUSTOMERS

Just as suppliers may know which businesses are for sale, businesses, in turn, can lead you to their own suppliers that may be on the block. Businesses have a big stake in seeing that major suppliers stay in business. Contact these sources through trade associations, as well as directly.

REAL ESTATE BROKERS

Most real estate brokers are a little overawed by the details, paperwork, and investigations intrinsic in business sales. There are a few who work in this area, but their depth of understanding varies. Real estate brokers involved in business brokerage are usually reputable, ready to admit their lack of knowledge, and willing to get necessary information. They are good at generating leads.

BUYER'S BROKER

Business brokers normally represent the seller. However, there is nothing illegal or immoral about a business broker representing the buyer. You will not want to hire a business broker on a percentage basis to help you buy a business, since his incentive would be to secure the highest price. Instead you may want to pay the business broker by the hour to bring you deals or perhaps by the number of qualified deals he presents. Incentive compensation could also be based on the improvement in sales price obtained by the broker.

Whatever the compensation arrangement, work closely with the broker, explaining in depth your criteria, and giving ample feedback on any and all deals you reject. Since brokers themselves have to develop a good deal flow to keep their business going, their flow can be a shortcut to your own deal flow.

BANKRUPTCIES

Just because a business is in bankruptcy is no reason for it to close—for instance, "Chapter 11" is used to continue the business while legally keeping creditors at bay. And just because a business is in bankruptcy is no reason to believe the business itself is bad (although it is a possibility you'll want to explore). A newsletter called *The National Bankruptcy Reporter* gives information on large bankruptcies. It is available through Andrews Publications, Box 200, Edgemont, PA 19028, but the price is stiff—about $1,000 a year. Your friendly local bankruptcy attorney or local library (or more likely the local law library) may have copies you can review.

Another source is the local bankruptcy judge. Not only will you want to let bankruptcy judges know you "have turnaround teams available" and are interested in buying businesses but you might also find it challenging to seek a position as a bankruptcy trustee for a company in order to help turn it around or liquidate it. Several famous venture capitalists started this way.

You should also plan to visit the clerk's office of the local bankruptcy court to check for Chapter 11 filings a couple of months old. These are companies in financial difficulties that have sought the court's protection from creditor lawsuits, while they try to turn things around. After several months they may have gotten worse. As an outsider you can perform miracles: You can buy assets free of creditors and usually at bargain prices. Insiders, on the other hand, need to find some way to deal with the mountain of debt they have built up before they can bring the company out of bankruptcy.

Another option you have is to wait until the company has closed its doors. You can pick up the assets for the proverbial song, but by then the customers and most valuable employees may have fled. You must weigh for yourself whether the low prices are worth what you must give up. But don't overlook the bankruptcy court as a place to cherry-pick a few good assets for the business you acquire outside bankruptcy. For these sales, watch the legal notices and classified sections of your newspaper for auction sales.

Another source of information is the credit report newsletters published in most large cities. These are put out by credit bureaus or other credit reporting agencies. Locate your local one through your Chamber of Commerce, or through your attorney. These newspapers report bankruptcies and lawsuits filed locally. Also, if you find a certain company is regularly getting sued, it may point toward an owner anxious to bail out, perhaps at a bargain price.

CORPORATE PARTNERS

Several large companies encourage entrepreneurs both inside and outside their corporate hierarchies. Prime among them recently have been 3M and General Electric. Both regularly create a slew of new inventions and businesses that for whatever reason they cannot cash in on themselves, so they sell or license them to small companies. Sometimes it is done in the form of whole operating divisions, and more often as just raw technology. Watch the business press for clues as to who is spinning off opportunities. Contact these companies and any other large companies in your fields to see if they have any interest in licensing. Some companies may have licensing departments, but it will pay to make friends with the switchboard operator and the head of Research and Development (R & D), to find out who is really the person to talk to.

YOUR OWN ADS

In the real estate field, there are promoters who suggest you put ads in the newspaper: "I buy real estate. Call Jim." If you do the same for a business your ads should be longer: Tell a little bit about yourself, and describe the type of business you are targeting. Make the ad sound professional. We haven't seen many use this technique with businesses, but there is no fundamental reason why it wouldn't work. Try it and send us a letter to let us know what happens. We might even be able to include your success story in the next edition of this book.

KNOCKING ON DOORS

It can be well worth your time to visit businesses in your targeted industry and talk to the owners. How do you go about knocking on doors? If the business is retail, first visit as if you were a customer. Browse a bit and keep your eyes open. Are the shelves well stocked, or is there a lot of dusty, shopworn or dated inventory? Is the cash register constantly ringing, or do the salesclerks sit around reading comic books? What is the attitude of the personnel? Are they anxious to help, or are they sloppy? These little things can be clues as to how well the business is doing and whether or not it might be for sale. For manufacturing concerns, you can learn a lot by sitting outside the gate at shift change, looking and listening for employee attitudes, and so forth.

Leave and come back another day. Check in the city directory to learn who the owner is, or just call the store and ask for the owner's name. City directories, the *Thomas Register of American Manufacturers* (New York: Thomas Publishing Co., annual), or calling again can get you the name of the owner of a nonretail establishment. Time your visit for less busy hours.

When you talk to the owner, be sure that you are businesslike and courteous. Demonstrate to the owner your knowledge about her industry, and explain that you are looking to acquire an operating business. Is it possible that she might know of some businesses for sale? The owner will probably not mention her own business unless she is particularly anxious to sell, but will talk about others in an effort to determine whether you really are someone who knows the business and are genuinely interested. The owner will be anxious to see if you are just a competitor seeking inside information. Once the owner is comfortable with you, there will be ample time to probe whether her own business is for sale.

We suggest a book by Joe as a useful tool during the deal flow building stage. It's just jammed full of useful information in its 540 pages. We really couldn't pull out all the good sources for you in this chapter—there are too many. Even that book doesn't have all *your* leads, because creating a deal flow takes not only information but hard old-fashioned thinking, pondering, plotting, and strategizing. But, you may want to get it for your library. It will prime your thinking pumps every time you open it. It is called *Mancuso's Small Business Resource Guide,* published by Prentice Hall Press, and it is available in most bookstores.

2

How to Get the Deals Flowing

Attempt the end, and never stand to doubt;
Nothing's so hard, but search will find it out.
—ROBERT HERRICK, *HESPERIDES, SEEK AND FIND*

Now YOU KNOW who to contact and where to go to turn on the spigot of your own deal flow. Precisely how do you start the flow? Do you call, write, visit, or something else?

TARGETING

Many people do themselves a disservice by looking at all deals that "might be interesting"; instead know what you're after. *Targeting* is probably the key word for the person or company looking to buy a business. Targeting makes your search more efficient and more likely to succeed. It is the most important thing you can do in a business acquisition (see Appendix A).

Once you have targeted one or two prime industries for your acquisition, rank the sources of deal flows in the prior chapter to noodle out just which ones have the best probability of turning up the exact business you seek, as efficiently as possible.

You might put an "A" beside each one of the sources apt to produce the exact business quickly, a "B" beside those likely to know of the precise kind of business but not react quite as soon, and a "C" beside those that would know of businesses that only approximate your requirements. If you have to choose between finding the wrong business quickly or the right business after a time, you should opt for the right business.

18

After you have your ABCs outlined, go through all of the entries in each category, and number them in order of strength. In other words, the strongest "A" will be "A1" and the weakest "A" will be "A5." Then the strongest "B" will be "B1" and the weakest "B" will be "B3," and so on. Then work your list in priority order.

Your search will be most productive once you have targeted the most likely sources for early contact. Your less valuable sources are still worth contacting, but later.

TARGETING CRITERIA

Here are some considerations to make when selecting an industry, and ultimately, a company for your acquisition (see Appendix A for a full listing of criteria for your targeting process):

For Corporate Buyers

1. Size of company.
2. Labor intensity of industry.
3. Stage of development—start-up, growth, maturity, stagnation, or revitalization.
4. High or low technology.
5. Compatible product.
6. Filling a hole in your current product mix.
7. Unionized or not.
8. Cost of living in the target's locale.
9. Dominated or fragmented industry.
10. Complementary busy season to present business.
11. High-quality versus price-sensitive marketplaces.
12. Level of return on investment.
13. Price range.
14. Use of purchase to acquire a particular large customer.
15. Fit of proposed acquisition with your goals and business plans.

For Individual Buyers

1. Your business experience.
2. Your training.
3. Your ability to concentrate on a project without getting distracted.

4. Areas of work you enjoy.
5. Your business skills.
6. Your ability to accurately pick out trends in certain industries.
7. Tasks you most dislike in your present job.
8. Your standards for product quality, service, and price.
9. Your ability to manage others.
10. Your physical and emotional energy levels for industries in which you have an interest.
11. Your hobbies, particularly those with commercial prospects.
12. The amount of time you are willing to devote to your business.
13. Your recurring daydreams and the likes, skills, and opportunities they hint at.
14. What skills you'll need to hire to complement your own.

STACKED LETTERS

Let's say you're an acknowledged expert in your field. It is well known you know what is going on in your industry. You are up on current industry trends. Out of the blue you get a letter from a stranger, asking you to help find businesses for sale in your industry. What would be your reaction?

If you're like most people, you'd have the following reactions in quick sequence:

"Who wrote this letter?"
"Do I know this person?"
"I like to be helpful to others, but why should I help this writer?"
"That's a strange letter!"
"I don't really have time to write a reply, let alone sit and think for five or ten minutes if I know of any businesses for sale."
"If this were a friend, I would probably take the time, but it isn't. I'll just go ahead and file this . . . in the round file."

"Okay, Mancuso and Germann. So letter writing's no good. Right?" Wrong. Letter writing can be very effective.

The problem is that you will get zero response to a single letter. Read up on the mail order literature today, and you will find that a response rate of 1 percent or even less is considered good. Doug recently did a mailing of 7,000 pieces with *no* response! So the answer is to mail effectively. Imagine what the response to your second and third pieces over three weeks could be:

"Here's another letter asking about businesses for sale. It's from that same person who wrote me a week ago. The letter mentions something about people approaching retirement age. Hmmmmmmm. If I remember right, old Sam over at PQR Company is probably close to retirement. Oh, well. I still don't have time to write a response. Out you go, little letter."

(One week later) "Another letter! This person sure is persistent. And I did remember about Mary at JKL, Inc. Is there a phone number on this letter somewhere? It might be worth a call to find out what this person's all about."

You will not get everybody thinking this way, at least to the extent of actually responding. But you have gotten some people thinking, if only for an instant, about your desire to acquire a business.

Instead of a single letter, have a series of mail pieces that work together well. It is relatively less expensive to print three, four, or five letters in your series simultaneously than to keep going back week after week. Then send them out, spaced about ten days to two weeks apart. Set a goal of sending out fifty to a hundred letters per week. The more you send as part of an overall strategy, the better your chances.

It also is less drain on your physical and mental energies if you write the whole "stack" of letters at one sitting. It is unlikely you will generate many great leads just from the letter campaign. An objective of your letter campaign, therefore, should be to "soften up" the resistance to your later contacts. Don't overdo the letter campaign. A set of three or four letters similar to the samples in Exhibit A should be sufficient. The important thing is to develop a system so you automatically have first letters and follow-up letters going out each week, and it's not a big hassle. The problem with doing a few at a time without a system is each mailing becomes an event, and you eventually tire.

Write each letter from the recipient's point of view and answer WIIFM—what's in it for me. Don't make the mistake of only describing what *you* want or what *your* qualifications are up front.

EXHIBIT A: STACKED LETTERS

Letter 1

Dear Mr. Owner:

Do you know any business owner who could use an infusion of cash or the help of a management team? I am looking for companies to acquire. Perhaps you, as an industry insider, might know of people who could benefit from the cash and management team I have available.

Who could benefit? Companies for sale because of

Retirement
Death
Divorce
Owner who is just plain "fed up."

Who am I? My name is John B. Uyer. My educational background is in electrical engineering, and for the last twenty-one years I have held increasingly responsible positions in the consumer electronics industry. I am currently group vice-president in charge of the consumer electronics division of a Fortune 150 company. I have cash and a team of managers available with experience commensurate with mine in the fields of production and finance.

What am I looking for?

• Consumer electronics manufacturer
• Sales range $1,250,000–$3,000,000
• 50–100 employees
• High-quality product
• Company established ten years or more
• Strong second-line management team

If you should think of such a firm, please give me a ring (collect, of course!).

Sincerely,

John B. Uyer

Letter 2

Dear Mr. Owner:

Did you get my letter last week inquiring about companies for sale in your industry?
    Have you thought of any consumer electronics manufacturers that might be for sale? If so, please call me collect.
    Enclosed is a summary of my criteria printed on the back of my business card, for your convenience.

Sincerely,

John B. Uyer

Letter 3

Dear Mr. Owner:

Remember me? I'm the guy looking for consumer electronics manufacturing concerns to buy.

Have you thought of any such companies? My cash and management team might be just what a friend of yours is looking for.

Please call me collect whenever you run across a company for sale.

Sincerely,

John B. Uyer

TELEPHONE

Remember the trite 'n true rule of thumb: "To get a 'no,' call; to get a 'yes,' go." Think back to your own experience. How many times have you bought something from the telephone salesperson who calls you at dinnertime? Or any other time, for that matter? Probably not very many times. For the same reason, you will probably not produce many top-rate leads over the phone. One or two maybe, but certainly not a large number.

Since you shouldn't expect concrete leads via the phone, you should change your goal. Instead of trying to persuade the person to give you a lead to a business deal, merely try to get him to meet with you. You will discover it is easier to "sell" a brief meeting than to persuade someone to let loose confidential information over the telephone.

EXHIBIT B: TELEPHONE SCRIPT

1. This is John B. Uyer calling. Is this George Executive?
2. Do you have two or three minutes to talk? (If no:) When may I call you back?
3. I'm calling about the letters I recently sent you about businesses for sale in your industry. Did you get my letters?
4. (If no:) Oh, I'm sorry! Perhaps I was using the wrong address. I was using 123

Main Street, Suite 456, Anytown, IL 99797. Is that the best address to use? I'll send you copies and call you back after you've received them.

5. (If yes:) The response from those letters has been low. Since you have been involved with the industry for several years, I was hoping you might be able to spend five minutes with me, to see if there is some way I could improve my approach. I'll be in your area next week. Would Tuesday at 1:40 or Wednesday at 11:25 be better for you?

VISITS

Clearly the way to generate the best-quality leads is an in-person visit. It may be easy to toss a letter into the wastebasket, or say "no" to a disembodied voice on the phone, but most people respond to in-person requests. And entrepreneurs like you have a certain unexplainable charm.

Don't begin by asking for leads. Remember the sensitive nature of such information. Instead, ask for advice in some area related to your subject, such as where the best leads might be found, or whether this region or some other region of the country would be more favorable to your chosen industry. Leads follow advice. Your purpose in visiting is to bring the person into your confidence and develop a helping attitude, as well as to generate information. After that confidence is established specific leads can be solicited.

But go easy. Give the person a way to save face, in case she can't immediately recall any businesses for sale. Remember, you have built the person up as an expert who knows what's going on. If you then put her on the spot and she can't remember anything for sale, you have just taken her down a peg or two. One of the best ways to handle this problem is to break your question down into very specific subcategories. For example:

1. Can you think of anyone who has told you he's planning to retire soon?
2. Has anyone in the industry died recently?
3. Has word of any divorces leaked out?
4. Can you think of anyone who has acted like she is just getting fed up with her business?
5. Is someone looking for a second career?
6. Who in the business seems to be in trouble financially?
7. Are there any partners who don't seem to be getting along too well these days?

Note that the questions are nonjudgmental—they don't give occasion for anyone to find fault if he does not know the information. Specific questions from different approaches will often uncover things that wouldn't be triggered by a more general question.

BUT DO I HAVE TO VISIT EVERYBODY?

Of course you can't visit all fifty state directors in each of the three associations in your targeted industries. But you can visit the ones closest to you to obtain whatever leads they have, and ask for their suggestions on how to make the best telephone approach to their cohorts. They might even be willing to contact their friends at other branches. Proceeding from a personal reference is always preferable to "cold" calling.

TIP CLUBS

If you have a "tip club," or similar informal business idea exchange group, invite one or two of your best local lead producers to join. Some Chambers of Commerce sponsor these, but it is best to find the ones put together from time to time by local business owners. Call your own life insurance person—these people often initiate tip clubs. Start such a group, if you don't already have one in your area. Tip clubs are places where a handful of people, or more, can get together over coffee and exchange business ideas and information about what is going on in business in your area, so you'll find them valuable after you have made your acquisition, too. Because of their informal fluid nature, there is no directory of such groups.

SHOULD YOU GO TO VENTURE CAPITAL CLUBS?

By all means go. Go to learn what the competition is doing. Go to learn what the venture capitalists are seeking. Go to rub elbows with the right people. Don't expect to land a deal the first time you go, or maybe ever. But the experience is helpful. Think of it as entertainment, like going to the movies.

The problem is most of the people who attend are entrepreneurs, so they only get to rub elbows with each other. But that is good. It's not unusual for a good idea in a totally unrelated field to prompt you to make an improvement in your own product or business plan or financing approach. Some groups that sponsor these clubs are the MIT Business Forum, which meets in most large U.S. cities monthly, and the American Electronic Association in Carmel, California, which has a similar program. The medical groups in Florida do the same thing. Ernst & Young, the CPA firm, has an annual state-by-state competition for the Entrepreneur of the Year. Go to these clubs, but don't go with very high expectations.

THE CARE AND FEEDING OF LEAD PRODUCERS

Make sure each of your lead producers knows your criteria. A one-page written checklist in the hands of your most important lead producers will help. Keep in contact. Take them to lunch. Call on their birthday; send flowers on special occasions. Send a newspaper clipping or magazine article they might enjoy. In a phrase, be a friend.

FOLLOW-UPS

You can keep your deal-flow pipeline full only by nurturing your contacts. Do so initially with any person who has given you a fair-to-middlin' lead, as well as anybody capable of giving you a lead in the near future.

Your follow-ups should include reporting on the status of your search, especially from the leads they generated, and any change in the acquisition criteria. Always send a thank you note for every lead, however valuable the lead might be. It's not the lead, but the referrer that is most important. As Henry Clay pointed out, "In all the affairs of life, social as well as political [and, we add, business], courtesies of a small and trivial nature are the ones which strike deepest to the grateful and appreciating heart."

Don't keep asking for new leads. Sometimes just give reports. And always express your appreciation. Contact your follow-ups by phone, by letter, and sometimes in person. You are trying to engage these lead producers in a confidential relationship leading to their voluntarily providing you with leads as they discover them.

WHAT INFORMATION SHOULD YOU SEEK?

Since you are receiving a favor from your lead producer, you don't want her to suffer through a full-fledged game of twenty questions every time she gives you a lead. Therefore, you need a reliable method to produce the most useful information, with the least time commitment by, and intrusion upon, your lead producers. If you are businesslike, she will appreciate it, and will contact you the next time she uncovers an acquisition candidate.

The following questions should help produce the desired information:

1. What do I need to know about the business?
2. How can I contact them?
3. Should I use your name? (Note that this is really two questions: Do you want to remain anonymous? Do you think it would help to mention you?)
4. Is there anything else I should know?

Note that all of the questions are open-ended, allowing your source to abbreviate or expand as her time permits. Taken together these four questions imply you trust her to keep you on the right track, another subtle compliment.

PRIMARY AND SECONDARY DEAL FLOWS

So far, we have discussed starting the secondary deal flow: the deals you generate through one or more intermediaries. Primary deal flow is what you uncover through your own efforts. Primary deal flow comes into play when you knock on doors, send letters directly to targeted businesses, make contacts at trade association meetings and seminars, and initiate similar direct buyer-seller contacts.

What is special about these direct contacts? Often, the need for confidentiality is more keenly felt. It is easier for a supplier to say "It looks like old Suzie is struggling to make ends meet," than it is for Suzie to admit to any problems or desire to get out. We're often the last to know (or at least admit) our own shortcomings. There is a fear that someone will view a "for sale" sign on a business as an admission of failure or an invitation to customers to go elsewhere.

Most important, the owner of a business, particularly if he started the business, is apt to consider the business as a child. Listen between the lines, and you'll hear it too:

"I started this business in my garage."
"I have grown this business from nothing to $3 million in sales."
"This business is my baby!"

The implication of this parental attitude is that the "parent" won't let just anyone adopt his "child." This is not just a quaint way of making a point. It is a deep-seated psychological fact of life. Buyers who have ignored it have found themselves with a failed deal.

The purchaser of a business in many ways becomes the seller in the transaction. As buyer, you must very early on sell the seller on the idea that you will be a good parent for his child. If you can't make this sale, you won't buy the business. It is not an issue of money but of emotion.

Given the hypothetical choice between a buyer with brains, energy, and all cash, and a buyer with less money but who will love the business, care for it, and cherish it, many small to medium business owners would prefer to sell to buyer number two. There is an Irish pub in Framingham, Massachusetts, that was sold in just this way. The owner had developed an emotional attachment to this pub, which was not a big cash generator. The new buyer was also Irish-American, and was a customer who really loved the place. It was the place he visited after work. Those were his friends he drank with. The business was sold with essentially no money down, even though the owner received a higher all-cash offer.

Even if you're buying in a corporate divestiture situation, be aware that it may have been the place the vice-president got his start before he was bought out by the big conglomerate, or maybe just the brainchild (see how "child" keeps popping up?) of one of the managers on the negotiating team. There are more Irish pub owners (parents of businesses) than there are Irish pubs (drinking establishments).

HOW DO YOU MAKE THE FIRST DIRECT CONTACT?

Whether it is the result of primary deal flow generation, or a lead developed through your secondary deal flow sources, you must develop a coherent, unified, systematic approach to the business owner or divestiture team.

Responding to Blind Ads

In cases where the seller does not give a name or telephone number in a newspaper or magazine ad, Doug gets a fairly good response by writing using just his name and a street return address. Letterhead might frighten the smaller company owner off, but it is necessary for most larger deals to show professionalism. Since you don't know which is which in this case, go without printed or fancy letterhead.

If you are reluctant to disclose your name to an unknown seller, you might use a friend's name and address. Don't use a post office box, because box numbers can be used as a "front" for a competitor who just wants to get the financial statements. They are perceived as the least reliable.

A short letter asking for a description of the business and copies of the financial statements (both balance sheet and income statement) for the last couple of years should get a prompt response. Sometimes you'll get the financial statements, and sometimes you won't. Be leery of ones who refuse to send financial statements—what do they have to hide? Try a second letter on a printed letterhead with a copy of your original low-impact letter and ask politely, "What happened?"

Telephone Savvy

If you're calling based on a referral, or if a telephone number is given in an ad, call rather than write: It's more personal. Below is a checklist that will get most sellers to open up during a phone conversation:

1. Introduce yourself. It is important to establish rapport with the people. Tell them why you are interested in their business. You often have to "sell" the seller on dealing with you before the seller will open up to you. You can say something like "I've worked as a manager in the wholesale automotive aftermarket for twelve years. An auto parts store like you've advertised appeals to me." In other words, go beyond the perfunctory name, rank, and serial number. Always phrase your conversation in terms of what's in it for the listener. Remember, at this stage you are "selling."

2. "Please tell me about your business." The important thing is to close your mouth and listen. Doug once responded to an ad for a "distributing business." What he thought would be a wholesale warehousing operation was really a retail office supply store. Don't let your preconceptions get in the way. If you close your mouth, the seller will often give you more information than you ever thought you'd get via an initial phone conversation. When they respond to open-ended questions, you should pay more attention to the subject they address (money, people, sales) than the specifics they relate.

3. "What differentiates your business from your competitors?" This question gives the seller a chance to put in his sales pitch. Meanwhile, you're listening between the lines to see if it meets your criteria.

4. "Is your business profitable?" Again, listen carefully between the lines. If she just says "yes," try a little silence or probe further. "In what product areas is it most profitable?"

5. "Has your business been going up or down in the last few months?" "Years?"

6. "How many employees do you have? Are you on good terms with them?" This question is key to many buyers. The number of employees will give you a feel for the size of the operation, and whether it is too large or small for you. It's a better initial measure of size than annual dollar sales.

7. "Is your business experiencing any particular problems?" Ask about any problems you know the industry, in general, is facing.

8. "Do you have a price range in mind?" The seller will often be reluctant to name an exact price. Perhaps he is afraid the price will scare people off. Or perhaps he hasn't a good idea of its value. Or more likely, he may know what he wants, but is willing to take more if you are fool enough to offer it. Most sellers don't think most buyers are on to that one. Therefore, asking about a range of prices may get you a feel for what the seller is thinking. Notice if he relates price to cash flow (six times cash flow) or to earnings (ten times earnings) or to sales (twice annual sales)—such factors are good fundamental clues of the nature of the business (see Pricing Formulae).

9. "What is your reason for wanting to sell?" This question is expected, and you ought to at least get the "advertised" reason on the record. There will be plenty of time later to explore the "real" reasons.

10. "How do I go about seeing the audited financial statements?" Try to phrase this question in these exact words, since you want to be as agreeable as possible. If the seller refuses to provide financial statements, find out why. Mark him low on your list if he tells you the financials do not tell the story, that there is more money there than meets the IRS's eyes. If he is willing to cheat the IRS, he is willing to cheat you, too.

There is a difference between an outright refusal to give financial information, and a reluctance to give it. You don't want to be too pushy this early in the analysis. If you feel this kind of reluctance, change topics and suggest a tour of the facilities. You will have an opportunity to build more confidence. Later you can renew your request for financial information. Just be careful about spinning your wheels running from place to place. Most serious buyers analyze the basic financial information before they get involved with plant or store visits.

PRICING FORMULAE

COMPANY	HOW PRICE IS TYPICALLY DETERMINED
Large companies with public shareholders	Price-earnings ratios
Private companies with a product	Multiples of cash flow
Small service companies	Multiples of sales

These are just rules of thumb. Rules of thumb are often inaccurate when applied to a specific set of facts.

TRENCH COATS

Once you've determined which places are worth visiting, stop. Ask yourself if anything would be gained by an anonymous investigation. We don't mean real cloak and dagger, breaking and entering stuff. But you may want to visit the place anonymously, or have someone else do it for you.

For instance, for a retail establishment you might park across the street and count cars in the parking lot at various times of the day; determine if the building and grounds are presentable for this type of business; see if many people walk out without buying anything. If it is a store, go in and browse, being alert for inventory too large or too small; dirty or shopworn merchandise; dirty or sloppy displays; customers complaining; employees lacking knowledge or giving misinformation; failure of clerks to try to raise the sale or be helpful; prices out of line with the competition; out-of-season or obsolete merchandise.

For a manufacturing or distribution business, the cloak and dagger stuff still has some value. You may want to visit with the independent manufacturer's agents or the various suppliers. Often it's wiser to visit before you announce your intentions as a buyer.

YOUR FIRST FACE-TO-FACE MEETING

You have two purposes in visiting: to gather information you need, and to give information about yourself. You give the seller the most important information simply in the way you present yourself. Dress in a fashion expected in the business you're investigating (jeans in an art studio; three-piece suit for the board room). Remember, body language and credibility are controlled most effectively by your attitude. Be confident, open, and businesslike. Above all, be friendly. Smile (try it now: When you are exhausted from the process of buying a business it is sometimes easy to forget to smile).

Have a résumé for prospective sellers. Make sure it's more than a listing of job titles. Even if you were an executive vice-president, informing the reader you saved your employer $500,000 in your first two months on the job is more effective. Use as much numerical and quantitative information as possible.

If you've been mentioned favorably in the press, a clipping or two will be useful, if it's related to this business. Perhaps a sort of press kit showing you in your best light would be useful.

One of the most effective ways to give information about yourself, one about which little is written, is to ask top-notch questions. Questions often give more information than they solicit! Here are the kinds you want to ask:

1. Questions that demonstrate your knowledge of the seller's business. Use the local buzz words. Computer firms love to use colloquial slang. Quote industry statistics and trends. Cite industry problems or changes and ask how the seller is dealing with them.

2. Questions that demonstrate your knowledge of business and management generally. Ask how the seller deals with employee absenteeism, or returned goods from customers. Then mention your similar experiences and (excellent, no doubt) solutions.

3. Questions that show your perceptiveness. "How do you keep a machine shop so spotless?" "It looked like your inventory of this product was a little low—are you experiencing supplier problems?"

What you're really after may not be written down on any paper the seller gives you. You're looking for good management practices, good employee and customer relations, the attitude of the owner toward his business and you, and potential liability problems. Those things you learn by keeping your eyes and ears open, and taking lots of notes. Don't trust anything to memory. Two businesses later, you won't remember one from the other.

So let the owner give you his shop tour first. Is he proud of the place? What is he particularly proud of? What areas did the owner steer you away from? Were the employees smiling? Helpful? Did the employees avoid you? Did the owner address the employees by name? In what tone of voice? Is the place neat and clean? Is the equipment up-to-date and in good repair, or has it been fixed with bandages and bailing wire? What do they do with their waste? What kind of waste do they produce? Could it be dangerous? (If you wouldn't eat off it or drink it down, it's probably "hazardous" to some bureaucrat.)

Meet some employees and ask them what they do and what they like about their work. Look at the books if you are given them, and ask questions. Don't be too rough and tumble: Remember, it's early and you're still selling yourself. If you've been given some financials before, have some prepared questions.

Always ask how the owner got started in this business—it's a great opening, and gets him talking. The only way you learn something is if your mouth is shut and the owner's is open.

Look around you: up, down, right, left, fore, and aft. Try to read body languag̶ Try to read the owner's attitude: go-getter, lax, negative, positive, friendly. Write down all your observations—maybe some private ones when you get to your car and before you drive away. Two people acting together often get more out of one visit than one person alone: Each sees the same thing in a different light.

GETTING THE FINANCIALS

By this time you should be asking for the financials if you don't already have them. If you have done a good job of creating rapport with the owner, this request is easy. Any remaining reluctance will probably be due to a fear that private information will get into the wrong hands or maybe that you'll start a competing business and use the information against the owner. To reduce this reluctance, consider a confidentiality agreement. There are many different ones in use. Here's one:

To: Dough Makers, Inc.
    ATTN: John Dough, President

Confidentiality Letter

I am requesting you to furnish me with information about the affairs and operations of your business so I can consider the possible purchase of your business.

I acknowledge that the information is in all respects confidential and that any disclosure of the same, or use of the same, except for the express purpose stated, can and will involve serious harm or damage to your business, its owners, and proprietors. Therefore, I promise I will not use or employ any confidential information for any purpose other than for consideration of a possible purchase and I promise that I will not disclose the confidential information, either in whole or in part, to parties other than my own officers, key employees, and outside professional advisors, as appropriate. I promise that I will advise those parties to whom the information is disclosed of these requirements for confidentiality and will require that each be bound by this agreement.

At the close of negotiations I will return to you (unless a transaction is consummated) all records, documents, and memoranda furnished and will not retain any copy, reproduction, or record thereof except for sales literature and publicly available industry data.

Signed: _____

Dated: _____

3

Preliminary Analysis—How to Screen the Flow

For many are called, but few are chosen.
—MATTHEW 22:14

How do you efficiently, effectively decide which of the thousands of deals now coming across your desk each month are worthy of further investigation?

THE VENTURE TIME-IST

First you must develop the information checklist to see whether this deal meets your basic needs. Just like the venture capitalist who, after five minutes perusing a business plan can decide whether to meet the principals or toss the proposal in the trash bin, you must be able to quickly size up a proposed deal. You, after all, are a venture time-ist.

The venture capitalist is someone who manages a fund of money, usually acquired from a group of investors, by placing it in appropriate business enterprises. Venture capitalists target an overall return on their money of 40 or 50 percent or more. However, in practice they are lucky to realize half that lofty objective. If they did not shoot for 45 percent, they surely would not be able to obtain a rate of return necessary to justify the risk.

A venture time-ist, on the other hand, does not have capital to invest, or if he does, he does not choose to invest the capital in new enterprises. Instead, the venture time-ist seeks to invest time, ideas, savvy, and brain work in an enterprise in order to obtain a return in the form of cash.

34

Be wary of becoming a venture out-of-time-ist. Careful thought and good ideas should stretch your time and make your search more effective, despite the numbers of deals facing you. Use your own brain power and experience to develop your own checklists. Custom design your checklists into a set of ever-finer sieves through which to run your deal flow. Initial sieves will relate to the broad questions of whether or not your needs are met. Later sieves narrow the flow by examining the specific deal in depth for potential sales levels, hidden opportunities or problems, legal and financial details, and similar due diligence factors. Your screening is a process of constantly narrowing your field, not a one-time event.

Now let's construct the first level or two of sieves. In Part Two we'll cover the more in-depth screens you'll want to build. Remember there is more art to the process than science. One person's good deal can be another person's problem.

What do you really need to know up front? First, you want to know if the business meets your own criteria. Second, you need to know whether the business can be financed, given your situation. Third, you need to know whether the business is a good deal.

DOES IT MEET YOUR CRITERIA?

Is it really in your targeted industry? Or does it take your team outside its expertise? If every manager quit when you took over, how comfortable would you be running the show? How long would it be before you were at 95 percent efficiency? Note we're looking for visceral responses, not numbers; you want to quickly screen the likely deals from the unlikely.

Include criteria about the number of employees and number of managers who will stay with the new buyer. This information can help you determine if the business is going to be manageable by your team.

Where is the business located? Is there a long-term lease? Why is the business located where it is? Most businesses are movable, many at a low cost. Don't initially get hung up on the idea that a business might not be located where you would want to live. Many are movable. Then again, a long-term favorable lease might more than outweigh the savings from moving the business closer to its suppliers or customers. What are the weaknesses in the management team? There is no such thing as a business without weaknesses. If the owner will not admit to any weaknesses, he might be unrealistic in other aspects of the negotiations, too. What you are really looking for is to see if the weaknesses in the business match the strengths on your team.

Is the profit level high enough to pay your team's salaries and give a good return on investment? Remember that your salaries are not part of your return on investment (ROI), unless you like working for nothing. Many buyers miss this point because of its simplicity. Buying a business is an expensive alternative to securing a job.

Is it a good deal even if it isn't profitable? First, many business failures are caused by "pilot error." Second, doing a turnaround in a business you know might be easier than taking over a profitable business where the owner's personality dominated the business and the customers are likely to disappear when the owner leaves. Finally, a losing business that has a patent you could use, or a distribution system in place that complements yours, or a key piece of property that fits your needs, or a product line that can fill holes in your own product line, might be worth buying because of your particular needs. In business, two plus two can equal five. Check for synergy.

CAN IT BE FINANCED?

You'll need to determine if the business can be financed readily, or whether an inordinate amount of effort and persuasion will be required. It is often easier to finance a business with a tangible product, as opposed to a service business. A product-oriented business has accounts receivable, inventory, and fixed assets, much of which can serve as collateral for a bank or other loan. A service business typically has little in the way of bankable assets. If you are buying a $10 million manufacturing facility that has $5 million worth of equipment and $5 million worth of inventory, you will find it easier to finance than if you were buying a service business for $100,000 with $6,000 worth of office equipment. For this reason, obtain a current balance sheet early. The seller will often initially send just the income statement, because he thinks you are only interested in current income. Insist on seeing the balance sheet, because you are buying a package that includes financing, and the balance sheet quickly gives you the most useful information about the business. By the time you are ready to buy, you must see all the financial statements, but as a first quick cut, get the balance sheet.

But are service businesses wholly unfinancable? If you reject out of hand all service businesses, you will have rejected 60 percent of all businesses in the United States today. That percentage will continue to grow. Aren't we all really in the service business? Take a look at IBM, one of the largest manufacturing companies in the world today. What have they traditionally advertised? Not their machines, but their people and what those people provide: service. So be careful not to sort out prematurely all service businesses, especially if your experience is in service businesses. Owners of service businesses know they aren't bankable, so they are often willing to take a few extra steps to provide the financing themselves.

There are several ways to finance a service business. For example, professional practices, such as accounting practices, are typically sold on a multiple of client billings. The price is often paid as a percentage of gross revenues actually received over two, three, or four years *after* the sale. The price might be, say, 45 percent of all receipts the first year, 35 percent the second year, 25 percent the third year, and 15 percent the fourth year. Doug, for instance, once sold a tax preparation business that he owned in just this manner.

Therefore, if you are evaluating a service business you should gauge the owner's willingness and ability to provide the financing. For instance, you might ask the seller, "How much cash do you need to have at closing?" Or you might ask what the seller plans to do with the sale proceeds. If the money needs to be used for pressing medical bills, you have a poor candidate to provide financing. You might politely inquire what levels of payment the seller would be likely to need, and for how long.

Whether the business is service- or product-oriented, you will want to determine if the income is subject to seasonal fluctuations. Since making level monthly payments is easier if you have level monthly income, the business without great monthly fluctuations will be easier to finance.

Is real estate included? Most people are pretty sophisticated when valuing real estate, so you seldom obtain a bargain price. If the seller is willing to separate the building from the business, and lease it to you with an option to buy, that can provide a big chunk of your financing. On the other hand, if there are not many tangible assets in the business, a piece of real estate might make your deal "bankable." Or you might be able to sell the building at a gain and move into less expensive quarters, using the cash from the sale to cut down your debt service burden.

Although it need not be a line on your checklist, be on the lookout for a business that is in or near bankruptcy. The business has creditors already in place. If you can increase their chances of getting more than 10 cents on the dollar, you just might be able to take over financing-in-place. Bankrupt companies can be good businesses. The bankruptcy might have been caused by "pilot error" and you might be a better "pilot." As a rule of thumb, with exceptions, many of the best leveraged buyouts (LBOs) are generated out of bankruptcy. Robert McCray, now an "angel" in New Hampshire, bought Worcester Control out of bankruptcy. He was a salesman who converted a lot of brains and a little money into a business he sold for millions of dollars years later.

IS IT A GOOD DEAL?

You want to get a workable overall view of the deal as quickly as possible, which involves not only running the numbers but doing an internal interest-level check on yourself and your team members. If after the initial review you can't get excited about the deal, you probably won't be able to later, and it's your enthusiasm and excitement for a deal that will sell your financing package, as well as make a go of the business in the long run.

You are not just looking for the seller's answers to questions, but for the reactions of the seller as well. Buyer and seller must develop a good rapport and trust. Some face-to-face contact is therefore essential and usually it saves time if undertaken early in the process.

Here are the questions that should be on your checklist:

1. **How long has the business been for sale?** The first few deals you uncover will be the ones on the market the longest. If it has been an inordinate length of time, say, more than six months to one year, there is probably something wrong with the deal. Most often it is an unrealistic attitude on the part of the seller toward price, or toward providing financing. This problem is not necessarily a go/no-go factor (very few of the questions you ask are), but it is something for you to weigh in the total balance.

2. **What is your lowest all-cash price?** The answer will give you an idea of whether the business is within your price and financing range. It will also serve to give you a psychological bargaining tool later, because the seller has already openly committed herself to a certain price range.

3. **Why are you selling the business?** Sometimes the advertised reason is the real reason, but often it is not. At the preliminary stage you are really not in a position to explore the real reasons so just listen and see if you catch anything between the lines.

4. **What were last month's sales?** Profits? What were the same figures for last quarter? For last year? From this information you can determine if the business is profitable, but you can also discover the owner's astuteness. The information can be useful in later bargaining. It also gives you a brief trend to see if the business is going uphill or downhill. A critical supplier could have gone out of business, or a large customer could have fallen on hard times or pulled a major order, or a product quality problem could have developed. Nothing ever stays level in life or in business.

5. **Are there any IRS problems?** Are there any other tax problems? This question is in all likelihood a surprise for the seller. The answer is one he didn't want to let out this early in the game. The most typical IRS problem is not having paid withholding taxes. Not having paid sales taxes runs a close second. It is so easy to keep that money in the till and operate on it that a lot of businesses get stuck. But once the tax man cometh, the situation becomes dire quickly. The seller has to do something *now,* or face an IRS agent who wants to padlock his doors. This situation puts you in a good bargaining position because you can become the potential white knight with the cash to relieve the pressure. Here you need legal advice. It is often possible to get a good deal from the seller, but an even better one directly from the IRS or state tax collector.

Payroll taxes are not relieved by Chapter 11 filings; they are then the owner's personal liability.

6. **If you're examining businesses in bankruptcy, does the business have a relatively high proportion of noncritical unsecured lenders?** A secured lender will usually get its money because of the liens it holds. A critical supplier, one who supplies a product that cannot be duplicated elsewhere without inordinate cost, is in a commanding position to stay on as a supplier if the business continues. The noncritical unsecured lender is at risk—at risk to lose the entire amount or at least 90 cents on the dollar of everything that is owed. This person is someone with whom you can negotiate. You may be able to work out a deal by which the supplier gives up his claim, and you agree to purchase all of your needs from that supplier for the next three years at 2 percent above market. Or maybe you can discount his debt by 50 percent or 75 percent. Examples would be printers, filling stations, restaurants, office supply stores, TV or radio stations, newspapers, or any other business where there is much competition for your orders.

7. **Is the business a corporation, a partnership, or a proprietorship?** If it's a corporation, is it an S corporation? The answers will help you determine the tax impact of your proposed purchase, and will help you structure it. You will also learn a little bit about the degree of sophistication of the seller.

8. **What differentiates you from your competitors?** Why is your product or service any better than theirs? This question gives the seller the chance to give you a sales pitch. But it is something you need to know for your own financing efforts, as well as to see whether the company is operated in a way that agrees with your business philosophy. For instance, if you are oriented toward high-quality products or services, and the answer comes out, "We provide the best price in town," you may not want to get involved with this particular deal.

9. **Who are your three most direct competitors?** The answer gives you people you will visit before you buy (you certainly won't be able to visit them *after* you buy). It also helps answer the following related question.

10. **What business are you in?** This question helps you determine if the business owner has thought about the business and has a plan for its future. If you get an elementary answer, you may be more able than present management to grow the business. On the other hand, if you get a sophisticated answer, and the business is losing money, chances are slight that you can do any better. If it is both a sophisticated response and a profitable business, you may have a winner.

11. **Who do you owe the most money to?** Is it personally guaranteed? The answers to these questions help you to determine the financability of the deal. If there is a large amount of money outstanding personally guaranteed, it might be difficult merely to assume that debt, because the seller often wants to be released when you

close your purchase. If the seller does agree to remain liable, you might find it easier to assume that financing, because the lender has two sources of repayment securing the debt. If the money is not personally guaranteed, it indicates a degree of confidence by the creditors in the ability of the business alone to service the debt. (For more details about getting off and staying off personal loan guarantees, see Joe's book, *How to Get a Business Loan.*)

12. **What makes this business a good opportunity for me?** Again you are giving the seller a chance to make a sales pitch. If you haven't heard any good news by this point, you might as well walk away.

13. **If I invested $100,000 in your business today, but required that it not be used to pay outstanding debts, how would you spend it?** The answer gives you an insight into the seller's dreams for the business and where it might be able to go. Good insider ideas on improving the business are invaluable. You will have plenty of your own, but the wisdom that comes from experience should always be sought.

14. **What do you plan to do with the money you receive?** How is your personal tax situation going to affect what you do with the money? The information here is personal, so it is often difficult to get in any great detail. Try a little finesse. The information is necessary to enable you to generate creative solutions to the problem of financing, and sometimes even to the question of the price. Even if you get it in bits and pieces, it's worth being persistent.

15. **What percentage of the purchase price must be cash at closing?** The answer is another clue to financing from the owner. Be careful to ask the question this way so you don't lock in the seller. If she says, "Read my lips—no financing" this early, you could have a tough time getting her to change her position later. Financing from an owner generally is easier to get the closer you get to closing. So the best bet is to be low-key and play a little dumb on this issue. Remember, you're still selling.

4

The Special Case of Franchises

Is there anyone so wise as to learn by the experience of others?

—VOLTAIRE

IF YOU HAD bought a McDonald's franchise when they were first offered, you would be a millionaire several times over today. Why? What is the magic in the franchise business?

1. With a franchise, you get national advertising.

2. You get a recognized business format and product; people new to your community already know your products, quality, signage, buildings, and maybe even prices.

3. You get know-how. Not only do you get training on the front end but as new techniques are developed or discovered by others, you benefit. You also have someone with experience to call when problems and questions arise. In short, it can be a fast track to success, since you do not have to make all the mistakes yourself. Depending on the franchise, assistance can be in some or all of these areas:

1. Feasibility studies
2. Site selection
3. Staff hiring
4. Staff training
5. Management training
6. Accounting
7. Supply sources
8. Supplier negotiations
9. Marketing

10. Management
11. Finance

Often this assistance comes from other franchisees or franchisee associations, as well as from the franchisor itself.

What are the downside risks?

1. Typically, there is a high entry cost. It is usually over and above what you would normally spend to start or acquire an independent business. You are paying hard cash for a name and a system of business.

2. There are annual dues, assessments, membership fees, national advertising contributions, and similar "extra" ongoing costs.

3. Evaluating a franchise can be a difficult and expensive task, with a lot of unknowns. If you're dealing with a new franchise, which most of the offerings are, your problem is exacerbated.

For instance, a client brought to Doug a franchise opportunity for a hair-care studio. (It was "headed up" by a man who was bald!) This company had several outlets across the country, but none within the client's home state. In addition, the franchisor refused to supply any statistical information about how well the other franchise holders were doing, which made it next to impossible to evaluate the franchise.

4. Because the franchisors normally want to control quality and format, the franchisee must give up a large measure of his business freedom.

For instance, you cannot vary the size of a hamburger or order of fries, nor can you paint your building red if all of the other outlets are yellow. You are merely following someone else's business plan. Even if you think the particular step you are being asked to take will lose you money, you normally have no choice but to follow instructions. Ordinarily, your only alternative is to resign the franchise, completely change the name of your business, redecorate, buy new signs, and so forth. This alternative is normally too costly to be practical.

5. The franchisee has less security than the independent business owner. Many franchise agreements are terminable by the franchisor after a stated period of time, with or without stating a reason. The franchisor can simply elect not to renew. The franchisor often reserves a veto power over whom you can transfer your business to, whether it be by will, gift, or sale.

This lack of security is not just contractual, but can arise from the acts of other franchisees. If harmful defects are found in products put out by outlets 500 miles away, your customers might be reluctant to deal with you.

6. You normally have a limited territory that restricts your ability to grow.

FINDING A FRANCHISE

Having a target industry in mind is the key. Newspaper and magazine ads in local and national publications are a good starting place.

However, you'll do best to concentrate your efforts at your library. Don't just look to the popular magazines and their rating services; rating services can't cover every franchise. There are many directories of franchises available, some privately published, some put together by government agencies. These directories are surprisingly detailed. They not only tell you what you can learn from ads, such as the type of business, but also the franchise fees, what services you get, and more.

INVESTIGATING A FRANCHISE

If you have decided that a franchise is something worth investigating, how do you evaluate what's available? It really is not a difficult task, but it is one that takes a lot of effort. With franchises, you usually have loads of information available to you, sometimes too much.

With the burgeoning numbers of franchises developed in the seventies and eighties, various governments and agencies saw a need for regulation. Most states today require some documents similar to a prospectus for a public stock offering, usually denominated "offering circulars," or "offering memoranda." The required information can push the documents to a hundred pages or more. By law, they are highly negative: They give you every conceivable reason why you should *not* buy.

If you happen to be in a state that does not require the registration of franchises, or if for some reason your franchise company thinks the rules do not apply to it, you should at the very least request this information:

A written description of the business and its market.

A written résumé for each of the officers and key management employees of the franchisor.

Financial statements for the franchise company and all of its affiliated companies, in audited form, for at least three years.

A copy of all documents you will be required to sign, as well as all documents to which you will be subject.

Here, then, is what you want to ask yourself and the franchise company as you investigate the franchise and review the stack of documents sitting before you:

The Business

1. What, precisely, is the business that you are being offered? Can you state in one or two sentences what makes it different from (and hopefully better than) other businesses? If not, the franchise may lack a clear sense of direction.

2. Is there already name recognition in the marketplace for the company? Or will you have to build it yourself in your own town? If so, what budget is the franchisor going to commit to your local market?

3. Is the demand for the product good both in economic ups and downs?

4. Is the product priced competitively?

5. Is the product a staple or a luxury? If it's a luxury, are people apt to stop buying if the economy turns down?

6. Is the product quality both high and consistent?

7. Did the company provide statistics as to the income of its present franchisees?

8. How long before the business breaks even? How long before it can support both itself and your family?

9. Who are the target customers? How many are needed in a single store's market area to make that store profitable?

10. What are the population trends in your area? Do you have enough of the target customers to support this business?

11. Are there any plant closings in the wind? What about new industries coming to town?

12. What insurance will the new business need? Can the franchisor (or a franchisee association) get it for you at lower group rates?

13. If there are warranties on the products, who backs the warranties? Who will pay for the repairs? You? The manufacturer? The franchisor?

14. Precisely what can the franchisor do for you that you can't do for yourself? This matter, after all, is the point of buying a franchise.

The Franchisor

1. Is the franchisor a one- or two-person operation? Is there much depth and experience in the management team of the franchisor?

2. Where does the company get its main income: from renewals, annual fees, and other recurring income, or mainly from new franchise fees? If from new franchise fees

for the most part, does this mean that the company has no solid base, and that it might not have staying power?

3. Is the company financially sound?

4. Are there so many subsidiaries and affiliated companies that you feel like you are watching a shell game, particularly when you are trying to find out where the assets and liabilities of the entire business reside?

5. Has the franchisor engaged in many reorganizations in recent years? If so, what are the reasons, both stated and probable?

6. Are there any state or government-imposed escrows of franchise fees, or administrative orders outstanding against the company? The answer may be a tip-off to problems.

7. Are there any hidden costs in your franchise? These often appear as special items in the financial statements of the company. (One trick most business advisors have learned is to look at the footnotes of financial statements. Quite often, particularly if you can read between the lines, you can discover in the footnotes much not-so-apparent information about the company.)

8. Has the franchisor investigated you to see if you are qualified to run the business? Will it? This inspection may be a good clue that you are dealing with a quality organization. A fly-by-night operator will want to get your franchise fee and keep moving. He won't care whether you have the ability to make it or not. But a quality franchisor will want to see that its good name is maintained in every marketplace. It has a large stake in your success. If it has too many closed outlets, its business will also suffer. The more thoroughly the franchisor checks you out, the better you should feel about the organization.

9. Does the company actively engage in test marketing to see how well its advertising program works and how well its products are received? Does it engage in market research to help develop new products and services?

10. What portion of the annual fees go to national and local advertising budgets? Many will commit to a stated percentage in writing up front.

11. Does the franchisee have a voice in deciding where national and local advertising funds are spent?

12. Does the franchisor have a history of responding and reacting to results in market tests and franchisee requests for changes in advertising?

13. Is the franchisor connected formally or informally with another organization offering similar or related products? What protections do you have against that organization competing with you?

14. Is the franchisor adequately capitalized so it can carry out its side of the deal? Even if it sells the number of franchises it plans on selling? Even if it sells no other franchises but yours?

The Offering Circular

1. Read this document at several sittings. If you try to comprehend everything at one time, you will miss things. You may also fall asleep reading the legal mumbo-jumbo all at once. Start with the overview section and try to get a mental picture of the entire franchise.

2. What kind and amount of litigation has the company been involved in, particularly recently? Doug once reviewed a franchise offering circular for a client listing fifty-seven different lawsuits against the company! What's interesting is to see how companies try to squirm out from under such obviously negative information; the "explanations" can be good for a laugh or two!

In Doug's case, each lawsuit had a similar explanation: This one was "frivolous"; that one was "without merit"; another was "immaterial in amount." The one that was "immaterial in amount" turned out to be an administrative order by a federal government agency requiring the franchisor to pay some $90,000!

If you run into a similar situation, run as fast as you can. Usually, if there are that many lawsuits there really is some underlying problem.

3. Has the franchisor attached three years' worth of audited financial statements? The emphasis is on *audited,* which means a CPA was employed so that creditors (you) could rely on the accuracy of the financial statements. These statements do not protect you against fraud (even CPAs cannot protect you against that), but they do indicate that the franchisor is willing to do a first-class job for you.

4. Will your note for payment of the franchise fee be discounted to a bank? Legal defenses available against third party note holders are fewer than against the original payee. Thus, you have less leverage with an outsider if (read, "when") a problem develops. Also, does the franchisor get a fee for selling your note to the bank? If so, the franchisor might be more interested in getting this fee than in helping you. When you pay the franchisor your money, it should be working for you.

5. Are all contracts that you are expected to sign attached in full? If not, what is being hidden?

The Franchise Agreement

1. What fees will you be required to pay? It might be handy for you to keep a list. Sometimes you will wonder at the inventiveness of your fellow man.

2. What assistance must the company provide to you? Must it provide education? Must it provide site selection assistance? Must it help you buy equipment?

3. What does the company do for you that you cannot do yourself? That you cannot do better yourself?

4. Do you get an exclusive territory? One franchise we examined did have an exclusive territory: one-half mile radius of the store! It was a business that the franchisor strongly recommended be in a regional shopping mall or in one of its satellite malls. A regional mall draws traffic from a 10- to 20-mile radius. It would be possible for a franchisee to open a store in one satellite mall next to a regional mall, and for another franchisee, or the company itself, to open a competing store in a different satellite to the same regional mall, since the stores would be over a half-mile apart! Is that a realistic "exclusive" territory?

As the saying goes, "Education is what you get from reading the fine print. Experience is what you get from not reading it." Read the fine print.

5. If you sell goods in addition to the franchisor's goods in your store, may you do so without them counting in the franchise fee calculations? Many franchise fees are calculated by a percentage of total sales. If this franchise is only a part of your business, do you have to pay a fee based on your other sales as well?

6. Must you be an owner-operator, or can you be an absentee owner?

7. Are you required to buy your equipment or supplies only from the company? In some states such a requirement is illegal. You really should have the ability to shop for quality and price elsewhere, assuming the resulting product or service to the customer or client is kept to company standards.

8. Are there additional costs for training? Some costs, such as meals and lodging while you're training at company headquarters, will not appear in the contract.

9. Read the contract for an overview perspective. Do you get the feeling that the contract leans one way or the other, for or against you? Is there a lot of language such as "in the absolute discretion of the franchisor"? If there is, it is entirely possible for the franchisor to become high-handed when dealing with you. It's not fun to be at the mercy of someone else.

10. If you want to sell your business, can you? Must you sell it back to the company at a preset price? Does any preset price compensate you for the goodwill you have built up?

11. Can you will your business to your children, or even your spouse?

Check with Other Franchisees

1. Call several other franchisees. Visit a few. Usually names and addresses of most of them are given in the offering circular. If not, the company should be willing to provide them.

2. Ask whether there were any hidden costs that the franchisee did not know about in advance.

3. Were there any disagreements between the franchisor and franchisee?

4. Is there an association of franchisees? Associations can be valuable, both in arbitrating any disputes between the franchisees and the franchisor, and in coming up with new ways to make your business more profitable. They might even give you the inside story before you sign with the franchisor. They might also be company-run, so be careful!

5. How long have you been involved with this franchise? Ask this question even if the company records show that the store has been open for fifteen years. You may find that somebody new just took over the franchise, which will affect how much weight you can give the answers you get.

6. Knowing what you know about the franchise and the agreement, would there be anything that you would like to see added to the franchise agreement? Any changes made?

7. Would you advise someone like me to buy this franchise? Why or why not?

8. Always ask, "Is there anything else I should know?" Most of the time you'll get a "no," because you will have thought of more questions to ask than most other prospective franchisees. But sometimes this question pays off big with something you would never have thought to ask.

9. Is this established franchisee or some other one you know about for sale? An established franchisee is less risky than one you have to start.

Consult the Experts

1. Be sure to get your attorney to review the documents for you. You are tying up your life savings and your life efforts for the next several years in one place. Make sure you head off as many problems as you can up front. Be aware that more of the preprinted forms are changeable than you might guess.

2. Another must is to have your CPA review the offering. As with the attorney, what she can tell you will pay for itself many times over.

3. Contact suppliers of local franchisees, such as the people who provide the hamburger or the nuts and bolts. Ask them what they know about the company. Ask them whether they think the company is financially stable, and how well it and the franchisees are doing.

4. Go to the library and check for directories, rating services, and similar types of references to see what you can learn about the franchise company. In this type of business opportunity just about everything is known and written down. Take the time to look.

5. Go over the opportunity with your insurance agent. As an outsider, she can come up with excellent business ideas, as well as tell you what insurance you are going to need, whether it is available, and whether the premiums will be affordable.

6. Contact your secretary of state, Better Business Bureau, and Chamber of Commerce. Find out if there are any complaints against the franchisor.

The fact that so much detailed information is so readily available to you is the only important difference between acquiring a franchise and acquiring some other existing business. In other respects, the process and the art need to be the same: You still need to read the financials with a jaundiced eye; you still need to sell yourself to the franchisor much as you would to a business-owner; you still need to use good psychology in negotiating with the "other side"; you still need to put your team together in the most effective, profitable way; and you still need to find financing.

II

Investigating Your Deal

5

Picking Apart the Financials

Round numbers are always false.
—JAMES BOSWELL, *LIFE OF JOHNSON.*

IN THE FIRST PART of this book we discussed methods to obtain information and sort out which deals are worth analyzing. In Part II we will discuss how to analyze the information and build rapport so that you (and the seller) are comfortable.

WHAT STATEMENTS YOU NEED TO SEE—AT A MINIMUM

In an ideal world, you would ask for and get financial statements for the prior ten years. That way you'd get a good idea of the trends in income and expenses and other categories over a long period of time, and what effects economic fluctuations will have on your target acquisition.

In the real world, ten years' worth may be a real burden for a small company, and no problem at all for most moderate- to large-size businesses. Ask for ten years' worth of financials and settle for five or six. Asking tells the seller you are serious about in-depth analysis, and are therefore a good risk to care for her "child" in the future. You have turned your request into a subtle sales message for you as a buyer, and as a credit risk.

Often, in figuring averages, you should drop off the high and low years, averaging only the years that are left. Thus, you need statements for at least five or six years. For instance, Doug once negotiated for another attorney's law practice. The seller said his

53

average income for the past five years was $80,000. Although he was literally correct, the actual numbers revealed there was one year in which the income was $120,000. Removing the high and low years resulted in an average of less than $60,000, a 25 percent lower income! Since the sale price of any business is to a large extent based on the income it produces (why else buy a business, unless you happen to be looking for a hobby?), a 25 percent differential in the income should translate into a sizable purchase price reduction.

Try to get enough financial statements to include at least one or two years from an economic downturn. The figures will give you an idea of the lowest sales you can reasonably expect from the business. These figures will be indispensable when you put together your loan package. Of course, you want to be realistic with yourself as well: Lower numbers can temper any overenthusiasm you may be experiencing.

When analyzing financials, another common method is to weight the results you see, on the theory that more recent results are more likely to recur. Here's how it might look (000 omitted):

YEAR	SALES PER YEAR	WEIGHTING	WEIGHTED AMOUNT
19X1	$ 1,000	1	$ 1,000
19X2	1,500	2	3,000
19X3	2,000	3	6,000
19X4	3,000	4	12,000
19X5	5,000	5	25,000
Totals	$12,500	15	$41,000

So, in the above example, the average sales over five years was $2,500,000 ($12,500,000 divided by 5), while the weighted average was $133,333 ($47,000,000 divided by 15). This example is only one somewhat elementary weighting formula. While we don't recommend any single technique as clearly better, we judge it important for you to be aware of multiple options for analysis.

One of the most active firms in the United States in the sales and buyout business is the Geneva Corporation in California. The first thing Geneva does in analyzing a firm to establish its value is to work only with the last three years of financial statements. The second step is to recast these financials to a "true form." Most entrepreneurial businesses have financial statements that need to be recast to eliminate any tax benefits to owners, and other peculiarities.

Get both the tax returns and the regular financial statements. In the smaller businesses, the owner may only have the tax returns. But with larger businesses you should also obtain the monthly and quarterly internal financial statements.

The tax return has been signed under penalties for perjury. Few people want to incur the wrath of the Internal Revenue Service, so even if they are "aggressive," they will draw the line at outright fabrications. In addition, most taxpayers list every conceivable expense, and reduce all sources of income to the extent legally permissible. Therefore, tax returns tend to show low profits (income).

The regular financial statements of the business contain more detailed breakdowns of income and expense data. These financials are designed as management tools. You can and should use them as such. Since they are used to obtain loans, they usually paint a brighter picture than the tax returns. In most cases it is a good idea to obtain the owner's personal tax return. This procedure is becoming more common. See "Personal Tax Returns" in Chapter Six.

INSIST ON COMPLETENESS

We don't mean to force the seller to have statements prepared that usually are not prepared. But if the seller has it regularly prepared and available to its managers, there's no reason you shouldn't have it, too. Doug once reviewed a set of statements presented by a seller. It contained a list of expenses that had a shadowy line about two-thirds of the way down the page, where someone had literally covered up part of the page before photocopying it for the buyer!

The solution to incomplete information is to keep asking for the statements you want, over and over again, if you think you've got a potentially good deal. If you are creative in your requests with an honest seller, you'll get them.

THE RETICENT SELLER

A few people seem to feel the financial information about the business is their private property, and neither the buyer nor anyone else is entitled to see it. Normally, you should walk away from such deals, but if the sellers are just inexperienced you may want to explain to them the facts of business life. First, if they withhold critical information, they could be sued by a buyer who was injured because information was withheld. For instance, if we understate a major business expense in our business, and you borrow money and make other plans based on the understated expenses, when you take over and discover you are coming up short, you could be indignant to the point of suing us for fraud or misrepresentation.

Second, if the seller will have to provide some of the financing, he needs to realize the relationship with you will not end on the date of closing. Withholding critical financial information can lead to a breakdown in that relationship, and make it hard for all parties to get along over a period of years.

Finally, if the seller provides financing, the first thing an injured buyer will do is withhold payment. If the seller had counted on a "retirement" check each month from the sale of his business, it only makes good sense to provide full and complete information on the front end to keep those checks coming regularly.

Joe once had a delicate impasse: a seller who fundamentally refused to give copies of his personal tax return because he said it was too personal. The impasse was overcome when it was agreed that Joe's CPA could see the tax returns but not Joe. The CPA verified the data and this compromise worked to everyone's advantage.

STATEMENT OF CASH FLOWS

Make sure you also obtain the financial statement called Statement of Cash Flows. (Older financials called it a Statement of Changes in Financial Position.) The purpose of this statement is to show what came in and out during the year, on a cash rather than an accrual basis (see "Accrual Versus Cash Basis Accounting"). It can prove extremely useful in planning your cash flows, probably the most critical step in your planning process.

Nonfinancially trained people need to be aware that it used to be possible to prepare Statements of Changes in Financial Position several different ways, and the results could be dramatically different for the same business and the same fiscal year, depending on which method was chosen. Some statements were based on net working capital (current assets minus current liabilities), and others were based on cash. The trend was to use the cash method, and the rules were recently changed to require it. The accounting rules are in flux, so be careful in comparing these cash flow statements from year to year so that you really have comparable items.

Accrual Versus Cash Basis Accounting

Most financials are prepared on the accrual basis. Thus, when a product goes out the door, it is assumed to be sold, and the income is recorded immediately, even though the customer may not yet have paid—even though the customer may never pay. Likewise, the accrual method assumes that the minute you receive inventory or a new typewriter for your business, it is at that instant an expenditure, even though it is not yet paid for.

The concept of accrual accounting is based on the logical, but theoretical, assumption that accounting statements should reflect the *activity* for the period, rather than the *cash* in and out. Therefore, accountants spend a great deal of time trying to "match" all income with its "proper" expenses. The idea is to make it possible to look at several statements side by side and see which way the business is really going, by comparing like items. Similarly, unusual items are stated apart from the normal income statement. That way, if you sell a building at a large profit, it doesn't look on the financials as if you had just doubled your product sales for the year.

However, because of this theoretical way of preparing financial statements, it is entirely possible for a business that shows a large income to be broke! It is also possible for a business that shows a loss to have a million dollars cash sitting in the bank. Many nonfinancial people in business aren't aware of this fact of business life, and continue to believe that income statements actually tell how much cash the business is making.

The Statement of Cash Flows is just a way to try to show what happened with the cash money of the business. It converts the accrual basis financials to cash.

LEVELS OF ACCOUNTANT'S REPORTS

There are three levels of accountant's reports. If you've been in "big business" all your life, you may never have seen two of the three. First among these is the Compilation Report. At this level of accounting service the accountant does little or nothing to verify the figures, so you have little outside assurance of statement accuracy. Quite simply, the accountant takes the numbers given to him by management, and puts them on a sheet of paper in the proper format. In other words, he makes sure that sales go on the top line and net income goes on the bottom line and that the math on the face of the report is accurate. Example A is a sample compilation report.

Example A: Accountant's Compilation Report

March 10, 19X1

PQR Company
123 Main Street
Profit Park, NI 99999

Gentlemen:

The accompanying balance sheet of PQR Company as of (12/31/XX) and the related statements of income, retained earnings, and cash flows for the period then ended have been compiled by us.

A compilation is limited to presenting in the form of financial statements information that is the representation of management. We have not audited or reviewed the accompanying financial statements and, accordingly, do not express an opinion or any other form of assurance on them.

Management has elected to omit substantially all of the disclosures required by generally accepted accounting principles. If the omitted disclosures were included in the financial statements, they might influence the user's conclusions about the company's financial position, results of operations, and changes in financial position. Accordingly, these financial statements are not designed for those who are not informed about such matters.

Greene, Eyeshaids & Co., CPAs

The second type of accountant's report is called the Review, which is the middle-level accountant's report. The accountant here will look at the numbers, perhaps reconcile the last bank statement, and see if the numbers make sense as presented and as compared with prior years' results. In some cases, the accountant will do even more work. The result is you have some assurance the numbers are accurate, but again the numbers are based largely on what the management has provided to the accountant, with limited outside verification. Because of cost, most medium-size businesses prefer this report. Example B is a sample review report.

Example B: Accountant's Review Report

March 10, 19X1

PQR Company
123 Main Street
Profit Park, NI 99999

Gentlemen:

We have reviewed the accompanying balance sheet of PQR Company as of 12/31/XX and the related statements of income, retained earnings, and cash flows for the year then ended, in accordance with standards established by the American Institute of Certified Public Accountants. All information included in these financial statements is the representation of the management of PQR Company.

A review consists principally of inquiries of company personnel and analytical procedures applied to financial data. It is substantially less in scope than an examination in accordance with generally accepted auditing standards, the objective of which is the expression of an opinion regarding the financial statements taken as a whole. Accordingly, we do not express such an opinion.

Based on our review, we are not aware of any material modifications that should be made to the accompanying financial statements in order for them to be in conformity with generally accepted accounting principles.

Greene, Eyeshaids & Co., CPAs

The third level of accountant's report is the full-blown Audit Report. An audit means that the CPA has verified the numbers on the report as being accurate in all material respects. It does not mean that the accountant has uncovered all fraud. (There is a move to push for more antifraud procedures by CPAs, but the fact remains that if a manager wants to hide something, even the most skilled CPA will only discover it by chance.) It does mean the accountant has verified bank balances, has sent for and received an adequate test number of confirmations for accounts receivable and perhaps accounts payable, and has done many other things necessary to give an opinion that the financial statements are reasonably accurate. Because of the level of assurance, most bankers prefer this report. This report is used by "big business." Example C is a sample audit report.

Example C: Accountant's Audit Report

March 10, 19X1

PQR Company
123 Main Street
Profit Park, NI 99999

Gentlemen:

We have audited the accompanying balance sheets of PQR Company as of December 31, 19XX, and the related statements of income, retained earnings, and cash flows for the year then ended. These financial statements are the responsibility of the company's management. Our responsibility is to express an opinion on these financial statements based on our audits.

We conducted our audits in accordance with generally accepted auditing standards. Those standards require that we plan and perform the audit to obtain reasonable assurance about whether the financial statements are free of material misstatement. An audit includes examining, on a test basis, evidence supporting the amounts and disclosures in the financial statements. An audit also includes assessing the accounting principles used and significant estimates made by management, as well as evaluating the overall financial statement presentation. We believe that our audits provide a reasonable basis for our opinion.

In our opinion, the financial statements referred to above present fairly, in all material respects, the financial position of PQR Company as of December 31, 19XX, and the results of its operations and its cash flows for the year then ended in conformity with generally accepted accounting principles.

Greene, Eyeshaids & Co., CPAs

HOW TO READ THE FINANCIALS

Don't abdicate the responsibility for statement analysis to anyone, not even your CPA! You will see things that no accountant will see, because you have been on-site, because you have experience with the industry and what numbers to look for, and because you have been talking with the owner or managers and you know things no other outsider does.

If you've never analyzed statements before, it is not difficult. It just takes doing it, and keeping your wits about you while you read. We'd like to recommend a wonderful thirty-two-page pamphlet by Merrill Lynch called "How to Read a Financial Report." It is often a giveaway in MBA classes and is both free and useful. Contact any Merrill Lynch office. Approach it not simply as an analytical project but as a stream-of-consciousness process. Look not just for financial data but also for scenarios or questions the numbers raise. Follow your hunches. Just keep asking questions. Read the financials in this order:

1. Accountant's report
2. Footnotes
3. Income statement
4. Balance sheet
5. Statement of cash flows
6. Other schedules and breakdowns, such as accounts receivable agings and schedules of debts owed to officers

In the accountant's reports you are looking for deviations from standard form (see the examples). If you find deviations, you have a clue something is unusual—not necessarily wrong, just unusual. Treat it as a signal to dig deeper.

The footnotes may at first seem boring, but they contain a wealth of information about how the financial statements were put together, and how the business is operated. Generally, you will learn about lease terms, loans to and from shareholders, insurance policies, and most of the unusual transactions. The footnotes will also tip you off to any unusual accounting practices. These are all clues you can use to adjust the information to reflect changes you will make.

Most buyers are anxious to turn first to the bottom line of the income statement. Remember that number is often an Alice in Wonderland number: It means just what the accountant said it should mean, nothing more and nothing less.

Most buyers (because most are not financially trained) are not interested in the balance sheet. You are. Hidden in the balance sheet is information the knowledgeable buyer can use to get the business at the best price, and to obtain financing for your purchase. Balance sheets are analyzed in the same way as income statements, but with an eye for relative values of assets. Remember that a balance sheet shows historical costs, not current values, so take asset values with the proverbial grain of salt.

A balance sheet is a picture of the company at a moment in time. A snapshot. The income statement is the picture over time. It's time-lapse photography.

The other financial schedules should not be skipped. They are usually included because they are significant in some way to this particular business. Often they are a management tool, or something the banker regularly insists on seeing. For example, get an aging of accounts receivable (if customer names are a problem, you can always get the aging with names removed) and ask yourself, How old are the receivables? Do they consist of many small accounts, or a few large ones? Are there two or three that make up 30 percent to 40 percent of the receivables? Is what you see healthy? If there are liabilities to officers, ask the seller, What are the terms? Are they all up-to-date, or in default? When was the last time the notes payable to officers were rewritten? Are they rewritten often? What were the changes?

You will be analyzing each number in each statement for all of these factors:

1. **Individual numbers.** Do they make sense by themselves; compared to other numbers; compared to what you have observed; based on your industry experience?

2. **Trends.** Do the numbers, compared with prior periods and compared with changes in other numbers, point to trends within this business? Are categories of income and expense being created or disappearing? Do the changes indicate operating changes in the business?

3. **Industry comparisons.** Compare the numbers against published industry data. Two good general sources are Prentice-Hall's *Almanac of Business and Industrial Financial Ratios,* and Robert Morris Associates' *Annual Statement Studies.* Remember Morris's data is slightly skewed, since it includes only bankable companies. But don't stop there. Get industry information from trade associations. You will make comparisons of the target's numbers to percentages of sales or total assets, and also standard industry ratios, such as inventory turns or quick ratios.

4. **Economic, political, and social scene.** Financial statements do not exist in a vacuum. They always have to be analyzed against the backdrop of the national and local economies and sociopolitical trends. Local and regional competitive environments need to be reviewed, as well.

5. **What you have been told about the business.** Consistency and the "smell test" are your clues.

6. **Financing.** An entire chapter (Chapter 8) discusses this subject.

7. **Your changes.** Will you need to hire more or different managers? Will you replace people with machines? Will you change employee benefits? Will you update equipment, machinery, buildings?

8. **Another day.** It is always a good practice to let the statements and your first-time-through analysis sit for a few days to "simmer" in your subconscious "cooker." Often, you'll come up with fresh insights when you get back to them.

9. **Cash flow.** Finally, convert the numbers to a cash flow basis by adding back noncash expenses like depreciation and amortization. Or simply use the Statement of Cash Flows as a starting point. Then account for changes you will institute, like additional debt service (both principal and interest), changes in labor and management costs, changes in rental costs, and the like.

The result indicates whether you will have enough cash flow to run the business. If the result is negative, you must cut expenses or increase sales. If you can't do either, forget this deal and move on—good deals are available every day. Many deals will show negative cash flows, particularly with heavy acquisition debt.

THE PREVIOUS ACCOUNTANT

One of the best ways to read a balance sheet is to approach your target's previous accountant or other financial statement preparer—not the current CPA firm but the one who had the account before the current one, or an accountant who was previously employed by the present accounting firm and worked on this particular account. He'll often tell you things that the current accountant won't tell you because there is no need to keep the account. You will need to get a release of information from the owner before you can talk to this accountant. Seek it out and get the inside scoop. This alone can pay for this book many times over.

GETTING YOUR QUESTIONS ANSWERED

How do you go about getting reliable and complete answers to your questions? This process revolves around something that is extremely important in acquisitions: your attitude. If you go to the seller with the attitude of "I've got a few questions, and I'm not sure how to interpret some of the numbers. Could you help me?" you will make more headway than if you are negative or accusatory. It is essential for you to be easy to get along with. At the same time you need to be firm and insist on answers to your questions.

It is important for you to watch how the seller answers your questions, as well as to listen to the words. If you are getting evasive answers, or if the answers are coming too quickly (like they are preplanned), or if for some unexplained reason you just don't trust the answers (probably because you are picking up body language that tells you not to trust the answers), then dig deeper and be persistent. If you still get the same kind of information, then you are better off saying good-bye to this deal. A skunk is always a skunk.

No one deal is worth making a bad deal. There are hundreds of thousands of businesses that change hands in this country each year, and most of them are good deals for both sides. There is no sense getting hooked into a bad one. Just write it off as a bad experience and go on to the next one. Even if it takes you a few more months to get a better one, it will be worth the wait.

Included in Appendix B are two examples of financial statements to help you get the feel for acquisition financial statement analysis. You will find the discussion particularly helpful if you are not financially trained, but you might pick up some ideas even if you are.

6

Investigations Checklist

Never believe on faith,
See for yourself!
What you yourself don't learn
You don't know.

—BERTOLT BRECHT, *THE MOTHER*

Y OU HAVE FOCUSED on one or two businesses that look promising. How do you perform your investigation?

There are no perfect deals out there. What you should seek is the deal in which you reduce your risks to a reasonable level, one in which you have most (but likely not all) of your requirements and desires met. To paraphrase Henry Ford, "To be successful, all I have to do is be right 51 percent of the time, and make many decisions." Carry that attitude into your search, and you may do as well as Henry Ford!

You will not want to do every one of the following things to investigate every deal, and for some deals you will want to do more. Don't follow any checklist blindly. Adjust each one to meet your particular needs.

FINANCIAL CHECKLIST

1. Make sure your attorney and accountant both check out the financials. They'll provide insights and points of view you couldn't on your own.

2. Has management or the owner prepared financial projections? If so, get as many as you can.

3. What bank or banks does the business work with? What services do they get from each bank? Contact these banks.

4. Are there any appraisals of the business or any of its assets made within the last five or ten years? If so, get copies.

5. Get an aging of accounts receivable, both current and at the end of each of the last three years.

6. Get a list of the principal suppliers of the business including how long each one has been a supplier and who the alternate suppliers are. What are the terms of sale for each? Are there any long-term purchase commitments?

7. Visit the suppliers of the business. Try to talk to the particular salespeople who call on this account. Ask them what they know about the business and whether it is worth buying. These people know how well the business is doing compared to similar businesses.

8. Check with noncompeting businesses in the area (such as the business owner next door) to see how well your target is doing.

9. Check with local business associations to find out how your target business is doing. The local Better Business Bureau might be a good stop, as well, to find out if there are many complaints against the business.

10. Check with former owners and with competitors about how well the business is doing. They might not tell you everything you need to know, but it wouldn't hurt to have a few extra clues.

11. Check with similar businesses in noncompeting geographic areas. They might be able to tell you what to look for in this particular business, and they might also be interested in selling if your deal falls through.

12. Sit down without benefit of actual financial statements in front of you and see if you can list what items you would expect to affect the sales in this type of business. Then list what should go into making up the cost of sales. List what would probably be the expenses needed to run the business and the necessary equipment. Then take your lists and look at the financials. Are there missing items? Additions? If so, you have new questions to ask.

13. If the postage meter is fat, the company is fat; if it's skinny, the company is skinny. Look particularly at the beginning of a month or the beginning of a year to see how much postage is in the machine. (It's easy to do—if you don't know how, the secretary who runs the machine can show you.) Some businesses have been known to use the postage meter to get a big tax deduction for postage at the end of the year, and then take the postage meter back to the post office for a refund early in the following year. It is also an easy place to save or even hide excess cash.

14. The backs of checks provide many little (and not so little) pieces of information about the business. You may find that certain checks to employees are always cashed at

the Country Saloon, or that business expense reimbursement checks made out to the owner are consistently cashed at a resort 500 miles away.

15. It is getting harder for purchasers to buy the tax loss carryforwards of the prior owner. But if they can be purchased, it can make a good deal even better. Don't go shopping for tax loss carryforwards, but be alert to their possible existence.

16. Look particularly for checking account deposits in round numbers. Customer payments are hardly ever in round dollars. Are they loans to the business? Are they transfers in and out? What is going on with these "odd" deposits?

17. Make sure you get the bylaws and minute books. Don't just hand them to your lawyer—you'll get more out of them than she will. If there is anything unusual or significant going on you will see it here. The bylaws are generally pretty standard, so get a set from your lawyer or the local library so you can isolate unusual provisions. Then start with the most recent minutes and work your way backward for three to five years, until you feel comfortable with what you're finding. You will see things such as authorizations of bonus or retirement plans, grants of stock options (who will you have to buy out?), awards of fringe benefits, leases of property to or from "insiders," and licensing, royalty, or franchise agreements. A quick skim is really all that is necessary.

18. Review internal and external audit reports and management recommendation letters.

19. Review tax audit reports and determine if there are any extensions of time to complete audits, or any audits still in process.

20. Review reports filed with any and all state and federal agencies.

HISTORY OF THE BUSINESS

1. When was the business founded? What was its original name, and what other names has it had?

2. What was the company's original line of business, and how did it get started with its current product line?

3. What are the names of all of its subsidiaries and divisions, when did each start business, and what is the function of each?

MARKETING AND COMPETITION

1. What is the company's main business? Be careful. This is a trick question. The business may be different from what management thinks it is. For instance, railroad companies that defined themselves as railroads in the early 1900s lost business to

trucking companies. Those that redefined themselves as transportation companies saw the possibility of additional markets, went after them, and kept their businesses alive and vital.

Ask this question not only of the management and current owners but also of yourself. If you are looking at a hardware store, is its business to supply hardware items? Or is it to provide information and supplies to people to improve their homes? The difference is more than semantics. It might be the difference between survival and failure.

2. Get copies of the sales literature and brochures of the company. What kind of an image do they portray?

3. What is the growth potential in this industry? Ask the seller's management, but also your own management team. If you don't know, then get someone on your management team to find out. Does the potential that you see match what the seller sees? What is the reason for the difference?

4. Who are the competitors? This may also be a trick question. For instance, if you are looking at a local office supply store, the competitors may not be the other office supply stores in town. The major competition might be the mail order house from the big city 300 miles away. Your seller may not have focused on this issue. If not, don't alert her.

5. How do the company's products or services differ from the competition's? What makes the products or services any better? What niche is the company aiming to serve?

6. What is the sales trend and pattern for each product or service? Is demand seasonal? Are the trend and pattern cyclical over a period of years? For instance, are the sales up for three years at a stretch and then down for one or two?

7. Is the market dominated by large companies or many small ones? If it's controlled by a large company, you might find yourself trying to fight a giant that can underprice you and sit back waiting for you to fold. On the other hand, a fragmented market might mean that there are no real leaders, and the business could be out the door the minute somebody undercuts your price by one-tenth of 1 percent.

8. How closely tied are the sales to the personality of the owner or key managers? If that person leaves, will the business leave with him or her? This situation is difficult to assess. A survey of customers or potential customers might provide clues.

A true story can help us see how serious this issue is, and how tough it is to spot. Ziggie P. owned a large auto repair shop. This shop usually had ten to fifteen mechanics and was extremely busy. It had a lot of innovative practices such as staying open evenings. Ziggie was getting the mortgages paid off and even finding time away from the business to go fishing.

But then Ziggie became extremely ill. There was a time when it wasn't known whether or not he would live. He was away from the shop for almost ten months.

Although the shop ran well when he was away, when word of his serious condition got out, business began drifting away. Ziggie's wife and management did much to keep the business going. They had sales. They ran ads in the paper. They contacted the usual referral sources. Nothing reversed the trend.

Then, just when it looked like the doors would have to close on Ziggie's shop, Ziggie started getting well. Almost as soon as Ziggie started coming back to the shop half-days twice a week, the business picked up. Ziggie's shop is now doing well, and Ziggie is back to almost full-time, but his case is instructive. In most small businesses, even when it does not appear to be the case, sales levels can be tied to the owner more than you suspect. It pays to be extremely sensitive to this fact. Because if you buy from a Ziggie, and your Ziggie flies to Florida with the cash the day after closing, your business may disappear almost as quickly as the jet stream from Ziggie's plane.

9. Check statistical information about the market from sources such as the *Wall Street Journal,* trade associations, and government reports. Contact the Small Business Administration for government reports. The public library has surprisingly detailed information, if you get some help from a reference librarian.

10. There is a magazine or newsletter for just about every occupation and business imaginable. Some get extremely specific when it comes to the group of people they serve. If you have a university library nearby, it would pay to visit the periodical section. If you can't find an actual copy of the magazine or newsletter, find out some likely candidates. Write the periodicals in question and ask for subscription information and sample copies.

11. Visit your local library and get a copy of the last two census reports. Page through and ask yourself questions about what you see in those reports and how they might affect this business. Is the population of your target county increasing or decreasing? Is the population becoming blue collar or more white collar? Is the income increasing or decreasing? Will this help or hurt your business? There are interim census reports available to update your research—don't rely on stale information.

12. Visit your local telephone company and newspaper advertising departments. Ask them for rate information for advertisers and for market data. You will find a wealth of information that these sources have spent a great deal of money and effort gathering. Some of it will be information that is not available through the local Chamber of Commerce, another good place to check.

MARKETING AND PRODUCT DEVELOPMENT

1. Does the company sell through its own salespeople or through manufacturers' representatives? If through its own salespeople, are they compensated by commission

or by salary, or both? What is the precise compensation structure? Just what does such a structure promote? Get copies of all contracts, peruse them yourself, and have your attorney review them.

2. Are the products distributed only locally, or nationwide?

3. Who are the principal customers? You might not be able to get the names until you get close to closing, but you might be able to get descriptions of the types of companies. Are the customers in an expanding or declining industry? How well do they pay? How well do the top five customers pay? Are any of the top ten customers in financial trouble? Are any old-time customers starting to pay more slowly than in the past?

4. Try to get the sales volume for the top ten customers for the last three years. Trace whether or not a particular customer is moving away from the company, or increasing its dependence. Is your target too dependent on one or two key customers?

5. Have any larger customers been lost? This question is different from the prior one, because a seller could just give you a list of only the current larger customers.

6. Do the sales usually involve maintenance agreements, or express or implied warranties? Has the company experienced any product liability claims? What are the rates of warranty and maintenance claims?

7. Have there been any new products introduced in the market that make the company's products less competitive or even obsolete? Have any new competitors entered the market?

8. Is the company involved in any research and development? Have the expenditures for R & D tended to grow or diminish over the last few years? What does the company expect to spend in the next few years? The answers can give clues to future sales potential.

9. What has been the bad debt experience of the company? Ask for a listing of sales and shipment dates by each of the major customers, along with the dates of payments of those invoices for the last year or two. This listing might point up some slow-paying customers. How does the volume of slow-paying accounts affect your cash flow projections?

10. Is the product potentially dangerous to the end user? One of the big problems these days is what happens if your product explodes or injures somebody in some way. Who is liable for it? If you buy the company, are you picking up liability for products that were improperly manufactured or designed in the past? This field is a quickly developing area of the law, and there are no black-and-white answers. The trend is to have products liability go with the holder of the assets. In other words, even if you buy assets (not stock) of the corporation, you could be held liable for improperly manufactured products, even though you were not the one who manufactured them. Two things you need to do are consult with your attorney about your exposure and what can be done to limit it, and consult with your products liability insurance carrier to see what coverages are available (if any). Make sure that you get coverage for past acts.

11. Does the company have a proprietary product, or is it a job shop? If you are manufacturing to specification, then you are essentially a service business. The personality of the owner in that situation could be a key element in the success of your target.

12. Review present and planned advertising campaigns. What are the costs and terms of the contracts, if any? What would you be bound to do? Review sales brochures for quality and effectiveness, but also for overpromising, which can lead to lawsuits. It might not be a bad idea to have legal counsel look at them, too.

13. Would you buy this product or service at this price? This question is always a good litmus test.

ASSETS

1. Get a complete depreciation schedule for all assets of the business. This schedule will tell you how old the equipment is, and will give you clues as to whether there will be any recapture taxes that may have to be paid by the seller. This information can help you to structure the tax treatment of the deal. Also ask for a list of all equipment currently on order.

2. Are there any leased facilities? If so, get a listing and copies of all of the leases. Actually read the leases. Sure, they're long and boring. But if you read them, and the seller goes from memory, you could know something the seller doesn't. This advice is particularly important for leased real estate, since the building and its lease may be essential to the continuation of the business. In many businesses, location is the main element of success.

For example, Gary H. used the lease as a backup to his negotiations to buy a small retail shop. There were no competitors in the vicinity, and no competitors could move in, because all of the other likely storefronts were occupied by thriving businesses. Gary found the landlord and negotiated a lease to begin in a few months when the business owner's lease expired. Was this ethical? You decide for yourself.

Also look for rights to sublease or assign the lease, if you expect to use the property.

3. Check the physical condition of the land and buildings even if they are only leased. Many leases require the tenant to make all repairs to the building. Even if the lease does not, you need to know whether the landlord is cooperative in this regard. An uncooperative landlord can mean having to pay for repairs yourself and hoping to get the expenses back later. Therefore, it makes sense to check the roof, parking, ceiling (you are looking for signs of leaks), heating, plumbing, equipment, and similar items to see what shape they are in. You don't need to be an expert; just keep your eyes open and ask questions.

4. Check out the premises and the inventory. Is the inventory covered with dust? Is it shop-worn? As the eminent philosopher Yogi Berra said, "There are a lot of things you can observe just by looking."

5. If you are buying real estate, get title insurance commitments and have your attorney review them.

6. Are there any patents, trademarks, or service marks on which the company relies? If so, have them checked out by patent counsel.

7. Are there trade secret or other nondisclosure agreements? Review them yourself and have your attorney do so as well.

8. Leasehold improvements are often written off when they are purchased or over a short period of time. Sometimes they are not recorded anywhere. There may be some real value hidden in leased premises. If so, and if the asset is removable when your lease terminates, you might have another asset available for financing.

RELATIONSHIPS WITH OUTSIDERS

1. Are there any licenses required to make the product, occupy the premises, or otherwise open the doors for business? Are all licenses valid, up-to-date, and without outstanding violations?

2. What is the company's safety record? Does it have any Occupational Safety and Health Administration (OSHA) or environmental problems? Most businesses are subject to environmental controls if the business produces anything, has by-products, or dumps anything into the water or the air. It pays to take a tour of the facility, including the back end of the lot, to see if any on-site dumping is going on, and that all environmental regulations are being met. If there are any underground storage tanks, there is a potential huge liability. The same is true if there were ever any underground storage tanks on the premises. According to the environmental laws, if you own the real estate where toxic waste has been dumped, even if you are not the one who dumped it, and even if the waste was dumped thirty years before you bought the place, you can be responsible for the entire costs of cleanup. There is no limit on your liability in environmental cases, so you need to be very sensitive to this problem.

In fact, if your target has dumped toxic wastes at an approved toxic waste disposal site, and the company running the disposal site is not handling the waste properly, you can be responsible for the full costs of cleanup, not just your share. You can be held responsible even if you did not buy the stock of the business. Bankers and other lenders are increasingly aware of these issues, and are taking a very close look at them. Be sure to review OSHA and Environmental Protection Agency (EPA) inspection reports and company filings.

3. Are the raw materials readily available? Are prices for supplies stable or volatile?

4. How stable are the relationships between the company and its suppliers? How long has your target been dealing with each of its major suppliers? If for too short a time, you could face defections as a new owner; if for too long a time, the prices being paid could have grown to be noncompetitive.

5. Have your legal counsel check for lawsuits, administrative or disciplinary actions, and review in-house litigation logs.

6. Check for contracts with outsiders such as the government, suppliers, customers, insurance companies, and independent contractors. Get copies of these agreements, peruse them yourself, and have your legal people check them out. All insurance policies should be reviewed by your own insurance advisors.

LOCALITY

1. Visit your local traffic department and see what traffic counts there are for the area of your business. These counts are particularly important for a consumer business.

2. Visit the planning department of your municipality and county and determine what changes are in the works. If that new highway is to be rerouted away from your location, will the change be good or bad?

3. Check for restrictions, liens, zoning, and licenses that might be necessary. Most of these things can be checked out with local municipal offices, starting with the clerk's office. When it comes to licenses, it makes sense to call the municipal attorney's office and find out what licenses are needed for your type of business. Speak to a deputy attorney, not the receptionist. It could be that your target has been operating without proper licenses, and when it changes hands, the city will want to make sure you have them.

EMPLOYEES

1. For each officer, director, key employee, and key independent contractor, find out:

Length of service
Business background (get a copy of his or her resumé if possible)
Compensation and fringe benefits
Age

2. Does management devote all its time to this business, or only 80 percent or 50 percent?

3. Do the key people plan to stay with the business? What can we do to help them want to stay (assuming that's what we want)?

4. Are there any employment contracts? Independent contractor arrangements? If so, get a copy of each of them.

5. Are there any noncompetition agreements or confidentiality agreements between management and the company? Between other people and the company? If so, get a copy of each one. Remember, when you're dealing with management, there is no such thing as a standard form. Many will have additions and cross-outs.

6. Get the organization chart for the business. If one is not already made up, try to get one or make one up with the help of current management.

7. Review actual management functions as well as job descriptions. Check out the personnel files of all the key people.

8. Review employee handbooks, vacation plans, bonus plans, severance plans, and early retirement plans. Do you want to be bound by all the terms?

9. Review claim and insurance files for workmen's compensation and unemployment. Are there many disputes?

10. Have a qualified employee benefits attorney review all health, accident, disability, deferred compensation, life insurance, pension, and profit sharing plans. This person should not be your regular business attorney: You need a specialist. Are you going to be bound to continue these plans? At what cost? Are the plans in full compliance? What will be the cost to bring them up to par?

11. How many employees are there? Get a complete census showing departments, ages, hire dates, and wages.

12. Is there a union? If not, have there been any moves to unionize? When? What were the results?

13. What is the historical labor turnover rate?

14. Try to keep your eyes and ears open for evidences of employee morale when you are touring the place of business. Ask questions of personnel along the way. Listen between the lines.

15. Are there any retirement plans, insurance plans, company cars, or other fringe benefits? If so, get a list of them, and of who takes part in each plan.

OWNERSHIP

1. List the owners of all outstanding stock, along with their relationships to each other (family, business partner, etc.).

2. Does anybody have a right to acquire stock under stock options or warrants? If so, get copies of these agreements.

3. Are there any buy-sell agreements? Are there any restrictions on the ability to buy or sell the stock, or on its use as collateral?

4. Are there any agreements with banks or other lenders limiting transfers of stock?

5. Are all shares fully paid?

6. Are there any agreements among shareholders, written or oral?

7. Does the person with whom you are dealing control at least 51 percent of the company, even if all options and warrants are exercised? If not, who else must consent before you know you have a binding deal?

8. Has the principal owner's stock been placed in trust or given away?

PERSONAL TAX RETURNS

1. Take a look at those personal income tax returns. Look in detail at the interest received and paid. If the corporation is involved, the corporation's name or address will appear on the return in several places.

2. Look for personal tax situations that might help you to put together a good package offer that has a better than average chance of being accepted.

3. Look for rents, dividends, leases, credits, and other entries that signify money going between owner and business.

How Do You Get the Personal Income Tax Returns?

More often than not you will hear objections from the seller to this "invasion of my privacy." You need to assure the seller that you are not really interested in any great detail in what her personal financial situation might be. But you are interested in making sure that you see all of the transactions that are going on and have a complete picture of how they might affect your own tax situation before you go ahead with the deal. This point is critical. If the seller has something to hide from you, the odds are strong that it is not visible in the financial statements—and you won't find it until after you own the business, and the problem.

A good way to answer the objection is to say, "I just want to satisfy myself there are no big problems. I don't intend to make any copies. Would it be all right if I just came over to your place or had my accountant go to your accountant's and look at the return without taking any copies?" More often than not, this request works. If not, we suggest you seriously consider walking away.

7

Analyzing Your Deal for Cash Flow

Ready money is Aladdin's lamp.
—GEORGE GORDON, LORD BYRON, *DON JUAN*

Hᴇʀᴇ's ᴡʜᴇʀᴇ ɪᴛ ᴀʟʟ comes together. Analyzing a deal for its cash flow potential is probably the most critical part of the investigation phase. Everything else is preliminary. Once you have established comfort and trust levels with "the other side," you will make your go/no-go decision based on the sufficiency of the cash flow.

In short, can you pay the bills of the business and still have enough left over to feed your family? You are not after income. You are after cash. For you (and most entrepreneurs), the hard cash payment for goods shipped or for services performed is what counts. Accounts receivable do not pay your bills. In fact, getting the order out the door will be more of a minus than a plus to you, because you have spent cash. Cash is not just king: it's crucial. Martin Edelstein, the publisher of *Boardroom Reports Newsletter,* sells a very popular T-shirt in each issue of the newsletter. It's the only one he sells and it's a quote by Fred Adler of venture capital fame, "Happiness Is Positive Cash Flow."

You should begin your cash flow analysis from the day you first see the financial statements, and constantly refine it for new facts and figures. Even after you put the deal together and close on it, you will still be performing cash flow analyses, probably for the life of the business.

When you first start thinking of "projecting" cash flows, and "predicting" what your cash position will be at any given point in time, you no doubt wonder about the cloudiness of your own crystal ball. In actual practice, there are two techniques you can use to make your view into the future much more reliable: (1) three scenario analysis; (2) break-even analysis.

THREE SCENARIOS

The first technique is to give yourself a range of targets at which to shoot on the theory, "The bigger the target, the easier it will be to hit." The first step is to construct separate projected income statements based on three scenarios: best case, worst case, and most likely.

Start off with the best case. Assume you will land that big account you intend to pursue. Assume you will keep a high level of the current customers and sales. Chart out your sales month by month for the next three to five years. Draw a line and stop.

Remember you are after cash, not sales, and the two are not the same. Therefore ask, For each $100 of sales I make in January, how much cash will I actually collect in January: $25? $100? How much in February? These projections could be based on statistical information collected by your targeted business over the years, or on industry data from the major trade association. From this information you will plot cash collections for each month, for the entire period of your projection.

Next, deduct your fixed cash expenditures. For nonfinancially trained people, this category contains those expenditures that continue the same, month in and month out, whether or not the business operates, whether you make one dollar's worth of sales or whether you make one million dollars' worth of sales. Examples include rent and insurance.

Next comes variable expenses, such as hourly payroll, commissions based on sales volume, and most cost of sales components. Remember that cost of sales cash outflows often lead sales, and therefore cash inflow, by several months.

The second scenario is to make the same projections based on what you see as the worst case. The purpose is to give you a baseline against which you can measure your performance and the actual effects of your efforts. It also serves to show you (and later, your banker) where you would be, if, for the first three years, income and expenses did not obey your every whim.

Finally, do a third scenario showing what is most likely to happen. For instance, most new owners will experience a drop-off in sales for the first few months. You might therefore want to plug in a 15 percent or 20 percent decline in sales. Perhaps figure in a higher reject rate as your new people learn the system. If the winters have been mild the past two years, you might want to project higher power costs this season. Be as honest with yourself as possible. The other two examples had just a touch of fantasy or nightmare to them. This scenario requires cool thinking. While the above is a synopsis of how to do cash flow planning, we'd like to recommend a fuller treatment in a book published by Upstart Publishing, written by David H. Bangs, Jr., entitled *The Cash Flow Control Guide*. This subject is somewhat boring and technical but it's important and this booklet details what are really cash and noncash items.

HOW TO MAKE YOUR PROJECTIONS

The best starting point for your three analyses is with the statement of cash flows. Most businesses you will be investigating already prepare this statement. If you have not seen one, ask for it. Most businesses that need statements for bank or shareholder use are required to comply with the American Institute of CPAs "Generally Accepted Accounting Principles" that require the use of the statement of cash flows. This requirement is called GAAP (pronounced "GAP"). If, for some reason, there is none, your CPA can probably convert the income statement for you (ask your CPA to use the direct method—it's more useful to you).

Having obtained two or three years' cash flow statements, it's easy to construct your own projections from them. As with your initial reviews of financial statements, and unlike actually preparing historical cash flow statements, do not leave this task solely in the hands of your CPA. There are things you know about the business and how to operate it profitably that the CPA would never discover. So you need to work through these cash flow statements and adjust them for what your changes will cause the numbers to do. Don't forget to add in your full debt service payments (principal and interest), your salaries (down because you'll work cheap, or up because the seller had too many people working for low pay), your special expenses (start-up for that new product line you intend to add), lower sales the first few months, cash generated by assets you intend to sell, and similar changes.

Once you are satisfied the numbers are reasonable, compare your statements to the same industry ratios to which you have been comparing the historical statements. Are your figures too optimistic? Do they make some modest and likely improvements on the ratios the business itself has been generating? The goal is to make your numbers as realistic as possible, in all three scenarios.

HOW MUCH CASH IS ENOUGH?

When you look at cash on hand, or your own working capital needs, how do you know whether you have a comfortable amount of cash or whether it's barely enough? In one company $50,000 might carry it through a full year's downturn in the economy, whereas in another company it wouldn't last beyond next Monday. One useful technique is to relate cash to number of weeks of payroll. It will give you some sense of how much time you have. "We don't have $50,000 in cash—we have six weeks of payroll" is the resultant thinking pattern.

BREAK-EVEN ANALYSIS

It is easy for the prospective business owner to predict what net profits after taxes (PAT) would be at a given level of sales. Casting projections in three scenarios will highlight your maneuverability between positive and negative cash flows. The practical problem with the three-scenario analysis is that it is theoretical and your projections don't really prove much of anything. The analysis is based on guesses as to inputs (sales), rather than starting with known values. However, the three analyses will be useful for your banker in selling your loan to the loan committee (bankers, like most people, don't like extremes and will sell themselves on your middle choice, the "most likely"). A much more useful buying guide is the break-even analysis. It is one of the most important tools in the manager's tool kit.

Note: We said *manager's* tool kit. Although break-even analysis is often thought of as an accountant's tool, it is really a way for you to get a quick grasp on what level of sales you need to move your company out of the red ink. From that vantage point you can more readily determine profitability. If your break-even analysis shows your entire sales force needs to be working twenty-seven hours a day for your target to break even, you know some changes must be made for you to do this deal.

Break-even analysis is a three-step process. First, determine the fixed costs of the business. Although all costs are variable over the long term, in most cases there will be some costs, such as rent, basic telephone service, insurance, and similar items that will not vary from month to month in the near term. The statement of cash flows, as well as the income statement, yield most of these items. Total your results and put them on a graph.

Next, determine the relationship between each of the other expenditures and total sales. For instance, commissions might equal 5 percent of sales, so that as sales rise, commissions go up at the 5 percent rate. Wages will likely vary with production, which may lead sales by a month or so. These costs are placed on your break-even graph, on top of fixed costs.

Finally, sales are plotted as a straight line. The point at which total sales equal total costs is the break-even point. Any sales above this mark will produce profit in the till. Below this sales level you can see how many days you have before you must file bankruptcy. (See the sample graph below.)

Sample Break-even Graph

Assume the following:

A. Only one product is made.
B. The fixed costs are $100,000 per year. These costs include:

Lights, power, and phones (utilities)
Rent
Insurance
Administrative salaries

These costs are fixed over 20,000 units to 40,000 units manufactured annually.
C. The variable costs over the 20,000–40,000 unit range are:

$2.00 material
$3.00 labor
$1.00 overhead (50% of material)
$6.00 per unit

D. Sales price per unit is $10.00.

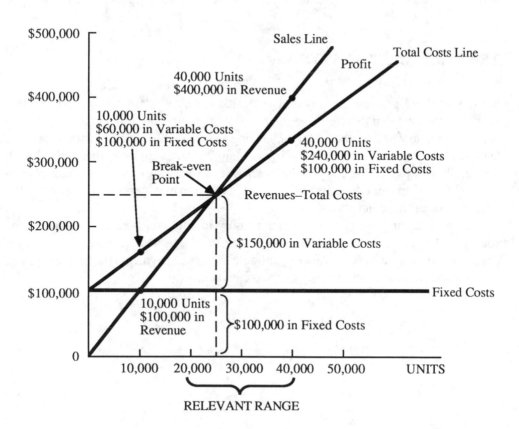

Break-even analysis is more accurately done by computer, so each item of variable expense can be plotted separately. The break-even analysis can be expressed as follows:

$$\text{Break-even Point} = \frac{\text{Fixed Costs}}{(\text{Revenue per Unit} - \text{Variable Costs per Unit})}$$

Always try to obtain the break-even analysis management is already preparing, if any. It will give you a good starting point. But you will need to adapt it to your own expectations for changes in sales and costs.

Remember, break-even analysis is only a tool of approximation. There are numerous factors that can throw it off. For instance, fixed costs are never really fixed and do vary in the real world. A changing product mix can throw the calculation off. Selling price is not constant. Many costs do not vary directly with production or sales, but with some other factors (a union settlement by a company clear across the country could drive your labor costs up). But the break-even analysis helps get you closer to reality in your financial projections. Use it to temper your three-scenario analysis.

TEAM MEMBER ANALYSIS

Having let these projections and analyses settle for a few days, each team member should re-review them to determine the psychological fit. Are things going to be tight at first? If so, do you have the financial backing to make it through the first two or three lean winters? Analyze yourself and your family: Do you have the ability, both financially and psychologically, to cut back your expenses to the bare bone, or even further, for an extended period of time? Each team member should consider the implications of these questions.

Each person can answer these questions only in cool and honest reflection in the silence of the personal study. Be sure to keep financial tightness in perspective. Things usually are tight at first. Remember your home mortgage payments the first few years? There often are unanticipated ways to make ends meet.

III

Finding the Dough

8

Analyzing Financing Sources

With money in your pocket, you are wise and
you are handsome and you sing well too.

—*YIDDISH PROVERBS*, ED. HANON J. AYALTI

Oᴜʀ ᴏʙᴊᴇᴄᴛɪᴠᴇs in this book now shift from seeing if you have a good deal to determining how you can finance the acquisition. How do bankers and other lenders analyze your deal and what will they lend money against? How can we uncover these other (sometimes little known) lenders?

The major share of the financing in most business acquisitions comes from some combination of the banker and the seller. Because sellers are usually more flexible to deal with, both before and after closing, they will normally be your preferred loan source. Even so, the banker will probably be involved, because sellers usually want some walk-away cash.

Sellers and bankers take similar approaches to loan negotiations and terms. Bank terms and conditions are what business owners and their advisors are accustomed to seeing, so common bank terms and conditions become the starting point in negotiating business acquisition financing.

Let's first see what can be financed, and then delve into how much cash can be raised against available collateral.

THREE KEYS TO SELLER FINANCING

Seller financing is probably the most common method of financing involved in most buyouts. Three factors distinguish seller financing:

1. The seller wants to sell the business and is less concerned about cash flow (timing) than collateral (being sure of payment). After all, she knows the business is a money maker; but if you run the business into the ground, she wants to be sure she can recover her business value.

2. The seller nearly always must provide financing in order to close the sale. Many sellers are aware of this common practice.

3. Usually you will not want to let the seller in on your plans for improving the business. The theory is, if the seller knows your plan, she might be tempted to do the same thing and not sell you the business. On the other hand, she might judge your ideas foolhardy, and not loan you the money or sell you her "child." All of these factors militate against giving the seller a full-blown business plan. But you still want to give her enough information so she has confidence in your management team's ability to run the business.

REVISITING THE FINANCIALS

You've already examined the financial statements to investigate details of the business: how it is operated, whether or not it is profitable, the state of the machinery and equipment, and so on. A good portion of the initial information came from the income and cash flow statements. Now we're looking for financing, and here is where the balance sheet is particularly telling.

Examination of the balance sheet will normally produce leads to several financing sources. The most typical are in (1) accounts receivable, (2) inventory, and (3) other fixed assets. For example, consider this simplified balance sheet:

ASSETS

(1)	Accounts Receivable	$ 800,000
(2)	Inventory	1,200,000
(3)	Fixed Assets	2,000,000
(4)	Total Assets	$4,000,000

LIABILITIES

(5)	Accounts Payable	$ 600,000
(6)	Long-Term Debt	1,400,000
(7)	Total Debt	$2,000,000
(8)	Equity	2,000,000
(9)	Total Liability and Equity	$4,000,000
(10)	Profit After Taxes	$ 500,000

Selling Price: $3,500,000 (1.5 Book Value or 7 ×
Earnings)

Most traditional lenders will base their loans on the cash flow of the borrower. Lending in the last half century has switched emphasis from the balance sheet (that is, asset values) to the income statement (that is, cash flows available for debt service). Still, the more collateral you can give your lender, the more confident he will feel about your cash flow. So, in the example, let's say your traditional banker would loan 75 percent against accounts receivable, 25 percent against the inventory, and 75 percent against the fixed assets. You would have a total loan of $2.4 million. An aggressive asset-based lender might go as high as $3.2 million:

			ASSET-BASED LOANS			
LINE	ASSETS	AMOUNT	TRADITIONAL		AGGRESSIVE	
(1)	Accounts Receivable	$ 800,000	$ 600,000	75%	$ 800,000	100%
(2)	Inventory	1,200,000	300,000	25%	600,000	50%
(3)	Fixed Assets	2,000,000	1,500,000	75%	1,800,000	90%
	Total Loan		$2,400,000		$3,200,000	

In either case, if you plan to pay $3.5 million for the business, you will have additional financing or capital to raise, between $300,000 and $1.1 million.

The balance sheet has just given you clues to financing sources for 68 percent to 90 percent of your purchase price. A little time spent analyzing balance sheets can pay off big in financing sources.

Once you have determined financing possibilities, make sure the business can support the debt service. In the example given, if you borrowed $3,200,000 at 12 percent over 8 years, your debt payments would total $624,000 per year. Unfortunately, the income available to service this debt is only $500,000. There is usually more cash than $500,000 because of noncash expenses, but can you increase sales or decrease expenses enough to make up any shortfall? We may be able to show you how to borrow enough money to buy the business, but we may not be able to show you how to pay back the loan! Raising the money can be the easy part, while paying it back presents the greater challenge. Organizations like the Center for Entrepreneurial Management, Inc., and the Chief Executive Officer's Club can help. See Chapter 7 for a discussion of cash flow analysis.

Your first task is to find assets against which you can borrow. These include hard assets like equipment, office equipment, automobiles, and real estate, and even intangibles (such as accounts receivable and cash surrender value of life insurance).

Second, you will scour the liability side of the balance sheet, looking for outstanding liabilities you can assume. It is easier to assume liability to an existing creditor than to create a new lender. Trade creditors' obligations, and even those longstanding notes to the owner herself, may be easily assumable. These are really sources of cash and can help in the acquisition.

Don't just stop with the current balance sheet. Get the balance sheets for the last five years or so to see if different creditors appear. The seller may have cleaned up certain debts just for the sale even though you might find it beneficial to draw on some longstanding credit relationships. For instance, if the seller normally buys $100,000 worth of supplies each month from PQR Corporation, but has paid off this account for the sale, you could set the closing for right after the regular monthly delivery from PQR Corporation, and assume the payable to PQR. Obtain a schedule of all major creditors over the last five years or so, as well as the balance sheets. Don't forget the accountant's footnotes are the most important aspect of the balance sheet.

Look into off-balance sheet borrowing possibilities. For instance, find out if assets have been written off but are still being used. Such assets can represent a hidden source of financing. Look also for a tax refund due from the IRS or a prepaid insurance item. Look around for things going on in the business—things you may only pick up by snooping around. You've heard of "managing by wandering around"? Well, try a small dose of "buying by wandering around." For instance, if there are vending machines on the premises, particularly if they do much business, you might approach the vending machine operator for a loan or an advance against the rental fee for the vending machine space. Then there could be obsolete or unused inventory or equipment or even plant space capable of being scrapped, sold, rented out, or otherwise converted to cash. How about that growing mound of scrap in the back? Is there some industry that might buy it? One of the best sources of these hidden assets are former accounting employees no longer working at the company. It can pay to trace them down. See Chapter 10 for more ideas.

Then take a look at the income statement and statement of cash flows. Do they suggest any potential lenders? Go through line by line and ask yourself these questions:

1. Is this number large enough that the vendor might be willing to make a loan?
2. Is there a customer who has no other economical source of supply? Would that customer be willing and able to make a loan?
3. Could I combine this item with some other and order it all from one supplier who would then be willing to "buy" my business by making a loan?
4. Who benefits the most from this line item?
5. Who would be harmed the most if this item were cut out or purchased from another source?
6. Could work being performed in house just as economically be done outside, thereby generating another lending source?
7. Does this line item suggest an asset against which some lender might make a loan?
8. Could I both save expense and create a lender by automating the work and buying equipment from someone?

Having once gone through this process, and each of your management team having done likewise, get everyone together and brainstorm additional possibilities. Remember, the purpose of brainstorming is to generate ideas in quantity, not quality. The more ideas, the better your chances of finding additional financing sources. Coming up with offbeat business financing sources might point you in the direction of the one practical source that will make the deal go. Joe saw one of these deals where the missing $100,000 was lent by the insurance agent who both liked the business investment and needed to protect the various insurance policies already in force.

HOW TO DO IT

One of the best ways to train your imagination to find hidden financing dollars is to work through actual examples. See the two examples in Appendix E. Many sources can be generated by questioning each number you see, and asking who would gain/lose from a change.

HIDDEN SOURCES OF BANK FINANCING

What asset appears in no balance sheet, could be worth about three percentage points off all bank interest costs, and is largely unknown to the small business community?

This hidden asset is easily found if you know what you're seeking, but is invisible to most managers. It is the total of average collected balances in all company bank accounts. ("Collected" has a special meaning to the banker, roughly equivalent to what a layman would call "cleared checks.")

Banks make money from their small business accounts in two ways: from loans and from deposits. The money made on loans is obvious, but the money made on deposits is less well known. Stripped of nonessentials, the concept is this: If a business deposits $100,000 cash in a checking account and never touches it, the bank has $100,000 it can lend at interest.

Take a look at the typical business checking account statement and you'll probably see a balance of the account for each day, and an average daily balance for the month. The bank doesn't compute that figure to see if it is charging enough service charge, or losing money on your account: Primarily banks compute this "wonder" asset figure to see how profitable the business bank account is, and therefore how much money the bank has available to loan to others.

Now compare the typical corporate checkbook balance against the bank statement—which is higher? The bank statement. It's always higher. Why? Because there are always checks outstanding that have not yet been presented to the bank.

A savvy business borrower, knowing banks make money on the average cash balance in the corporate bank accounts, is in a better position to compute the worth of her account to the bank (more on this point in Chapter 9). Knowledge of the worth to the bank of cash balances in your account can be converted into a better bargaining position with the bank.

Therefore, you will find it beneficial to obtain all monthly bank statements for all accounts of your target acquisition for the last three years. From them you'll compile annual and three-year averages of bank balances, for use in your bank loan negotiations. You don't want to clue the seller in to the financing possibilities, but you can justify your request by normal investigative reasons: The bank statements give you a backup to income statement figures, and it's an easy way to search for and find unusual transactions. (Look especially for large round-dollar amounts, keeping in mind the advice about round numbers that opened Chapter 5.)

BANK FINANCING RULES OF THUMB

Once you've determined which assets might be bankable, you need to know how bankers might look at the financials. Let's get a quick idea of how financable your deal might be, and how you can put together a proposal that will look reasonable to the bankers. Today this procedure is growing in complexity.

What will the bankers lend you? The answer varies from banker to banker, and the differences can be great. Often, banks can vary by up to 50 percent. However, in the past, most bankers had an ingrained psychological block against taking risks much above 50 percent of any business deal, so keep that figure in the back of your mind. Today, they will go beyond, to 80 percent or higher, depending on your presentation and how badly they want your business. The figures that follow should give you a good starting point in dealing with nonbank lenders, as well.

Cash and Liquid Assets

Cash can be used 100 percent for loan purposes. The cash sitting in your target business can qualify you for a bridge loan. Say there is $100,000 cash in the business over and above working capital needs, and you are short $200,000 for closing. You can use the $100,000 cash in the business to help acquire the loan by borrowing $100,000 from the bank and then using the cash in the business to pay off the loan a day later. This is simple.

Marketable securities present another problem, since there are margin requirements to prevent loans above 50 percent or so of the value. These margin requirements vary from time to time. But these requirements only apply if the purpose of the loan is to acquire and carry the securities that serve as collateral. If you sign a "purpose statement," the banker is often willing to go to 75 percent to 80 percent of market value. Here again a bridge loan coupled with a quick sale of securities held by the business can increase the percentage to nearly 100 percent.

Accounts Receivable

Accounts receivable can serve as collateral for a loan between 60 percent and 90 percent of the value of the receivables. Standard is about 80 percent for receivables under ninety days. It depends on such things as the size of the accounts (the smaller the account, the more valuable, based on a theory of safety in diversity), their age, the company's bad debt history, how the customers of the business will fare in a recession, how good the collection efforts and collection department of the seller have been, and similar factors. The real point of negotiation is how your lender makes the computations: Certain accounts may be more valuable to the banker if you can explain why they have higher value. Don't be afraid to delve into the banker's computations.

Let's say during the final few negotiating sessions that you're still a few dollars short of making the deal. Rather than borrowing against the accounts receivable through normal sources, you might instead negotiate to have the seller guarantee the collectibility of receivables. With that guarantee a bank might make a larger loan against the receivables, because the bank now has not only the collateral of the receivables to rely on but also the seller's guarantee. This is a good negotiating ploy, since it can tell you a great deal about the seller's real view of the receivables. If the seller refuses to guarantee the receivables, then maybe you should take a second look at whether the receivables are worth their price. In most cases there will be some losses in the receivables, so you should be willing to drop back a little on the guarantee to say 97 percent or 95 percent of the face amounts. If the seller still won't go along, you can offer instead to let the seller keep the receivables so you have less cash to raise. That way you don't have the risk, and if the receivables are so good, the seller ought to be willing to keep them. It's almost a "heads I win, tails you lose" argument.

Inventory

There are three kinds of inventory: (1) raw materials, (2) work in process, and (3) finished goods. Unless you are accustomed to thinking differently about each, it will seem like an exercise in Alice in Wonderland when the banker tells you how much she can loan against inventory. As a rule of thumb, it is rare for any banker to advance more than 50 percent of the inventory value, in total or in individual categories. More aggressive lenders may go higher. Raw materials can support upward of 50 percent to 75 percent of their cost, depending on marketability. On the other end of the spectrum, finished goods can support between 40 percent and 80 percent of their cost, also depending on marketability and the aggressiveness of the lender. If the finished goods are easily marketable without spending much on selling costs, they may support a loan toward the higher end of the scale.

The problem comes with work in process (WIP). What if you have an 80,000-gallon vat of chemicals on the day you fire your chief foreman? The foreman has mixed in some chemicals but not all those necessary to make the final product. You just don't know which ones he has dumped in and which he hasn't, since there is no particular order in which they need to be mixed. What is the value of the chemicals in the vat? There is some valid argument for a value less than zero, since you need to dispose of what's in the vat before you can mix another batch.

Again, if the company manufactures component parts for automobiles, and you have 112,000 parts on the floor, on the average 60 percent complete, how can you know the parts will pass inspection when they are fully complete? These are questions running through your banker's mind, since he does not know anything about manufacturing chemicals or automobile parts. Nor does he know how to sell half complete parts or chemicals. Therefore, it is rare to see a banker lend anything at all against work in process. You may want to have the seller convert all WIP to finished goods just before the moment of sale to optimize your ability to borrow.

Machinery and Equipment

Bankers tend to be conservative in this area, but there are degrees of conservatism. Loan values may run anywhere from 25 percent to 200 percent of book values because book value seldom represents the true value of the equipment. If there is a significant amount of equipment, it will pay to get an appraisal. Even so, many banks will use 75 percent of the liquidation auction "hammer" value as the loan value.

If it has been a while since the assets were acquired or refinanced, there is often sufficient gap for the purchaser to renegotiate and raise additional funds for the acquisition. This gap can arise through increases in value, inflation, and pay-downs on the debt. But figure that 75 percent of the appraised value is a good estimate. If the bank doesn't go with the 75 percent rule of thumb, it's possible to search for a wealthy individual in the community interested in a sale and lease-back of the assets to help you generate cash. Just get good legal counsel to protect you in case the deal doesn't go as the person expected.

Real Estate

Generally banks will lend 70 percent of the value of the real estate, although 80 percent is possible. Again, an appraisal is in order. You usually need an MAI (Member Appraisal Institute) appraiser. Bankers like to hire their own appraisers and tack on the appraiser's fee as part of the loan costs. Even so, it can be helpful to have your own appraisal, particularly if the banker is trying to find ways to make the deal work. In that case, what the banker really wants is something to put in the file to justify the loan. So if your appraiser comes in with a higher figure than the bank's appraiser, the banker may just use yours.

Other Assets

Things like patents, trademarks, and other intangible assets do not usually command a high loan value from bankers, so count them as zero. But you may be able to sell some intangibles (such as foreign rights), giving you a nonlending source of cash.

Commitment Capital

Bankers like (let's use the word *love*) to see some money put in by the buyer. Their reasoning is if you don't have the confidence in the deal to risk your own funds, why should they? It's commonly called earnest money. The amount of commitment capital is not a function of the size of the deal but of your own financial capacity. If you are worth several million dollars, and you have a million dollars in liquid assets, they may want to see you put in $500,000 to $750,000 to prove that you mean business. However, if you have only managed to save $5,000, and are willing to commit that amount and your home equity, it can be sufficient. Both deals could involve the same purchase price. However, bankers will not necessarily increase their loan just because you put in more of your own funds.

IS DEBT BAD?

Most of the methods of financing we're discussing here and in the next two chapters rely heavily on debt. Debt is often easier to obtain and cheaper than risk capital. But by leveraging your transaction you face the risks of the leverage working against you as much as the opportunity it will work for you.

Ask any accountant or consult any venerable business text and you'll find undercapitalization high on the list of causes of business failures. It might bear one of a dozen names: lack of risk capital, high debt to equity ratio, or underfunding. Whatever the name, the conventional wisdom is the same: Too little cash backing doomed the business from the start. There's nothing wrong with conventional wisdom—except it misses the underlying problem.

It's like the hot air balloonists who got lost. So they dropped down low enough to inquire of a man standing in a field, "Where are we?" The man in the field called back, "About 50 feet in the air, 10 feet south by southwest from me." One balloonist turned to the other and said, "Just our luck to ask a lawyer!" "How'd you know he was a lawyer," asked the other, incredulous at his companion's keen deductive ability. "Simple," he replied. "Everything he told us was absolutely correct, and totally useless." Calling the business problem undercapitalization amounts to the same thing.

For every business failure caused by inadequate capital, you can read about one that faced the same and greater problems, and survived to become an industrial giant. So what causes businesses to fail?

1. A product the market is rejecting
2. Ineffective salesmanship
3. Poor management of limited cash
4. Incomplete or nonexistent accounting information
5. Lack of imagination of where to look for funding
6. Choosing the wrong banker or other financier
7. The big killer: a broken spirit

Many businesses fail because the owners got tired and discouraged and threw in the towel. They may have been inches away from success. After the combatant is beaten back for the seventh or eighth time, and is bloodied and weary beyond fatigue, it's the extra effort that turns the momentum of the battle and provides undreamed-of successes. Owning your own business is 1 percent inspiration and 99 percent perspiration.

Every rich and powerful business today started from humble beginnings. No business ever started big. Many were as undercapitalized as the ones that failed. Even those that were "adequately" capitalized by wealthy people can trace their roots to people no more highly capitalized than you.

Now it is true that if you had the wealth of the Ford family behind you, you would stand a better chance of success than if you started out with only $53.27. But even money won't overcome the real problems (remember Ford's Edsel?).

Undercapitalization is not so much a cause of business failure as it is a symptom. (Worse yet, it is often an excuse for not making the necessary second effort.) Undercapitalization is a symptom of an underlying problem for which there is always a solution. But you must seek it out.

Remember, a business of your own is like a bacon-and-eggs breakfast: The chicken makes a contribution, but the pig, our real hero, makes a commitment!

9

Negotiating with Your Banker/Lender . . . Without Signing Your Life Away!

If you would know the value of money, go and try to borrow some.

—BENJAMIN FRANKLIN, *POOR RICHARD'S ALMANAC*

NOWHERE DOES PREPAREDNESS pay off more dramatically than in loan negotiations. Ask any commercial loan officer: Most business borrowers are unprepared for loan negotiations. No wonder there are so many turn-downs! If you approach the lender prepared, you will get more money and better terms than the average business borrower. Those terms might include staying off personal loan guarantees.

Your preparations started with the discussion in Chapter 8 about what percentage bankers will normally lend against which assets. Be aware that the seller is often willing to lend you the difference between what the banker will lend and the market values.

GETTING TO *REALLY* KNOW YOUR BANKER

Next, we direct your attention to the species that bears the name, *Conservatatus bankpersona*. Despite its ubiquitous nature, few people know much about its habits inside its natural habitat, the *Bankus cavernous*.

Normally a docile creature, the *Conservatatus bankpersona* has been known at times to rear up on its hind legs and dash to pieces many a businessperson's hopes with the most dreaded call of the species: "No!" (It is not true, as some wag once

94

remarked, that as morning exercises all entrepreneurs get up and practice saying "yes," all venture capitalists get up and practice saying "maybe," and all bankers get up and practice saying "no." Real life is not that simple and there is a large contingent of bankers who get up and practice saying "show me everybody else's 'bad' deals.")

Novice stalkers often take such occasion as a time to make a hasty retreat from further confrontation. Others, more experienced in the hunt, have stood their ground, and after some maneuvering, bagged their quarry. The difference between novice and experienced hunters turns out to be only a bit more knowledge and time spent preparing for the hunt.

First, the experienced hunter studies the habitat. Much is published about the *Bankus cavernous* and its individual manifestations, but in a jungle language with which few *Homo sapiens* are familiar. For example, here is a description of a particular specimen, which we will call "Neighborhood Bank." Note the strange-sounding language:

Neighborhood Bank Balance Sheet

ASSETS		LIABILITIES	
(1) Cash and Due from Banks	$ 74,621	(9) Deposits	$480,555
(2) Federal Funds Sold	9,460	(10) Federal Funds Purchased	12,186
(3) U.S. Gov't. Securities	106,450	(11) Other Liabilities	19,452
(4) State and Munic. Securities	21,610	(12) Capital Stock	33,302
(5) Other Securities	9,569	(13) Surplus	25,422
(6) Loans	341,682	(14) Undivided Profits	14,221
(7) Other Assets	21,746		
(8) Total Assets	$585,138	(15) Total Liabilities	$585,138

We now call your attention to three ratios, even stranger sounding, to help us predict the reactions of our quarry when confronted by an armed hunter (you). These will help us plan how to stalk our quarry: head on, from the flank, or from the rear.

1. What is our quarry's loan-to-deposit ratio? (average: 75 percent). This ratio is easily obtained by dividing deposits into loans (line 6 divided by line 9). In the case of Neighborhood Bank, the ratio stands at 71 percent ($341,682 divided by $480,555). By today's standard, this amount is rather conservative. The norm is around 80 percent, compared to 50 percent to 60 percent in the 1960s. Rural banks have lower ratios than city banks.

2. What is our specimen's liquidity ratio? (average: 30 percent). The liquidity ratio measures the amount of liquid assets, or assets easily convertible into cash, standing

behind each dollar of deposits. First, add cash on hand (line 1), federal funds sold (line 2) and U.S. government securities (line 3). Next, add to your total 70 percent of state and municipal securities (line 4). Then subtract federal funds purchased (line 10) from the total.

Finally, to obtain the liquidity ratio, divide your total by deposits (line 9). In the case of Neighborhood Bank, the liquidity ratio would be $193,472 divided by $480,555, a ratio of 40.3 percent. In other words, Neighborhood Bank has just over 40 cents in liquid assets standing back of each $1 of deposits. Again, that's fairly conservative. A typical liquidity ratio for a commercial bank today would be in the 25 percent to 35 percent range. Of course, the hard-hit savings and loans (thrifts) are usually less liquid than commercial banks.

3. What is this bank's capital ratio? (average: 6 percent). The capital ratio measures the amount of capital assets behind each dollar of deposits. Merely add together capital (line 12), surplus (line 13) and undivided profits (line 14). Then divide the total by deposits (line 9). For Neighborhood Bank, the capital ratio would become 15.2 percent ($72,945 divided by $480,555). Relatively few commercial banks maintain a capital ratio above 10 percent, with most falling in the 5 percent to 7 percent range. Federal law is slowly raising this ratio to help alleviate the banking crisis of the late 1980s.

So what? Why are such arcane ratios important to the prospective borrower/business buyer? Besides being a measure of the degree of conservatism of your particular specimen, they are big fat clues to how the bank policy will cause your banker to view your loan package.

In Chapter Eight we started you thinking about a subject bankers study and talk about over coffee every day: deposits. Banks are really like most business-to-business distribution companies; the difference is their inventory is cash, not lift trucks or computers. So when they get a fresh supply of inventory at a low price, it's almost as good as money in the bank (forgive the pun) for them! That's because they can always find a renter (a business borrower who will pay interest) or somebody else who will put it to work for them (the U.S. government, another bank, the Federal Reserve System, or a large corporate issuer of commercial paper)—all at a profit, albeit a small one.

Let's sharpen your banking focus a bit more. Say your target regularly has a collected balance in all its corporate bank accounts of $200,000. That's not its average check book balance, which is probably lower.

Now the Federal Reserve System requires each bank to keep in reserve 12 percent (at this writing) of all demand deposits (checking accounts) above $41,500,000 and 3 percent below, and 3 percent of all business time deposits (savings). Thus, 12 percent, or $24,000, of the average collected balance can't be loaned out: It must be kept available to cover checks and other possible withdrawals.

At the least, the bank should be able to loan the rest of the money out overnight to some other bank at the federal funds rate. At this writing, the rate is about 8.5 percent. So the bank can take your target's average collected bank balances and earn $14,960 annually ($176,000 × 8.5 percent).

Assuming normal service charges and target yield rates for loans established by the bank cover overhead, moving your acquired company's accounts from bank A to bank B moves almost $15,000 bottom-line profit out of A's profit and loss and into B's. Would bank B be willing to entertain your loan proposal (never say "request" again!)? Might bank B even be willing to negotiate its loan interest rate and share some of this $15,000 with you, just to get the account? And what would bank A be willing to do to keep the account?

There are three other key factors affecting the habitat of your *Conservatatus bankpersona* of which you must be aware:

1. Is this bank currently considering a merger with another bank? You need to know this because it is what your *Conservatatus bankpersona* is thinking about and talking about all day long, since it will affect his salary next month or next year.

2. Does this bank have a Small Business Investment Company (SBIC) or a venture capital company? Many of the larger banks do, and you ought to know whether or not yours does. If you get turned down, there may be an opportunity for you to get a referral to the venture capital company inside the bank and do a joint venture capital/bank transaction—you might be in a situation that falls right between the two.

3. Does this bank make the kind of loan you seek? Lawyers, accountants, and doctors specialize, and so do banks. Some (like savings and loans and credit unions) do little or no commercial lending, but those that do commercial lending break down by small versus large business lending, industrial versus retail customers, asset-based versus traditional lending, conservative versus (relatively) liberal lending, and so forth. The best way to make this determination is to review all the banks in your geographic area in *Polk's Bank Directory*. Give a list to your attorney or accountant to check. Using a professional helps assure you will get more complete answers. You will ask your attorney or accountant to call the head of commercial lending at each institution, supply without names the broad outlines of your transaction, and assess the fit of the loan to the bank and the enthusiasm of the banker for your deal. And you'll get responses about banks from other entrepreneurs. Usually these responses provide the best practical information on banks and bankers. But we say never pick a bank—pick a banker. In practice, the banker is more important than the bank.

Having studied the habitat, the skilled stalker studies his particular *Conservatatus bankpersona* to know that individual well. In fact we recommend that you actually make your banker your best friend, and a key person in your company. Learn your banker's likes, dislikes, abilities, authorities, and how your banker fits into the bank hierarchy/habitat.

BANKERS' QUIZ

Total Possible—200 Points

1. Can you draw an organization chart of the bank with your banker in the chart?
   ☐ Yes ☐ No   25 Points
2. Did you give your banker a small Christmas present last year?
   ☐ Yes ☐ No   20 Points
   Add five points if he came to your company's, or your target's, Christmas party.
3. Do you know where your banker went to school?
   ☐ Yes ☐ No   10 Points
4. Do you know the first name of your banker's spouse?
   ☐ Yes ☐ No   10 Points
5. Do you know the first and last names of your banker's boss?
   ☐ Yes ☐ No   15 Points
6. Do you know the names and backgrounds of at least two other members of the loan committee?
   ☐ Yes ☐ No   40 Points
7. Do you know your banker's hometown?
   ☐ Yes ☐ No   10 Points
8. Do you know your banker's birthday?
   ☐ Yes ☐ No   15 Points
9. Have you had your banker or his boss (or both) for a facilities tour of your company or target company in the last six months?
   ☐ Yes ☐ No   25 Points
10. Have you been out socially with your banker (not as part of a loan request) in the last six months?
    ☐ Yes ☐ No   30 Points

Scoring the Bankers' Quiz

The correct answer to every question is *yes.* To be your bank's best customer (the easy way to get your loan approved), you need to score 175 points or better on this quiz. Here's why:

1. These days, so much of banking is branch banking. You need to know where the decision-making power is and where your banker fits into it. Most business lending is done from the main office of the bank, not the branch.
2. When we say a small gift, we mean something like a book: If you know he's got a

hobby, like boating, give him a book that is relevant. It lets him know that you think of him as a human being, not just another *Conservatatus bankpersona*. Now we're not suggesting you bribe your banker; just give a small gift that shows you're on the ball, say less than $25.

For the last ten years or so bankers seem to have been playing a game of musical chairs. What do you do if, every time you call the bank, there is another banker assigned to your account? What's happening is that the large banks are going after smaller ones, and bankers are improving their operations and pursuing business development (their term for "sales"). Consequently, good bankers are in great demand.

Here is what you need to do as soon as you feel you are on the road to a good relationship with your banker. Privately say: "Pat, it's so obvious to me that you are the rising star in this bank, and I worry sometimes at night because you're such a crucial part of our little company. We wouldn't be where we are today if it weren't for you. Your help and cooperation and especially your advice has been very important in our development. (Remember, money follows advice.) Now it seems to me, looking at you and the other people in the bank, you're probably about ready to get promoted. And you're probably going to jump a couple of levels. And if you don't, you'll start looking elsewhere for a bank that will recognize your talents and abilities. What worries me is if you leave or move up, it could really hurt our business. What I'd really like to ask is a special favor: I understand when bankers get promoted, they sometimes take a few of their special clients with them. And I'd like to ask you to do that with our account. Now I realize that we're not the largest account you've got, but it would make a great deal of difference to me personally if you would consider keeping us as one of those few clients that you will continue to handle. Would you be willing to do that for us?"

3. One of the first things two people do when they get to know each other is to look for common ground. Knowing what school your banker attended will tell you something about him. It can often provide an opener like "We played you in football," or "My brother did his undergraduate work there."

4. Again, people trust familiarity, so it helps if you know the spouse's name of your banker and inquire after her once in a while. It's an American custom.

5. It's the nature of the banking business that bankers tend to move up quickly in their jobs, either changing banks or bouncing from one branch to another. If you know your banker's boss (and she knows you), when your banker moves, it's possible your account will be passed up to the boss rather than down to the new loan officer. And the higher the person you're dealing with, the better off you are. If you're really sharp, you'll know your banker's boss' boss' name (and he'll know yours). It's easy to meet the president of all but the largest banks—just ask. Your banker will be delighted to introduce you. It gives her more visibility. Did you know that most banks encourage their officers to meet their customers?

6. Ninety percent of the time, your loan officer will make the decision on your

loan, but he still has to get it approved by the loan committee. If you know who's on the committee (and again, if they know you), you will smooth the process, not to mention speed it up. Try to find out what your particular loan officer's lending limit is, both secured and unsecured. This knowledge will help you in negotiations, and it will tell you something about how the higher-ups perceive the strength of your lending officer. In order to have a win-win negotiation, it's important you know as much as possible about the other party. For sure the banker is going to know a lot about you: your financial situation, business and personal; your business plans; what life insurance you own; maybe even your medical condition.

7. Again, familiarity and common ground are the keys to a good relationship. And the more you know about your banker, the easier it is to strengthen and develop those ties. Negotiations are usually won by the side with the most information.

8. Whenever we suggest that it's a good idea to give your banker a quick phone call on her birthday, people laugh and say that's too corny. They laugh, that is, 364 days a year, but on their birthday they get a kick out of the fact that someone remembers. Calling your banker on her birthday tells her that you have a good memory for dates and you just might remember the date your loan payments come due. It's a nice touch for your best friend.

9. It's amazing the change in attitude a banker has when he actually sees a product being produced, sold, and shipped. (If you're in a service business, like real estate, more important than showing your banker your office is driving him past houses you've sold, as well as houses you currently have listed. If you can't take your banker to your facility—for instance, it might be too far away—how about bringing the facility to him? Bring in a videotape, or some snapshots.)

10. When we suggest taking your banker out socially (for instance, for dinner), we mean *socially*. No business. And especially don't make the mistake of asking touchy questions after a pleasant meal, such as, "My wife is a little worried about the bank wanting her signature on the loan, and she thinks it would be a good idea to discuss it with you while your wife is here." Let your banker do 90 percent of the talking. The more he talks about his interests, the better impression you'll make. And if you don't take your banker to lunch (without asking for money) at least once a year after you have made your acquisition, you won't be doing your job as a chief executive officer.

SHOULD YOU BE A SMART MONEY MANAGER?

Consider being a "dumb" money manager. Don't set up accounts that sweep all the money out of corporate checking and into a money market fund every weekend. Instead, leave the money in a "dumb money" checking account with your bank. Why? Because if you are sweeping the money out of your accounts regularly, it is not readily available for your bank to lend out. The bank must pay out interest and spend clerical or computer time to post your "extra" transactions. In short, offering to forego the "sweep" account could help your negotiations with your banker.

OTHER BANKING TIPS

Make sure your banker knows and meets with your accountant, lawyer, consultants, and key employees. All of you should have lunch together regularly. Your banker is not someone you can afford to ignore and approach only when you need money. Your banker can be a key business advisor (really!). That's why you need a good banker: for advice. Don't worry. Money always follows advice. Get the advice; the money will come. The banker is the heartbeat of the business—easily the most important of the outside advisors. Your lawyer and accountant are paid help. Bankers are to be loved and cared for in a special way.

Now don't go thinking that the relationship alone is going to make any particular loan for you. What it will do is make the going easier in any particular situation. Each loan stands on its own merits. The good relationship with your banker increases your odds of getting terms a shade better or doubts resolved more easily in your favor.

Go to one of your bank's seminars. Make yourself visible to your bankers. Go to your bank's stockholders' meeting. Sit up front and ask friendly questions like "What accounts for your stronger liquidity ratio this year?" This is a wonderful opportunity for you to meet the key executives in your bank, be it a small bank or a large one. Later, in the board or committee meetings, somebody will ask, "Who was that person up front who asked so many good questions?" And your *Conservatatus bankpersona* will say, "Well, that was one of my customers."

Get a copy of your own credit report. See if your banker will share it with you when you apply. If not, you can always go to the credit bureau and get a copy by paying a few dollars.

Be sure you create a letter trail in your bank's files. Send copies of updated financials you receive from your target. Send your banker periodic progress reports. When you take your banker to lunch, send him a note saying you enjoyed meeting with him and intend to see him again next week. And if the banker should happen to buy lunch (advice to the wise: you should always buy), don't skip the opportunity to send a thank-you note. Maybe you don't send letters like that to other business acquaintances. Why would you want to send them to your banker? Because your banker has a file. Every letter and piece of paper you send your banker goes into that file. When your banker leaves the bank, and a new officer comes in and picks up your file, you want her to say, "Gosh, look at all this great correspondence. This customer really makes an effort to keep on good terms with us." No entrepreneur in history ever gave a banker too much information!

Loans are made by people to people. Find your strongest weapon—your strongest selling point. For instance, which description of your target's product do you think would stand a better chance of gaining bank loan approval: a device that by motion and sound monitors the aspiration of infants, or a device that monitors a child's breathing to cut the rate of crib deaths? Aristotle said people make decisions emotionally and then justify them rationally. Bankers, contrary to popular entrepreneurial opinion, are people too. They make decisions the same way. Your job, as a prospective loan applicant, is to find the emotional issue and then construct the rational arguments to support it.

HOW LOAN DECISIONS ARE MADE

Do bankers really think like businesspeople? Yes. The difference between a banker and a "normal" businessperson lies in the nature of the inventory. In this case, the inventory is cash, and it is not sold, but leased. And it is more mobile than any other businessperson's rolling stock.

As a result, a banker has two business decisions to make for every "lease" he considers making: (1) Will the "lessee" misuse, abuse, or lose the "leased" cash (that is, what is my risk of loss)?; and (2) Can I make a profit on this "lease"?

Let's talk about the first question here, and leave the second one for later (see "Pricing: The Second Decision the Banker Makes," later in this chapter). The decision process is not unlike that used by the computer lessor. The differences are a matter of degree only—for instance, a large computer is hard to hide, and even if it is abused it can possibly be put in good condition with a minimum of expense. However, if cash is abused (at the racetrack, say) it is not retrievable.

In assessing risk, bankers have traditionally relied on the six Cs of credit:

1. Character
2. Cash flow
3. Capacity to earn
4. Conditions in the marketplace
5. Capital
6. Collateral

Character easily carries 50 percent of the weight in the risk decision. It revolves around your history on previous loans, your honesty, your reputation in the community, your credit rating by others, your goals, motivations, cooperative attitude, and determination to pay back your loans. In short, your moral character is under a magnifying glass. It also concerns itself with your business acumen and abilities: Just how savvy and perceptive and hard working is this potential "lessee"? What experience and training does this person have to run this business? If it were my life savings, would I trust it to this person in this enterprise? Remember, this analysis will be applied stringently to each member of your inside team, and even somewhat to your external advisors, so choose your entire team with care.

Cash flow is the second most important factor to a banker today. Ever since the Depression, bankers have shied away from collateral as a guarantee of performance, and relied more on the earnings stream to make sure they'll be repaid. If you can show a strong historical cash flow in your target, you have gone more than halfway to reducing your banker's fear of losing the "leased" cash (and his job). Capacity to earn (and therefore, to repay) often serves as a reminder of other ways to assess potential cash flows and the experience/ability component of character.

Conditions in the marketplace are those external factors that may hurt your plans or cash flow. (Unless you point them out, the typical banker will not consider, or at least not heavily weight, positive factors in the economy.)

Capital refers to commitment capital: Just how much are you, the borrower, willing to risk on the proposition? As we discussed in Chapter 8, commitment capital is a function of your financial picture, not the size of the deal. It is also a function of the quality of the assets your capital has purchased. If you have little or no cash to put in, or if you want to limit the cash you tie up in this deal, you will need to handle this factor up front. For instance, you might stress the commitment of your full working time and efforts to this project, when you could be content to sit back in a "safe" job in business or industry. You might remind your banker of your willingness to allow the family homestead that has been in your family for three generations to be mortgaged because you are committed strongly to making this deal go (no need to call to mind the shining office building you won't put up).

Collateral is last because it is least. Is that a surprise? It is to most businesspeople. But it shouldn't be. Repossessions and bankruptcies can net the banker 10 cents on the dollar, or less. Your banker has no practical idea of what to do with a factory full of metal parts except to sell them the fastest way possible, often to the scrap dealer. Nor does she care to be put in the position of having to make that how-to-sell decision or any of the other countless decisions. True, the lien can help relieve some of her anxiety, and it might have some *in terrorem* effect on the borrower, but (and mark these words well) it is axiomatic in banking that more collateral does not make a bad loan good. So if your banker starts demanding what you reasonably consider is too much collateral, haul out this information and use it to your benefit. Remember, 99 percent of all loans are repaid from cash flow, not collateral.

THE RISK MATRIX

To see how your banker views your loan package in analyzing risk, consider placing your package within this matrix:

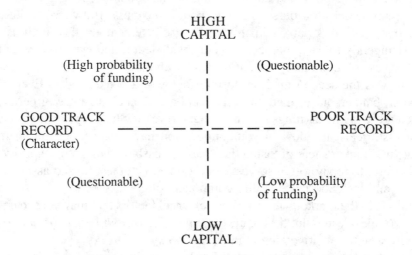

Cash flow, capacity to earn, market conditions, and collateral need to be added as well, making the matrix 6-dimensional. In practice, only 2 or 3 dimensions will be key to any particular deal.

What do the six Cs mean to you, the business buyer? Simply that if you know how your quarry thinks, and what is on your quarry's mind, you can prepare your proposal to take advantage of what you know.

YOUR LOAN APPLICATION PACKAGE/BUSINESS PLAN

After first studying the habitat, and then the quarry, the experienced hunter prechecks the equipment to be taken on the hunt. Chief among the weapons is the hunter's own mental preparedness. For if the quarry is aware you know all about him and his habitat, and if you exhibit the self-confidence that comes from such knowledge, the quarry is likely to actually help you bag the limit.

Your second most important weapon is your loan application package, which consists of modules of information that describe the pluses and minuses of your deal, as well as its salient features. Pulling this information together in the form of modules allows you to present the most telling information to each potential lender, in the best possible order for each one. For instance, the banker will need financial statements and a detailed narrative telling what changes you plan to institute to turn the business around; you might not want to share this same information with the seller.

The loan application package is sometimes called a business plan. Since you are acquiring an established entity, your business plan will contain information different from that in a start-up's business plan, and probably more of it. For instance, you would most likely include:

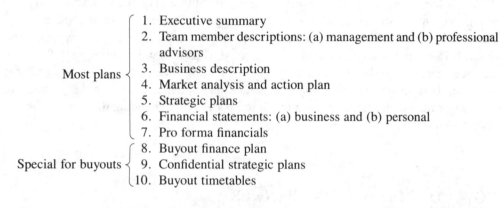

Most plans
1. Executive summary
2. Team member descriptions: (a) management and (b) professional advisors
3. Business description
4. Market analysis and action plan
5. Strategic plans
6. Financial statements: (a) business and (b) personal
7. Pro forma financials

Special for buyouts
8. Buyout finance plan
9. Confidential strategic plans
10. Buyout timetables

The key to obtaining financing is simple: hard work and preparing as completely as possible. There is no such thing as a mini-business plan. Put yourself in your lender's place: You're being asked to cut a check for significant monies and the person who is asking for the dough either won't, can't, or refuses to give you the complete picture you need to make an informed decision. Won't your decision be to take the safer course of action and deny the request?

A note about the personal financial statements you may be asked to give the bank when you apply for the business loan: don't inflate the assets or values. Keep in mind that what you are doing is giving a directory of your assets to the bank's lawyer in case they should have to pursue you on your guarantee. Don't hide anything, either. That could be a ticket to prison.

WHO ARE YOU WRITING THE BUSINESS PLAN FOR?

The question is less stupid than it seems, because it is so easily lost in the rush to prepare a plan to "sell" your loan. You are, after all, writing the business plan for the reader. So why not write it so it is easy for the reader to evaluate (favorably)?

Most professionals reading business plans initially average less than five minutes per plan. They may not study it in detail, but they can certainly get a sufficient grasp of the facts to know whether or not to go further. Also, most business plan readers grew up in the banking industry. Those who grew up in the banking industry grew up professionally around Robert Morris Associates forms. Robert Morris Associates (RMA) is an association that provides financial information and training for commercial lenders. They provide forms for bankers to use. One of the forms they provide is a simplified combination income statement, cash flow and balance sheet all on one page. (See example.)

If your lender is going to take your numbers and put them on the RMA form in order to study them, wouldn't it make sense to make your banker's job easier, and increase the positive information you communicate? Don't forget RMA's *Annual Statement Studies.* Use this book aggressively to project your own future income, cash flow, and balance sheet data to improve your chances of getting financed. In other words, keep your numbers in the middle, where it is nice and warm for your banker, lender, or venture capitalist. Remember, raising capital is the art of reducing the risk factors for your financier.

HOW TO FIND A GOOD BANKER

Joe has done research among venture capitalists and bankers to determine who generates their deals. Contrary to expectations, their deals were not generated by people calling to request money. Their deals did not come to them via the mail. They did not come from advertising or seminars. They came from existing companies in their portfolio. In other words, someone in whom they had already invested gave them a referral. Fully 55 percent of the venture capitalists and bankers Joe surveyed indicated referrals were their main source of deals.

You can turn this information to your advantage in dealing with bankers. You stand a much better chance of doing a quality deal when you are referred to a banker by a good client. Therefore, in seeking a banker, you should work through other entrepreneurs who are in similar, but not competing, businesses. Use their names when you first contact the banker. Bankers have told Joe, hands down, that the single best thing a good customer can do for them is to refer a good depositor.

And the best way to get that referral is to ask for advice in preparing and improving your business plan. Remember, money follows advice. Never go after money; always seek advice. Get the advice and the money will follow.

Sample Robert Morris Associates form.

PROJECTION OF FINANCIAL STATEMENTS

SUBMITTED BY _____

		ACTUAL	PROJECTIONS →										

SPREAD IN HUNDREDS ☐   DATE
SPREAD IN THOUSANDS ☐   PERIOD

PROFIT and LOSS

1	NET SALES												1
2													2
3													3
4	Less: Materials Used												4
5	COST OF GOODS SOLD												5
6	GROSS PROFIT												6
7	Less: Sales Expense												7
8	General & Administrative Expense												8
9	Depreciation												9
10													10
11	OPERATING PROFIT												11
12	Less: Other Expense												12
13	Add: Other Income												13
14	PRE-TAX PROFIT												14
15	Income Tax Provision												15
16	NET PROFIT												16

CASH PROJECTION

17	CASH BALANCE (Opening)												17
18	Add: Receipts: Cash Sales & Other Income												18
19	Cash Sales Plus Receivable Collections												19
20													20
21													21
22	Bank Loan Proceeds												22
23	Other Loan Proceeds												23
24	TOTAL CASH AND RECEIPTS												24
25	Less: Disbursements: Trade Payables												25
26	Direct Labor												26
27	OPERATING & OTHER EXPENSES												27
28													28
29	Capital Expenditures												29
30	Income Taxes												30
31	Dividends or Withdrawals												31
32	Bank Loan Repayment												32
33	Other Loan Repayment												33
34	TOTAL CASH DISBURSEMENTS												34
35	CASH BALANCE (Closing)												35

BALANCE SHEET

36	ASSETS: Cash and Equivalents												36
37	Receivables												37
38	Inventory (Net)												38
39													39
40	CURRENT ASSETS												40
41	Fixed Assets (Net)												41
42													42
43													43
44													44
45	TOTAL ASSETS												45
46	LIABILITIES: Notes Payable-Banks												46
47	Notes Payable-Others												47
48	Trade Payables												48
49	Income Tax Payable												49
50	Current Portion L.T.D.												50
51													51
52	CURRENT LIABILITIES												52
53	Long-Term Liabilities:												53
54													54
55													55
56	TOTAL LIABILITIES												56
57	NET WORTH: Capital Stock												57
58	Retained Earnings												58
59													59
60	TOTAL LIABILITIES AND NET WORTH												60

© 1984 Robert Morris Associates - Form C 117 Rev 8 84
ORDER FROM Bankers Systems, Inc. St. Cloud, MN 56302

These forms are intended for use in commercial lending transactions. Where any other use is contemplated, it is suggested that a careful review be made to ensure compliance with applicable laws and regulations.

Sample form (*continued*)

HOW TO USE THIS FORM

RMA's Projection of Financial Statements, Form C-117, may be completed by the banker, the customer, or both working together. It is designed to be flexible and may be used as a:

1) <u>Projection</u> tool to provide a picture of the customer's present and future financial condition. **Actual** and **estimated** financial data form the basis of the calculations.

2) <u>Tool for analysis</u> of the customer's borrowing needs and debt repayment ability.

3) <u>Budget</u> to aid in planning for the customer's financial requirements and repaying the banker's credit accommodation.

INSTRUCTIONS: In the first column, enter the actual PROFIT AND LOSS STATEMENT and BALANCE SHEET of the date immediately prior to projection period. Then, in each subsequent column, covering a projection period (e.g., month, quarter, annual):

- Enter on the "date" line, the ending date of each projection period (e.g., 1/31, 3/31, 19_____).
- Enter on the "period" line the length of each projection period (e.g., 1 mo., 3 mos., 12 mos.)
- Then, follow the line-by-line instructions below:

Line No.	Title	Instructions
PROFIT AND LOSS STATEMENT		
1	NET SALES	Enter actual or beginning net sales figure in the first vertical column. We suggest you project future net sales based upon a % sales increase or decrease. Estimate acceptable % figure and record here _____%. (This % is generally calculated based on historical changes in net sales. However, consideration must also be given to factors, such as general business conditions, new products and services, and competition.)
2 through 5	COST OF GOODS SOLD	Enter all relevant components of customer's cost of goods sold calculation. Project future cost of goods sold based upon % increase or decrease. Estimate acceptable percentage figure and insert here _____%. (This figure is generally estimated as a percentage of sales based on prior years.)
6	GROSS PROFIT	Line 1 minus line 5.
7 through 10	Sales Expense; General and Administrative Expenses; Other	Enter all items. Project future expenses based on an increase or decrease. Estimate acceptable percentage figure and insert here _____%. (This figure is generally estimated as a percentage of sales based on prior years. Anticipated increases in major expenses, such as lease, officers' salaries, etc., should also be considered.)
11	OPERATING PROFIT	Line 6 minus the sum of lines 7 through 10.
12 through 13	Various adjustments to Operating Profit	Enter all items and estimate future adjustments.
14	PRE-TAX PROFIT	Line 11 minus the sum of lines 12 through 13.
15	Income Tax Provision	Common methods used for calculating Income Tax Provision include the most current year's tax as a % of the Pre-Tax Profit.
16	NET PROFIT	Line 11 minus the sum of lines 12 through 15.
CASH PROJECTION CALCULATION		
17	CASH BALANCE	Enter opening cash balance. For subsequent periods, enter the closing cash balance (Line 35) from previous period. Or enter an adjusted amount to reflect a <u>desired</u> cash balance.
18 through 21	Receipts	Enter total cash sales & other income plus receivables collected. Receivable collections must be calculated separately. This requires an analysis of the customer's sales and collection patterns:

(1) Estimate the portion of each month's sales collected in that month and subsequent months.

(2) From the sale's figure last month and the previous month(s), calculate how much of the existing receivable figure will be collected in the current month.

(3) Deduct the collected receivables balance calculated in (2) above from the month-end balance of accounts receivables.

(4) Add this month's sales figure to the remainder of receivables calculated in (3) above. This figure is the new accounts receivable figure for the end of the current month.

EXAMPLE   Assumptions:
Projection calculation - monthly

Monthly Net Sales:	9/30 - $250M
	10/31 - $300M
	11/30 - $150M
Accounts Receivable balance:	9/30 - $250M
	10/31 - $367M

The average collection period is 45 days. This means that 66.7% (30 days ÷ 45 days) of each month's sales will be collected the following month and the remaining 33.3% in the second month.

To determine receivable collections for November --

Accounts Receivable balance, 10/31		$367M
Deduct: 66% of 10/31 sales	200M	
33% of 9/30 sales	83M	283M
		84M
Add: 11/30 sales		150M
Accounts Receivable Balance, 11/30		$234M

Line No.	Title	Instructions
22 through 23	Bank Loan Proceeds/Other	Enter actual or projected bank loan proceeds on line 22. Enter any other receipts on line 23.
24	TOTAL CASH AND RECEIPTS	Enter sum of lines 17 through 23.
25 through 33	Disbursements	Enter actual or estimated cash disbursements on these lines.
34	TOTAL DISBURSEMENTS	Enter sum of lines 25 through 33.
35	CASH BALANCE (Closing)	Line 24 minus line 34. Note: The closing cash balance on line 35 may be entered on line 17 in the next column. However, if the closing cash balance is negative, or below the desired opening cash balance, then bank loans (line 22) may be needed to raise the closing cash balance to zero, or to the desired opening cash balance. The bank loan necessitates planning for repayment (line 31 and 32) in subsequent columns.

Sample form (*continued*)

BALANCE SHEET

(36 through 44)	ASSETS	
36	Cash and Equivalents	Enter cash and readily marketable securities--current year only. For subsequent years use the closing cash balance (line 35).
37	Receivables	Enter actual receivables in the first column. To project, use previous receivables figure plus projected net sales (line 1), minus projected cash sales and receivables collections (line 19).
38	Inventory	Enter actual inventory in the first column. To project, add purchases to beginning inventory. Then, subtract materials used to calculate the ending inventory amount (lines 2 through 4). If the inventory purchase figure is not available, balances can be calculated based on historic turnover ratios.
40	Current Assets	Enter sum of lines 36 through 39.
41	Fixed Assets (Net)	Enter fixed assets. To project, add previous year's fixed assets and any fixed asset additions. Then, deduct estimated accumulated depreciation.
42 through 44		Enter other non-current assets (stockholder's receivables, intangibles, etc.).
45	TOTAL ASSETS	Add lines 40 through 44.
(46 through 56)	LIABILITIES	
46	Notes Payable-Banks	Prior period balance plus loan proceeds (line 22), less repayments (line 32).
47	Notes Payable-Others	Prior period balance plus note proceeds (line 23), less repayments (line 32).
48	Trade Payables	Prior period balance plus purchases less payments (line 25). If the inventory purchase figure is not available, balances can be projected based on historic payables turnover.
49	Income Tax Payable	Add prior period balance to income tax provision (line 14) and deduct income taxes paid (line 30).
50	Current Portion Long-Term Debt	Estimate current maturities by entering the sum of prior period debt's maturities and additional bank loan proceeds scheduled repayments.
51		Enter the sum of any other current liabilities.
52	CURRENT LIABILITIES	Enter the sum of lines 46 through 51.
53 through 55	Long-Term Liabilities	Enter long-term liabilities here. Calculate long-term debt by adding previous period long-term debt (line 53) to loan proceeds (line 22 & 23), and subtracting current maturities (line 50).
56	TOTAL LIABILITIES	Enter sum of lines 52 through 55.
(57 through 59)	NET WORTH	
57	Capital Stock	Enter current capital stock figure. An increase will occur if capital stock is sold; a decrease will occur if existing stock is repurchased or retired.
58	Retained Earnings	Add prior period retained earnings to projected net profit (line 16), and deduct dividends or withdrawals (line 31).
59		Enter other equity items.
60	TOTAL LIABILITIES AND NET WORTH	Enter sum of lines 56 through 59.

ANTICIPATING NEGATIVES

The biggest problem most would-be buyers encounter is that they have not reduced the lender's risk sufficiently. If a banker thinks the risks are too high, he will not do the deal. Therefore, your number one priority if you are to finance your deal is to reduce and eliminate the negatives as much as possible. It is the third weapon in your arsenal of preparation.

Here's a technique we have found works well to reduce risks: Gather together a handful of people who don't like you or your business idea. Find out precisely what they do not like about your new business. Get them each to give you their strongest objection. You're not after things like "The color of the product isn't right," or "The business name is goofy." Get the substantial objections, such as "The whole marketplace is changing and there will soon be no demand for your product." As soon as you've determined these objections, condense them to one or two sentences each. Make them concise and hard-hitting. Read each objection into a tape recorder.

Replay the objections several times until you begin to find both emotional and logical answers to them. Sometimes you will find solutions to hidden problems, and sometimes you'll concoct arguments to show why the perceived problem is really an opportunity. For each of the objections, come up with as many plausible answers as you can. Don't stop with one or two. Refine and rework your emotional answers and reduce them to the top two for each objection. Try the answers out on your don't-likers for their reactions. Listen—really listen—to their responses.

Then, when it comes time to answer the banker's objections, you will have considered the very worst, and come up with the very best solutions and answers. In short, you will have reduced the risk to your finance source, and increased immeasurably your chances of a successful financing. Put these objections and answers into a section of your business plan called "Risks." If you set out objections your banker has not yet considered, along with clear, concise, and cogent solutions and answers, you show yourself to be an above-average business person (and credit risk).

THE ANSWER SHEET

Remember the student from your school days who didn't show up in class all semester but who waltzed in for the final exam, and walked away with a better grade than you? What was his secret? He understood the concept of the answer sheet. This sheet might have been compiled by his fraternity or by friends who had taken the course the year before, and therefore he knew all the answers. Whether such an answer sheet actually existed, and whether these star performers ever really studied at all, is a question for the ages.

But what if we had a shortcut when it came to business plans? There are indeed shortcuts that will help your presentation. They just aren't the answer to the whole course. They will not construct your entire business plan for you if you just copy them into your documents. But they might just get your plan read in the first place. And if it's read, it's a lot closer to success than those that got summarily thrown in the round file.

1. "It's just like. . . ." If you are dealing with a venture capitalist or banker who missed the chance to invest in some highly profitable deal, an offhand remark like "It's just like Big Hitter Corporation" could get you an interested audience. Steven Job's new venture, which he called "Next," is merely a subtle way of saying "It's just like Apple Computer." How would you like to have backed Apple Computer?

2. "The other guys have deep pockets." In essence, if you can show other investors that investor 1 has deep pockets or special investing know-how, chances are they, too, will commit. If you knew H. Ross Perot or General Motors had put money in an investment you were considering, wouldn't you be inclined to give it a second look? Big guys by their very presence will encourage the smaller investors to jump on the bandwagon. Even when they don't invest, but are merely on the board of advisors, it helps.

3. "If it goes bad. . . ." You need a plan for what happens if the deal goes bad. Sale of assets, sale of patent rights, or foreign manufacturing rights, licensing, franchising, and selling off of profitable lines or similar ideas should be considered and suggested in your business plan. Obviously, you don't want to dwell too much on this factor or your potential investor may get the idea that you don't think the business will succeed. Joe often jokes that certain bankers in a rural area preferred to lend aggressively to liquor stores. When Joe pressed them for why they were being so aggressive with so mundane a business, one of them said, "If it goes bad, my bank could at least consume the inventory and pay off my position."

4. The question of past business failures. Most people who have grown significant companies have, at some stage in their history, experienced some failure. If you have just come off a failure, how do you handle it in your business plan? It seems to be a sticky issue. You might be tempted to just ignore it. As the old saying goes, "Success has many fathers, but failure is an orphan." The danger in ignoring it is that if it is discovered, the situation will be worse.

The better way is to turn that failure around and make it a plus. Full disclosure instills confidence, so it's actually a risk reducer. There's nothing more frustrating for an investor than to have gone through 95 percent of your analysis of a business opportunity, only to discover that there was an earlier company and an earlier problem that was never disclosed. We strongly suggest you bring it up early. Did you know that Henry Ford, before the success of the Ford Motor Company, experienced bankruptcy twice? Walt Disney had a similar experience. And Milton Hershey, before he founded the Hershey Chocolate Company, went bust. In fact, a taste of failure seems to be a prerequisite to a big success for many entrepreneurs. Henry Ford said, "Failure is a resting place on your destiny to success. Failure is a camouflaged view of success as viewed by a blind person."

SHOPPING A LOAN

Should you submit applications simultaneously to multiple banks? The arguments run both ways. Some people say the banks don't work as hard to make a loan if they know somebody else is involved. Others say the competition gets you a better deal. Competition has heated up among banks in the last few years. Banks are hungry for new business, particularly from small companies. We suggest today it's advantageous to deal with multiple banks, as a rule of thumb.

Much depends on the individual bankers involved. If the individuals are "institutional" people of the "old school," used to dealing in a standard framework day in and day out, the idea of competition might slow them down or even turn them off to your deal. This person is probably not the kind of banker you want, anyway. Luckily, he is a dying breed. Most bankers today expect that you, as a good businessperson, will shop the loan. One banker Doug interviewed said customers should shop the loan! You will ordinarily want somebody who is inventive. Check out the loan officer with other business borrowers and watch closely for clues. Look for signs of inaction or over-reliance on old formulae or bureaucratic committees. Always ask both "Will you support it?" and "Will you push for it?"

Don't hide from the bankers the fact that you are shopping the deal. They will find out anyway, since they will all be calling the same credit agencies for information about you. Tell them up front: They will appreciate your honesty.

MANCUSO'S SEVEN-WORD PHRASE TO CLOSE
ANY FINANCIAL NEGOTIATION

"You get all your money back first." This phrase will act as a litmus test to let you know whether the deal is closable. If not, it gives you the freedom to get up from the table and go seek your money elsewhere.

Let's illustrate the principle involved by this example: Inez Investor bought a twenty-acre parcel of land in the north woods three years ago for $100,000. Today, she has an opportunity to sell part of the parcel. She wants to divide it into two pieces of equal value. She wants to keep part of it, but is willing to sell half. So she puts the eastern ten acres up for sale. Here comes the test: What price does Inez Investor want for this ten-acre parcel? If you have been following along, you have probably guessed the answer. The answer is not based on mathematics but on human nature. Human nature dictates that Inez Investor will want $100,000 for this parcel of land. Why? Because she wants to get her original investment back at the earliest time.

Everybody is willing to gamble with winnings, but investors are anxious to get back their principal intact. This holds true as well for an outside investor, for the seller, and certainly for the banker. Your finance source is willing to gamble with the increase in value, but wants to get his original investment back safely as soon as possible.

Therefore, your job as a person seeking investors is to reduce the risk to the investor by getting his principal back as quickly as possible. It's one thing to lose your money. It's quite a different matter to lose your principal.

If you have arranged to get the investor's funds back, with as little risk for as short a time as possible, you have increased your chances of doing the deal. If, after plausibly explaining why the investor gets his money back first, he still waffles or does not want to proceed, you can safely get up and walk away from the table: That person will likely never do the deal. The litmus test saves time because a short "no" is better than a long "no," and maybe even a long "yes."

GETTING THE BANK'S ANALYSIS

Be sure to get a copy of the account analysis the present banker keeps on your target's account. Because banks are being pressured from all different directions, they are becoming more and more profit conscious. Everything they do must return a profit. That's why you rarely see "free" checking accounts and there are fewer "free" savings accounts. You can't even get a verbal report of your checking account balance without paying a fee for it at some banks!

So you shouldn't be surprised to learn your bank rates you as a customer on whether or not you are a profitable customer. The account analysis says this customer has deposits with us, has a line of credit, has compensating balances, sends us VISA and Mastercard business, has us handle his payroll, has the trust department handle his pension plan, and so forth. In other words, the account analysis shows that your target is making money for the bank, that it's a good customer of the bank. This analysis can help you find strengths and weaknesses of the account (from the bank's point of view) so you can leverage the "good" and correct the "bad" in your proposal. The analysis can be helpful if you later run into trouble, because you can point to your account analysis and say, "Look right here, in 1985 our business made $23,000 for your bank, and in 1989 it made $47,000. Our business has been a good and profitable customer for a long time. We're not the kind of customer you want to toss away." The same arguments hold when you go to a competitive bank.

Also, you should ask for copies of the bank's spreadsheet analyses of your target. The spreadsheets are the bank's translation into its standard format of the accounting figures your target has sent the bank over the years. The spreadsheets (or green sheets) will typically include balance sheet and income statement data. The spreadsheets might show ten years' worth of information on your target. They are prepared by the bank so that when a new banker takes over your account, the information is in a format he understands.

How do you get these documents? Basically by being persistent, yet nice. If you are told it's bank policy not to show these statements, ask who made the policy. Ask if there is somebody who can authorize you to see them. Ask if you should call that person, or if your loan officer prefers to ask on your behalf. You might also argue that seeing the spreadsheets will help you verify facts and figures given by your target's management. Call back periodically to ask how much progress is being made, until you do get at least a glance at the account analysis and spreadsheets. Always leave the banker an opportunity to save face so he doesn't feel trapped by your pressure.

What are you going to see on these spreadsheets? Much of the information is just a reformatting of numbers you've already seen. But you may see a number over here that's circled, one over there that's got a star next to it, and one in the middle that's been erased. Also you'll see the ratios banks love to track on your target. You're going to get your loan (and get off personal loan guarantees) by being the best customer the bank ever had, which means being the best-informed customer the bank ever had.

GOING FOR "THE KILL"

In the first five minutes of your negotiations with a banker, answer these questions:

1. How much money do you need?
2. What for?
3. For how long?
4. How will it be repaid?
5. If that plan doesn't work out, what is your backup plan for repayment?
6. What will you do if you don't get the loan?

You might consider scripting out your first loan-proposal meeting with your banker. Given adequate time (is there ever?) you might do a dry run with the outside members of your team. We suggest you can't prepare enough. Remember, practice doesn't make perfect. Perfect practice makes perfect.

Don't trust anything to the banker's memory. How much of that seminar you attended last month do you remember? Researchers say the correct answer is 2 percent. If it's not in writing, it doesn't exist. Be safe. Put all crucial facts in writing. Especially the obvious. What's obvious to you probably isn't to your banker. If you don't have it in writing, you just plain don't have it.

Be physically rested and mentally alert for your conference. Appear relaxed and in control even if you don't feel it. First impressions are lasting impressions. Ask lots of questions; the person asking the questions has the greater power. It's an old rule of negotiations. Ask for feedback to make sure you're understood. Check out the banker's understanding; then put it in writing to be sure.

THE TURN-DOWN

Don't take "no" for an answer. "No" may not be an absolute "no" to the deal, only a "no" to the structure. "No" might be a reflection of the individual bank's policies or financial condition at the moment. There might be a mismatch between one of your team members and the banker. Or it might just be a stall: "Nos" are reversible. Bankers sometimes say "no" before they give you the real answer.

With so many possibilities it pays to clarify all problem areas. If it is a turn-down, the banker is at his weakest. The expectation is you'll tuck your tail between your legs and leave. Asking questions in sequence is a surprise. The banker has his guard down; the deal is off, so now the banker can relax and just be friends with you. Finally, the banker might feel a bit guilty about getting your hopes up and then having to turn you down. You don't want to be pushy (you may be back here a few months from now). Just find out what you can to help you take the next few steps. Here's a checklist you may want to use:

1. "So then you're turning us down?" You may have read the signals wrong. Verify.
2. "What was the main reason for the turn-down?" Hopefully there's a misunderstanding you can clear up now. If not, strengthen your approach to the next banker, and shore up your negatives.
3. "Is there any other reason in the back of your mind why this would not make a good loan for you?" This back-of-the-mind question is to get at the real reason behind the logical one. Practice keeping your mouth shut and listening. Say "um-hmmm" and listen some more. Repeat the banker's last three or four words and put a question mark

at the end: "Not enough cash flow?" "The product is weak?" The lengthy silence is your ally—don't break it. He who speaks first loses.

4. "What would you suggest I do next?" Learn how to strengthen your case from the bank insider across the desk from you.

5. "Is there another finance source you think might be interested?" If it's a matter of a bad fit with this particular institution, this banker will likely know where you can find a better fit (long- versus short-term, asset versus cash flow lender).

6. "Why them?" Learn what your strengths are relative to the new bank. What do you have that fits this source particularly well?

7. "Who should I ask for?" If the other bank is a good fit, there will be a banker within it who can make the shoe supple. Because of the musical chairs constantly played in banking, this banker probably knows the better ones at the other bank. Always pick a banker, not a bank.

8. "Why him?"

9. "What factors of my deal should I stress to him?" Get clues to how you can mold your deal to fit the new bank's program.

10. "What shall I tell him about why you turned us down?" Banks have policy changes often. Suggest that as a nondamning answer to the first question on the new banker's mind.

11. "I'll probably authorize him to talk to you. What will you say?" Will it be hot, cold, or lukewarm? Get your banker committed to a response now—before he has a chance to cool further to your proposition. Once committed, the response is not likely to cool a whole lot by the time the new banker makes his call.

You'll get surprisingly helpful information by sticking to this checklist, even though you will feel like getting out fast. In addition to the questions, ask for and get (1) the spreadsheet on the loan application and (2) the profitability analysis of this account for this bank. This information will help you prepare your next loan proposal, and may show a glaring error that will get you back in the door of this bank.

PRICING: THE SECOND DECISION THE BANKER MAKES

Not every loan a bank makes is at the same rate: Car loans have one rate, mortgages another, unsecured personal loans a third. The differences often come down to relative degrees of risk and length of loan terms.

But even commercial loans of the same class, term, and size carry different rates. Why does your neighboring shop pay prime plus 1.5 percent while yours pays prime plus 2.5 percent? It may indeed be your neighbor is a more able negotiator. But it all starts with the question we all ask ourselves for any business deal: Will it be a profitable deal?

Say you're working up a quote in your job shop. What goes into your computations? First, you check your labor and overhead ratio, your material costs: What will the job cost? Then, if you're really pushed to give a low quote, you compute any savings you think you'll have because of economies of scale. You may even factor in future profitable business you can get by landing the account.

Guess what? The banker does the same. She even works through an estimating sheet for loan pricing. Consider the following worksheet:

LOAN PRICING WORKSHEET

INCOME		
Requested loan	$	
Interest rate	_____ %	
Annual interest earnings		$ _____
Other loans outstanding, average balance	$ _____	
Average interest rate	_____ %	
Annual interest on O/S loans		
Annual fees & service charges earned		_____
Average collected demand deposits net of 12% reserve	$ _____	
Average collected time deposits net of 3% reserve	$ _____	
Total	$ _____	
Return available on funds	_____ %	
Earnings on deposits		_____
Total Income		**$ _____**

EXPENSES	
Cost of loan funds	$ _____
Interest on these accounts	_____
Costs of providing services	_____
Taxes at assumed _____ %	_____
Other expenses	_____
Total Expenses	**$ _____**

YIELD	
Net Income (Income − Expenses)	$ _____
Gross yield (Net Income ÷ Total Loans)	_____ %
Target yield	_____ %
Over (Under)	_____ %

Now if your banker goes through a computation like the one above for every loan (some banks aren't this sophisticated yet), why do the rates come out as 12.95 percent or 10.5 percent, or 2 percent over prime? Is it possible that there is a fudge factor or cushion thrown in? Is it possible that if you point out other areas of profitability (such as other deposits you bring with you or control or even influence) you can actually improve on the quoted interest rate? And if you know how the computation is done, aren't you in a better position to negotiate interest rates than the horsetrader who blindly offers to "split the difference"?

In the Loan Pricing Worksheet, the return available on funds is often a conservative number. The concept is to say, "If we don't have any loans we can always stash this cash over here and at least earn X percent." Your banker may be required by bank policy to use a certain number like the Federal Funds Rate (rate charged to bankers by other bankers for overnight loans) or the London Interbank Offered Rate (LIBOR—the rate offered for dollars deposited in five London banks).

The cost of funds is also usually set by bank policy. Typically, this will be a certificate of deposit (CD) rate currently paid by the bank. And the target yield (sometimes called the hurdle rate) often is based on assumptions as to overhead, risk factors, and a profit. A high risk/low risk can add/deduct from the interest rate. A fairly high target yield to use for planning or negotiating might be 1.65 percent. Although that sounds low, a typical bank invests only 8 percent of its capital in any one loan, the rest coming from deposits. A modest rate of return on capital of 14 percent, multiplied by the original 8 percent capital, results in a target of only 1.12 percent.

There is plenty of room for banker judgment and therefore for good sales work on your part. Even if policy dictates a special number to be used here and there, you can highlight how your special case warrants another line entry around the corner. Just don't get so hung up on negotiating loan rates that you lose sight of the goal—to acquire your target. Take the long view: A little higher rate now gets you into the business that makes it possible, in a few years, to buy out the bank making to-day's loan!

STAYING OFF PERSONAL LOAN GUARANTEES

Upon the foundation of a good relationship with your banker you will build the structure that can keep you and your spouse off the personal loan guarantee. Getting off personal loan guarantees is not the object: It is the result and the reward of being the best customer the bank ever had. Here are the steps to follow:

1. Decide how much it is worth to you to get off the personal loan guarantee. This is key. How much in dollars? How much in terms of interest rate? Would you take a smaller loan if it were sans personal guarantees? Would you be willing to put up a larger compensating balance to get the loan? Would you be willing to go with a shorter maturity? If you don't know what it's worth to you, you get emotionally wrapped up in the issue and lose your perspective. The personal loan guarantee may not be worth all that much to you after you really consider it. If it comes down to getting off the guarantee or not getting the money, which would you do? It may be that getting off the guarantee is not that important to you. (You can bet it's initially very important to your banker.) But you'd better not change your mind later.

2. The best way to get off the personal loan guarantee is to ask. Start with, "Does everybody who borrows here sign a guarantee?" Suppose you get a "yes"? Then your response is "Aww c'mon. Not all the big companies sign guarantees, do they?" First establish that not everybody signs a personal guarantee and then determine what the criteria are by which the bank draws the line between signers and nonsigners. What do they have that you don't have? Keep asking!

3. Practice your answers to their questions. The bankers practice questions they're going to ask you, and they anticipate you will reel when they hit you with them. You must be ready. They'll ask, "Why don't you want to personally guarantee the loan—don't you plan to pay it back?" That question would blow most borrowers away. Being prepared, you will not get blown away.

One answer (when you invent your own, don't forget that your job is to reduce the risk factor for the banker—beware of the flippant answer) is to say "Yes, of course, I intend to repay it. But you know business and life isn't always as simple as we both would like it to be. It isn't strictly a game of dollars and numbers. The other day, in fact, my wife raised this very issue. You know we've struggled for years to build up what we have now: a successful business of our own, a nice home. And my wife said 'For once in my life I would like to live in a house that does not have a mortgage.' Of course, I tried to explain to her the dollars and cents of the situation. But that doesn't really hold any water against the lifelong desire she has to be free of this liability. And if she's nervous about it, that's going to make me nervous about it. If I lose sleep over this personal guarantee the business could suffer. Now neither one of us wants that. Can you identify with how my wife feels?"

Your basic approach is that life is not just a matter of cold hard facts: The issue of the personal guarantee is an emotional one. And a strong one. One that you will not give up easily.

4. Timing is important. If your alma mater called you on Friday and asked you to come over on Monday morning to spend the day making telephone calls to raise money, chances are that you'd say "no." But what if you were called six months ahead?

You would probably at least consider the request. What you are willing to do is sometimes a function of how far in the future you commit. The same is true of your personal loan guarantees. It's easier to get the banker to agree to take off the guarantee at a time in the distant future than it is to get him to do it at 7:30 tomorrow morning. Start off by asking, "If this loan were 95 percent paid off, and I was always on time and paid up-to-date, would you take me off the guarantee? Could my wife get off at 50 percent repaid and I get off at 70 percent?" It's a starting point. It is worth repeating: The way to get off a loan guarantee is to ask.

5. What if you have no track record? Does that doom you to a personal guarantee forever? Remember, you're better off than the person who has a poor track record. If you can win your banker's vision, and get him to believe in your dream, you have a better chance of avoiding guarantees than the person with an average track record. The problem is that many times your sales effort falls short and the banker does not believe in your dream.

A wonderful story is better than a good loan request. Did you ever see anybody get excited by a loan request? Remember the infant monitoring device? Isn't there just a little bit of human warmth in that company's products? Isn't it the responsibility of the entrepreneur to point out this human warmth to the banker? Won't the entrepreneur have a better chance of getting the loan if she points out the human factor. Don't just say "We'd like to borrow money to produce an electronic oscilloscope." Say "Our company needs these funds to save babies!"

6. The next technique is to chip away at the personal guarantee. A few legal distinctions are important here. Is the banker asking you to guarantee collection or performance? Under a collection guarantee, the bank has to pursue the corporation first and come up dry before it can sue you personally. Under the performance guarantee, the bank can go against both you and the corporation at the same time. Obviously, the bank wants the second. This point can be negotiated, if you are aware of it.

The second distinction regards joint and several liability. If there are several people on the team being asked to guarantee the bank debt, say four of you, does the bank expect each of you to guarantee 100 percent or 25 percent? Here the bank is most apt to give you some leeway. But only if you ask. The bank may not go all the way down to 25 percent, but it might be willing to go to 60 percent or 40 percent.

7. Get the milestones for when you'll come off the guarantee in writing. If you can't get the bank to put it in writing, then have your lawyer write the letter and get the banker to initial it and send it back to you. Make it clear ahead of time that without the milestones in writing you will not sign the guarantee. Then you've got a stronger chance of getting your document signed, if for some reason the bank's is not ready at closing.

8. Make it clear the guarantee is not being signed lightly.

KEEPING YOUR SPOUSE OFF THE GUARANTEE

We suggest you tell the banker, "I understand about your bank policy requiring the spouse to sign a personal guarantee. It's just that Mary doesn't understand your bank policy. And it's a big deal to her. So if you don't mind, I'd like to have you talk with her personally about this sticky issue, one on one, so that you can explain your positions to each other."

Your spouse will do a better job than you of presenting her case. Did the bank ask Lee Iacocca's wife to personally sign for Chrysler's debt when Chrysler was having troubles? The likelihood of Iacocca turning Chrysler around was less than the likelihood of you keeping your target company profitable for the next few years. The banker will tell you it's apples and oranges, but just what is the purpose of the guarantee? To show your commitment? Well, what is 60 hours per week, if not commitment?

This technique puts a great deal of pressure on the banker who is not comfortable trying to argue a logical point with someone who may be approaching the issue emotionally, who is not necessarily concerned about the details of the loan. It's your best shot.

LOAN TERMS TO EXPECT—AND SOME TO REJECT!

If you are doing a major deal, you should expect more in the way of loan paperwork than a simple note and a mortgage or security agreement. In some deals, the loan documentation may be thicker than that for the deal itself! Here is a quick rundown of what you can expect:

Positive Covenants—Things You Must Do

1. Furnish financial statements to the banker periodically.
2. Keep assets in good repair and adequately insured.
3. Maintain certain balance sheet and income statement ratios.
4. Notify the banker of any change in management.
5. Notify the banker of probable or pending legal actions, particularly those against the company.
6. Advise the banker of any change or circumstance that might negatively affect the financial condition of the company.
7. Use the loan proceeds only for the purposes stated in the loan application.

Negative Covenants—Things You Are Prohibited from Doing

1. The company will not dispose of or lease its assets, other than in the normal course of business.
2. The company will not repay loans from shareholders, or pay dividends or purchase or redeem any of its stock.
3. The borrower may not obtain loans from other institutional lenders.
4. The company will not make capital expenditures over a certain dollar amount.
5. Compensation to officers will not be increased. However, make sure that you have the ability to make increases to nonshareholders for any reason, and to shareholders to keep up with cost-of-living increases.
6. The company may not consolidate or merge with any other business.

Warranties—Things to Be True on the Loan Date

1. All financial statements are true and correct.
2. You have good title to the assets.
3. You are up-to-date with your taxes.
4. You have complied with all laws and regulations and you are not currently involved in any lawsuits.

Other Agreements

1. You may be required to carry certain life insurance on key employees and owners.
2. You may be required to sell off certain assets within a given period of time, or divest yourself of certain business lines.

Some Terms to Fight

1. Commercial bankers used to want to have you out of the bank once a year. That is, they wanted you to pay off your loan completely right after the "Christmas rush," to prove to the examiners that your 90-day renewing notes were not a disguised long-term loan. Even today, they are only comfortable with risks under about eight years. They don't like to make longer-term loans. The length of the loan is actually a way bankers can ration money. The tighter the money, the shorter the terms of loans tend to

be. Money was not truly tight during most of the 1980s. Bankers like to lend you money for seasonal needs.

If the banker suggests the best he can do is a seven-year loan, don't be afraid to turn it around and suggest it be amortized over fifteen years with a balloon at the end of seven years. That way you get the benefit of the lower cash payment, and after seven years of good loan history, the bank might be very interested in continuing the arrangement. Besides, inflation and other appreciation in value may have increased their security. In addition, seven years may be a good time to start looking at increasing the loan.

2. Some "standard" form clauses allow the bank to foreclose or otherwise lower the boom on your company with five days advance notice. Have you ever seen a letter take more than five days to go from point A to point B? Probably so. Or you might run into a clause that gives you one week to cure a default, after notice has been mailed. For all of these clauses, shoot for fifteen business days. It might take that long to get things straightened out, if there is a snag; or require all notices be sent by overnight carrier.

3. Default provisions not allowing for minor discrepancies should be avoided. Instead, hold out for the word *material* to modify all causes of default. Otherwise, a clause preventing you from leasing capital equipment prevents you from renting a tiny photocopier.

4. A requirement of a certified audit is expensive, and often a review will provide the bank with the information it requires (see Chapter Five for a complete discussion of the differences between these accountants' reports). The larger companies will be having certified audits annually anyway, so there is not much problem, but if the company's books are normally only "reviewed" (see Chapter Five), the expense could be a burden. This issue you may fight strenuously, but give up later to get something else more valuable. Then you can just chalk up the audit fees as additional interest.

5. Unclear or hard-to-define, calculate, or monitor terms should be challenged. The classic example is the clause that allows the bank to foreclose when it "deems itself insecure." If you don't know what a particular term means, or how to calculate the ratio required, get it fixed before you sign.

6. Try for a thirty-day exception to ratio or working capital requirements that don't take account of seasonality.

7. Inequitable provisions should be questioned. For instance, bank mistakes against you that you fail to call to the bank's attention within thirty days are forfeited, whereas bank mistakes in your favor can be corrected by the bank at any time. Another common example is attorney fee clauses against you if you breach the agreement, but no similar clause against the bank if it breaches its side. The attorney

fee clause is easy to get fixed, because the bank doesn't think it will ever give you cause to sue it.

ULTIMATELY, FINANCING IS YOUR RESPONSIBILITY

Make sure you seek enough financing to cover both working capital and acquisition needs. Doing so shows the banker you have thought things through, and also prevents the problem of pleading for more funds in a few months.

You are the one who must come up with solutions and ideas for your cash need. You cannot abdicate this responsibility to your banker, no matter how creative he is. Bankers are trained to study the figures you give them and see if your proposal fits their mold. After years of climbing up the ranks and being trained in the bank's way of doing things, few are able to switch mental gears and try to find innovative ways to make loans.

Many banks today are trying to break out of this trap, but with varying degrees of success. With the recent spate of lender liability suits for wrongful loan terminations and turn-downs, most of those who were willing to be innovative are drawing in their horns. So you be the innovative one. (For more ideas on raising capital, you might want to consult *How to Get a Business Loan* (*Without Signing Your Life Away*), by Joseph R. Mancuso, Prentice Hall Press, New York, 1990.)

10

Nonbank Money Sources

Few things are impossible to diligence and skill.
—SAMUEL JOHNSON, *RASSELAS*

Imagination is more important than knowledge.
—ALBERT EINSTEIN, *ON SCIENCE*

IT DOES NOT take $1 million cash to buy a $1 million business. Nor does it take $100,000 cash to buy a $100,000 business. Is the idea of buying a business with little cash down unrealistic? We have all read about the no-cash-down techniques in real estate. There are many real estate books, and even more seminars in this genre. The fact of the matter is statistically very few real estate deals get closed with no cash down. The reason? In most cases too many rules have to be bent or broken to make it happen.

Is the same thing true with businesses? No one computes these statistics so it's hard to say for sure. One recent source says about 80 percent of all business purchase deals are done with substantial seller financing, and more than half are done with little or no buyer cash. Of those deals we've worked on that closed, fully 75 percent have been done with little or no buyer cash. But don't be misled by statistics as it still depends on how well you can bring it all together.

We have personally been involved in dozens of business deals involving creative buyout financing. These experiences convince us there are literally hundreds of ways to finance a business. If you mix together the right ingredients, you can buy just about any good business with little or no cash out-of-pocket at the closing.

125

DISCOVERING YOUR BEST NONBANK SOURCES OF CASH

The key ingredients to buying with little or no cash, in fact the key ingredients for business success, are hard work and imagination. Anybody can make an offer on a business. Anybody can start a business. The difference between the successes and the failures is often only a nose.

The winning recipe is to put a pinch of yourself into your financing stew. For instance, if you picked up on the seller's keenly felt love for his business, you might find that allowing the seller to continue working and contributing would be the keystone of your deal. So propose a plan that gradually eases the seller out, relieving his very real pain of selling out. You might put it to the seller in the form of a "requirement" to actively consult with you. Your perceptiveness and subtle "selling" increases the chances of getting your offer accepted.

But don't get too detailed in your offer. There are seldom good reasons for complicated or overly sophisticated terms. Simplicity sells. Complications turn people off, even the sophisticated seller. Stick to basics: You have a better chance of making the deal work.

Hard work and imagination have always been the key financing sources. Our minds resist both. You'll be more productive if you approach the problem of financing from two different perspectives. The first is analytic, linear, left-brained, and the second is multidimensional and right-brained.

First, approach the situation logically. Define the need in dollars and cents. Write down a closing date (a time by which you need the money), even a temporary one. Then ask yourself the following questions:

1. Who would benefit from your purchase and improvement of the target business? Who stands to lose if the deal doesn't go through?
2. Where could you move the business? Would the municipality like to get/keep the business?
3. How can you change the business to make it more attractive to people with cash (customers, landlords, suppliers, other entrepreneurs, etc.)?
4. Does when you close affect the amount of cash you'll need at closing?
5. Why does the seller want to sell? Why at that time? Why on those terms?
6. What are necessary elements of your purchase? Which items are essential to survival of the business? Is there any slow-moving inventory, any equipment of marginal utility?

Second, set your analysis aside, sit back, kick your shoes off, and relax. Try to think of your acquisition in purely a visual and kinesthetic frame of mind. (If you're analytically minded, this might seem uncomfortable at first, but the ideas you generate using this method may be invaluable.) Picture a crowd of people who are interested in your target business. Here are the managers, over there are the blue-collar workers, here are the major suppliers, in the foreground are the customers, in the background are the minor suppliers, and so forth. Each person is holding an object or gesturing, charade-like, in an effort to demonstrate his interest in your target business. Each has cash sticking out of every pocket, out of his collar, even out of his shoes! Each person will readily part with the cash if you can help satisfy each one's wants and needs vis à vis your target business.

Look at the picture you've created more closely: What money do you see? What money has the name of your business on it? What object is each holding? What does that object have to do with your business? Perhaps it's a tool only you can make for your customer, one that's crucial to his operation. Maybe it's a pension check your employees want to begin receiving from your target business twenty years from now. Spend at least twenty minutes with this exercise, even if at first you don't seem to be getting anywhere. Then—and this is essential—turn to other things and let your ideas cook a bit. Come back to your analysis fresh a couple of mornings later. Ideas will come to you in the wee small hours, in the shower, when you're doing mundane things. These ideas are always fleeting. Make sure you always write them down.

At all times, keep yours eyes open and keep looking for sources. Keep thinking. Sit in another chair and look at it physically from a different angle. (Honest, it works.) Turn the thing upside down and look at it, bottom line first. Describe the deal aloud to several good friends. Sometimes saying what you've been thinking triggers new ideas. If you really want to make a deal work, you will.

SELLER FINANCING

Often the most important piece of buyout financing comes from the seller. It is nearly impossible for an owner to sell a business for more than $100,000 or so, without taking back at least some of the paper. The reasons are varied: Banks get nervous about assuming more than one-half the risk of a business acquisition; the buyer often insists on some "hold" over the seller in case part of the deal is not as represented; suppliers and others can't or won't lend the full difference; very few buyers have large sums of cash available. So if your seller insists on a certain percentage down, you can remind him, as does Henry S. James, a seller's broker with Corporate Finance

Associates of Northern California, Inc., in Orinda, California, "The issue isn't all cash; the issue is getting paid."

Thus, it will behoove you to develop a good rapport with the seller from the start and to nourish the relationship up to and beyond the time your note is finally stamped "paid." Remember, throughout your transaction you are the "seller" and the owner is the "buyer." If you keep that attitude in the fore your buyout should be successful.

1. **Rapport with the seller can be the whole foundation.** This is often the key in insider buyouts, both large and small. For instance, Bill M. was manager of El Rancho Grande, a local restaurant. The owner was involved in a construction company, a drive-through restaurant in another town, and several rental properties around the state. The boss was too busy to keep up with all his holdings, so he turned management of the restaurant over to Bill.

Bill had about ten years experience in restaurant management and had started at El Rancho Grande six months earlier. It was a middle-class full-menu restaurant serving lunch and dinner, and grossing about $400,000 per year.

The purchase price for El Rancho Grande was $95,000 plus the inventory. It was handled in two simple steps:

Note to Sellers	$60,000
Note to Parents of Buyer	35,000
Total Financing	$95,000

The inventory of about $5,000 was offset by a similar amount of payables. At closing, Bill M. agreed to take over the liabilities in exchange for the inventory.

What made this deal work? Clearly it was the trust that had grown between Bill and his boss over a six-month period. The owner knew Bill could make a go of El Rancho Grande. And Bill knew what he was getting into, because he had run the business as if it were his own for six months. He knew the employees, the liabilities, the pluses and minuses of the business. Trust is something you can take to the bank.

2. **Give something back to the seller.** Concentrate on simplicity. If you buy less of your target, you have less financing to find. One of Doug's clients bought an auto parts store by giving the seller some of the inventory to use in the seller's auto repair business.

Another, whom we'll call Winston, bought an operating business in one purchase and its hard assets (real estate and machinery) in a second transaction. The business manufactured a product found in most kitchens. The homemaker bought it for $3 or $4 at the dime store, and replaced it when it wore out. It cost about 90 cents to make, and was sold to the retailer for about $2.00—almost a textbook case.

Here's the deal Winston worked out:

1. The Business

Inventory	$ 460,000
Patent	1,000
Business Name	1,000
Consulting Agreement	310,000
Noncompetition Agreement	110,000
Accounts Receivable	500,000
Total	$1,382,000

2. The Hard Assets (fixed assets)

Real Estate	$ 35,000
Machinery	80,000
Tools	28,000
Total	$ 143,000
Grand Total Price	$1,525,000

The seller agreed to keep the accounts receivable. Why? Winston argued the seller knew the value of the receivables and he didn't. Further, the seller was assured he would receive most of his $500,000 in receivables over a sixty- to ninety-day period, without risking the receivables in the hands of the new management. The buyer, in turn, was relieved of having to come up with $500,000.

The rest of the purchase price was financed by an eighteen-month note to the seller for $420,000, and a bank loan for $730,000. The financing was secured by assets and personal guarantees. Because of the sales and profit history, the personal guarantees were of secondary importance to the lenders.

Winston did the deal on only $2,000 cash out-of-pocket! (State law required a minimum capital of $1,000 for each of the two corporations Winston set up to make the acquisition.) Adding the numbers, you will see Winston also wound up with $123,000 cash in the till from the borrowings! But that contributed to the logic of the personal guarantees.

Of course, Winston needed that cash to be able to run the business over the sixty to ninety days until his receivables began turning into cash. The note to the seller was payable quarterly, not monthly, to give him time to accumulate the first payment. Thus, when looking for financing, don't overlook assets you can return to the seller.

3. **The seller guarantees the intangibles.** As we pointed out in Chapter Eight, if the seller does not want to keep the receivables, or some other intangibles for that

matter, suggest instead that the seller guarantee their collectibility or value in writing. Another lender can use this guarantee to increase the amount loaned.

For deal closing in 1990, one of Doug's pharmacy clients is getting the seller to guarantee the first 25 percent of the selling price. The guarantee to the bank terminates as soon as 25 percent of the principal is paid off. Principally, the seller is taking back the risk on the blue sky or goodwill/going concern value.

4. **Lease the business.** If coming up with the downstroke is a problem, or if you're just not sure the business is something you'll enjoy, ask the seller to lease it to you. If you get credit toward the sales price for some or all of your payments you actually get a free peek, and the seller gets rid of her headache (the business) immediately. Yes, it does happen in real life. A client of Doug's sold a print shop just this way. It's a variation of the option-to-buy method.

5. **Be a part employee, part buyer.** Instead of leasing the business, it might be better for both buyer and seller to initially leave control in the seller's hands. For instance, Ken negotiated to buy a septic tank and sewer cleaning service run as a summertime retirement project by another man. It turned a $20,000/year profit. Ken had managed to save a few thousand dollars in an IRA that he didn't want to touch if he could help it.

In the midst of negotiations the owner died. His widow had no interest in digging holes or cleaning sewers. Because she had no idea what the business was worth, she was reluctant to name a price. Faced with this dilemma, Ken proposed to the owner, Marilyn, an unusual business deal: He would run the business for Marilyn for one season, about eight months. Marilyn would pay Ken $1,000 per month salary. Ken would also be entitled to one-half the profits. At the end of the season, if everything worked out to Marilyn's satisfaction, Ken would buy the business from Marilyn, at a price to be determined by an appraisal of the equipment plus an amount equal to the average profit of the business over the preceding five years, for goodwill. The terms were 50 percent down, and the balance over five years.

Ken had great confidence in his ability to run the business and to sell himself to Marilyn. Marilyn knew if Ken didn't make a go of the business in the first year, she could still sell the equipment, but Ken had every incentive to make it really go. Ken calculated that, after one year, the equipment would be worth more than half the purchase: Consequently, he could get bank financing for his down payment.

Ken used good buyer psychology by not rushing the widow/owner's decision to sell. You can work this kind of deal if you are inventive enough to mold your offer to fit your seller's needs and business. The worst that can happen is for the seller to say "no deal."

6. **Your good track record is "bankable."** To bankers your ability to run the business is paramount. The same is true of many sellers, only more so, because you are going to walk off with their "baby." It's important in the pure corporate divestiture, as well.

Victor Kiam's book, *Going for It!,* provides a case in point. Victor Kiam (you remember, the man who liked the shaver so much, he bought the company) purchased the Remington Company for $25 million with only $500,000 out of his own pocket. Kiam first went to the sellers and said, in effect, "You know about my management history, and how I've run profitable companies of similar size before—loan me part of the price." They did: $13,500,000 worth. Then he convinced an outside lender to commit to $11,000,000 worth of loans.

With all this in place, Mr. Kiam found himself $500,000 short of what he needed for closing. Glancing around his home his eye happened upon some oil paintings on the wall, owned by his wife. (His biggest sale was probably convincing his wife to let him sell her paintings.) The proceeds covered his $500,000 down payment.

Now let's bring those numbers down into the region where you or I might be able to relate to them. Consider this chart:

$$\frac{\$500{,}000}{\$25{,}000{,}000} \quad \begin{matrix} \text{down} \\ \text{price} \end{matrix}$$

If you merely take a zero off the numbers, you will see that what Victor Kiam did was the equivalent of buying a $2,500,000 business, with $50,000 down:

$$\frac{\$50{,}000\cancel{0}}{\$2{,}500{,}000\cancel{0}} \quad \begin{matrix} \text{down} \\ \text{price} \end{matrix}$$

Or take two zeros off, and find he bought a $250,000 business for $5,000 down:

$$\frac{\$5{,}000\cancel{00}}{\$250{,}000\cancel{00}} \quad \begin{matrix} \text{down} \\ \text{price} \end{matrix}$$

Your everyday surroundings may hold tremendous financing possibilities (like Mrs. Kiam's artwork), and therefore they shouldn't be ignored. However, the key, as Mr. Kiam points out, was his strong experience managing companies like the one he bought. He was a good risk for his lenders. In other words, the biggest loan value in your deal is you. Work on a business you know and one in which you can demonstrate a strong track record. Look no further for collateral.

7. **Earnouts are a method to bridge an impasse in price negotiations.** They might also be a way to obtain financing. The seller gets a higher price if the company meets preset profit goals in future years. In other words, the seller tells you about tremendous potentials and fantastic cost savings you can institute. So you say, "Okay, you take my price, but if the company produces the 50 percent increase in profits in the next three years you've been projecting, you get some percentage of the increase."

Here the earnout helped you bridge a price impasse. It sounds great on paper, but three problems make it difficult in real life. First, it is relatively easy to manipulate financial results. Say the seller gets a percentage of the bottom line. There are many numbers that can be manipulated between the first line and the last line of an income statement. Expenses can be accelerated and maybe even run up needlessly. Salaries to the new owner can be increased. Compensation to the owner's children and family members can be paid even when little work is done. Inventories can be manipulated in ways that result in direct charges to the income statement. When the seller starts thinking about the possibilities of manipulation, he will run to his attorney to "draft up something airtight so they can't sneak one past me." Unfortunately, that's easier said than done. Witness the Internal Revenue Code that keeps getting thicker and thicker as Congress tries to plug loopholes. No matter what you put in the contract, the other side can figure out a way around it.

The second problem is a tax problem. A contingency in an installment contract may actually accelerate the taxable gain. The seller could be taxed on all the gain at closing, without having received enough cash to pay the tax!

The third problem is an accounting one: You may be prevented from using the "pooling of interests" method of accounting. The problem only arises if you already own a business and buy a second one. As a result, your ability to borrow at the bank could be impaired.

In real life, earnouts are seldom used for small and medium-size businesses. When used they are usually keyed to numbers as high on the income statement as possible. For instance, the earnout may be based on gross revenues or gross profit on sales. Even then, the problem of manipulation still exists, particularly in the last year of the earnout: The buyer decides to ship less product in the last month, or not to bill in December of the third year. These manipulations can skew the results, shortchanging the seller.

More important, an earnout can put the buyer and the seller in adversary positions. You don't need a lengthy court battle while your business is relatively young. You need the seller's help to make things really click, at least during the first few years. If you are adversaries, your business won't prosper as it should. No one wins legal battles.

8. **Know the seller's hidden hot buttons.** Find out as much about the seller and the seller's personal financial situation as you can. Usually you don't have to ask outright; just listen between the lines. Obviously, every seller expects you to ask him why the business is for sale. And every seller has rehearsed an answer. But as Mark Twain said, "A person has two reasons for doing anything: the one he tells you, and the real one."

Try asking questions like "In addition to that, are there any other reasons you'd like to sell?" Or "Do you have any other reasons in the back of your mind?" Or perhaps, "Why do you think most entrepreneurs sell their businesses?" Encourage the person to talk by paraphrasing what he just said, agreeing with him, or repeating the last few words adding a question mark on the end: "Retirement in Florida?" "Trying a different business?"

For example, Alice was the key salesperson of a large local office supply store that sold only to a specialized market segment. Alice was single and the store's main salesperson for twenty years. She had managed to save about $40,000 through diligent efforts and the magic of compound interest. The seller was sixty-three years old, but his health was not very good. Sam, the seller, was willing to go the extra mile for this long-time loyal employee. So he offered the business to Alice for $500,000, with 15 percent down, and the balance payable over six years at prime plus 2 percent (the rate at which the company borrowed from its bank).

Although the negotiations went through several stages, the one thing that never changed was Sam's demand that his medical insurance be paid by the company until he reached age sixty-five. Sam feared a break in medical insurance coverage because of his preexisting poor health. Alice was sensitive enough to recognize this as a key concern for Sam, and although her accountant and Doug both kept telling her how expensive the insurance could be, she would not let them propose dropping this provision from the contract. As it turned out, that one clause was probably what kept the negotiations on track through several tough meetings.

The price of a business is often of secondary importance to the seller. If you are careful to learn all you can about the seller, you may be able to provide that little something extra that makes the deal go. In Alice's case, the extra health insurance might have cost her $10,000 or $15,000 a year for a few years, but weigh the cost against the income she was buying herself ($35,000 to $45,000 a year over and above her regular compensation), and you can see why the price was worth paying. It does pay to know your seller's hot button, because you may need to push it.

9. **Add a perk.** Knowing your seller can pay off in big ways. Take a break from your negotiations, and get away to the local coffee shop, just the two of you. No professionals allowed. Sort of like George Bush and Mikhail Gorbachev deciding to go for a breath of fresh air. You know, a single walk can improve the health of the whole deal.

Sometimes, just a little additional perk is what you need to make the deal go. Perhaps your seller has always wanted to take an around-the-world cruise. And it just so happens you have a credit card with enough remaining credit limit to buy that cruise. So you go to your friendly travel agent, buy the tickets, and staple them to the top of your offer. The offer just happens to include your favorite terms too, like requiring the seller to finance the purchase price.

10. **Pay full price.** Most sellers expect to haggle over price, and some relish the game. You can turn this to your benefit by haggling a little and then giving in . . . on price. A good negotiator many times gives in on price but stays firm on terms. A real estate developer in the Midwest used this technique to build a portfolio of several hundred rental units, but with a twist: He offered *more* than the asking price! And no less a person than the late Royal Little of Textron used this technique to buy some of

the 300 companies he acquired. He started buying these businesses when he was fifty-seven years old and continued until he died in January 1989 at the age of ninety-two.

11. **Reduce the inventory—hold a "sale."** If your target has unwanted or slow-moving inventory, a one-time sale can generate cash. If held before closing, you have less to buy (and finance); if held after, you can use the proceeds to pay down a short-fuse note to the seller. Perhaps you could give a series of notes due fifteen days apart, as (part of) your down payment. Maybe the seller would agree to no interest on the down-payment notes. See how your imagination can work for you?

12. **Offer the seller an employment contract.** Used properly, it can be a subtle compliment to the seller: She's still needed to make the business go. It's also a way to stretch your payments.

13. **Have your escrow check held uncashed.** This can be your earnest money, part of your down payment, or tied to an earnout or similar conditional payment. The idea: Your check won't be cashed until the condition is satisfied. Sellers accept it more often than you'd guess, and this allows you to use the same money for two things (but only for a short time), such as earnest money and working capital.

14. **Give a series of postdated checks.** Legally, they are treated as promissory notes, but psychologically and functionally they have more value, because the seller doesn't have to ask for payment: She just deposits the check. The good part is you pay no interest and the seller provides part of the financing, through the "back door."

15. **Get a balloon at 50 percent.** After a small down payment, there is a short period of payments (five years or so) and then the balance, about 50 percent of the original price, is due in one lump sum. The balloon limits the seller's risk to a short time. With a good operating history you should have no problem financing 50 percent (perhaps only 30 percent, after growth) of the value of the business.

16. **Let the seller know the bank is out.** Open communication is almost always the best course. If the bank will only commit to 50 percent, then you may have a tool with which to approach the owner, to get her to take more paper.

17. **Lease, don't buy, the hard assets.** It's normal to acquire buildings with a lease-and-option-to-buy package. You can creatively apply this technique to machines, equipment, and other hard assets. With a little imagination, the technique could be applied to "softer" assets, like contracts or leasehold improvements.

AVOIDING PERSONAL GUARANTEES

Often, owners and their counsel will suggest you personally guarantee your notes. All of the discussion in Chapter Nine about bank personal guarantees applies here. In addition, consider whether these techniques might satisfy your seller:

Give a lien on company assets: Argue that the lien is more valuable than your personal guarantee.

Pledge your stock, eliminating the seller's need to foreclose.

Limit your guarantee to a specific dollar amount.

Allow the guarantee to trigger only if you fail to meet certain promises.

Show the seller that his risk is small—for example, you've committed your life and all your assets to the company already.

Argue from fairness about your need to have some room for additional financing as needs arise.

Give a mortgage on another asset, you own, instead of the guarantee.

SUPPLIER FINANCING

1. **Get a straight loan from a supplier.** If your target is a major customer of some of its suppliers, or can be, the supplier might make a direct loan of the needed cash. This practice is common in some industries. Doug had a client buy a drug store with 95 percent financing from his drug wholesaler. Two days after closing, another wholesaler offered to take over the note at a lower rate, and finance the buyer's new home, as well!

Look for the major supplier, but also for smaller ones for whom this account is a big chunk of their income. Typically, a wholesaler is willing to finance about one year's worth of gross profit. Therefore, it'll pay to research profit margins and gross profits in your supplier's industry (use Prentice Hall's *Almanac of Business and Industrial Financial Ratios* and Robert Morris' *Annual Statement Studies*) before making your approach. Don't hesitate to shop such financing among competing suppliers.

2. **Get the lease.** The lease is the oft-forgotten key to location: The person who controls the lease controls the location, and ultimately the business. This is particularly true of retail establishments, where business is volatile—tenants come and go regularly. Landlords are anxious to sign that next lease. As we have seen, a buyer holding a new lease has at least one ace in his hand when it comes to negotiating with the recalcitrant seller. Be fair, if for no other reason than you have to live with the seller for the duration of your note! Just knowing when the lease expires can be a potent tool in negotiations. The person with the deadline (in this case, the seller/tenant) is in the weaker bargaining position. The secret to negotiations is being prepared.

3. **The landlord is a source of cash.** If the target is a key tenant in the shopping mall, the landlord is a party anxious to please. The same is true of the individual who owns a large industrial property. If you vacate that building it may be vacant for a long while.

Not only is the landlord a prime candidate for buyout financing but also for plant improvements. It is easier for a landlord to justify such expenditures than to justify a straight-out cash loan, particularly when it improves the value of her own property, and the cost can be recovered over the term of the loan.

4. **Bankruptcy can be your key.** It is axiomatic among creditors that once a company is in bankruptcy, even a Chapter 11 reorganization, you'll be lucky to get 10 cents on the dollar. Remember the noncritical supplier (Chapter 3 of this book), and how you can turn such a supplier's position into credit. Consider that supplier a potential source of cash, too.

There are at least two other ways you can use bankruptcy to your advantage. One is to negotiate with a major secured creditor for a key piece of operating plant or equipment, or with a key employee for customer contacts and know-how (assuming these items aren't proprietary or subject to noncompetition or nondisclosure contracts within the bankruptcy court's control).

The second is to negotiate directly with the trustee or debtor-in-possession (DIP) to purchase key assets or the entire business. Time payment plans, often quite liberal, can be negotiated. Keep in mind when you buy an asset out of bankruptcy, you often do so free of the claims of creditors.

5. **Assume trade credit.** This is relatively easier to do because usually it takes no prior creditor approval: The trade creditors become your involuntary lenders. The technique is usually valuable only in an asset purchase: The stock purchase deal, by definition, includes all the debt. But have you considered number 6 below?

6. **Negotiate with the creditors for a discount.** What are their prospects for quick, full payment without you on the scene? A quick discount and bank loan might free up additional capital.

7. **What if there are no liabilities to assume?** Say you have a seller who is averse to debt, and pays the invoices the day they arrive. In these cases, schedule the closing a few days after the major shipments for the month arrive. The seller delays payment under normal trade practices, and you assume the liability at closing. You now have less money to raise, and the seller gets the same walk-away cash because he didn't pay the bills ahead of schedule, having pocketed the cash instead. What if the seller still won't go along? Delay part of your down payment a couple of weeks (postdated checks could do the trick), and hold closing before the major shipments come in. Then you do what the seller would have done, using the vendors' cash for your down payment.

8. **Defer rental deposits.** Try a series of postdated checks to gain that last chunk of meat to throw into your financing stew.

9. **Check tax lien notices.** This nasty creditor carries a one-two punch favorable to the business buyer: The seller has a short-fuse deadline; and the tax authorities (or the secured creditor with a position ahead of the tax authorities) are often easy to bargain with. A quick check at the bankruptcy court and local county recorder's office is all

you need to get the inside scoop. Out of time? Title insurance companies will do the search for you for a low fee.

10. **Get a discount from suppliers for increased orders.** Can you switch from a half-dozen small suppliers to one or two larger ones? The discounts could give you better cash flow. Or the supplier might loan cash for larger orders.

11. **Get a little credit from many suppliers.** Or get cash loans.

12. **Give a seat on the board of directors to a large supplier or potential supplier.** Money follows advice. Put the supplier's president on your present board before you actively negotiate for a target company. Or put her on the board today looking toward financing a year or two down the line. The savvy chess player is always thinking five or six moves ahead. But set a finite period for this goodie, like two or three years.

CUSTOMERS AND OTHER DEPENDENTS

1. **Employee loans.** There are more people than just the owner who could be hurt if a business closes. Many can be good sources of financing. One source might be the employees. In several business acquisitions employees have either foregone raises or taken a salary cut, or even actually lent cash to the owner to make the transaction happen.

2. **ESOPs** (Employee Stock Ownership Plans). Congress in recent years has added sweeteners to ESOPs in the form of reducing the tax on interest received from loans to ESOPs (in turn, reducing the interest expense of a buyer using an ESOP as a acquisition tool), allowing sellers to roll over gains into other companies' stock, and giving an estate tax break to shareholders. But the key benefit is that principal payments (as well as the interest) can be tax deductible.

Think about it—you get to depreciate the building and equipment, and then you get to deduct the principal payments too! How? The ESOP borrows money from a bank to purchase company stock, and the company guarantees the obligation. The ESOP services the debt out of annual qualified retirement plan contributions made by the company to it. The contributions (within the ubiquitous limitations) are fully deductible.

ESOPs are not used in many small-to-medium-size acquisitions because they are complicated and take several months to install. But if there is already a qualified retirement plan in place, it may be relatively easy to convert it to an ESOP. So if you see a retirement plan in your target, think of it as a little red flag with "potential lender" painted on it.

Remember, ESOPs mean transferring the company to the employees. Don't get involved with one if that's not really what you want.

3. **Customer prepays.** This is a natural for a service business (because of high margins), but it can work anywhere. A discount for payment before the service or product is delivered to a large regular customer can secure your last chunk of financing.

Scotty B. was negotiating to buy a local franchise of a national office cleaning firm. The seller was willing to take back 50 percent of the $98,000 price, and Scotty had arranged to assume $22,000 of the payables. That still left Scotty $27,000 short. Scotty went to one of the larger customers of his target and offered this deal: If the customer would prepay his entire next year's cleaning bill (then running $1,800 per month), Scotty would give him a 5 percent discount. The customer did some quick math and figured the 5 percent discount worked out to a little over 11 percent interest, and the market rate for one-year CDs at the time was about 8.5 percent. The customer readily accepted. This gave Scotty $20,520, and left him with only $6,500 to find. He quickly made the same offer to a couple of smaller accounts and was able to come up with another $8,000.

Naturally, Scotty had some scrambling to do his first year in order to meet his payroll, but he had other ideas to cover that shortfall, such as foregoing his own salary and getting new business.

Do you remember when the video movie rental stores were getting started? They charged you a "membership fee." What do you think they were doing with the membership money?

Have you ever gotten a letter from a restaurant offering you "membership" in some sort of an executive club? For example, send in $150 now, and you are entitled to twenty meals priced up to $10.99, special preference for reservations, and a free bottle of champagne every fifth visit. Because it's an exceptionally good deal, people sign up and send their money. If you get 100 people to sign up, you've just raised $15,000 of your down payment!

Another twist on this idea is the business that regularly collects in advance, such as a health spa or a magazine publisher. In essence the cash received is booked as a liability when it comes in, because the cash doesn't become income until it is actually earned—meaning each month as the services are performed or magazines are mailed out. If you close your purchase a day or two after the largest group of renewals comes in, you can assume the liability, in turn reducing your cash needs.

INVESTORS AND OTHER "OUTSIDERS"

1. **Investors and partners.** Go slowly with investors or partners. First of all, there is a thicket of legal rules to trip you: It is easy to wind up in jail over something you didn't even know was illegal.

Second, investors and partners are expensive. If you need $25,000, and you agree to pay an exorbitant rate of interest, you have to start paying interest at a time when you can't afford cash outflow. But if you take in a partner and you make $10,000,000, your partner is going to want half. That $5,000,000 is certainly more expensive than the exorbitant interest, whatever it was, on $25,000.

Third, and often the real problem area, investors and partners often expect to have a voice in how the business is run—perhaps even outright control or a veto power. So think twice before you seek investors or partners.

Investors expect risks and rewards to go hand in hand. If your enterprise is a stable one, it should be easy to find investors at a relatively low rate of return. On the other hand, with a risky venture the investor will expect a large return. Typically, the high-risk investor will want 30 percent or more per annum, compounded, and will expect to be in control of your company for the three- to five-year period in which he is involved. Is giving up control bad? Not necessarily. Half of a winner is better than all of a loser. Perhaps the real plus is the investor may bring your company the needed skills to make it a winner.

Your best investors are usually the current investors in the business. If people are already loaning money to your target business, they are a prime source for continuing and possibly even increasing their participation. Why? First, they are familiar with the company, and second, they know the risk involved. Third, they have already accepted the risk. Fourth, they might not have any choice in the matter. Fifth, if they have no choice but to continue, investing in you as the new owner might be logical because it helps shore up any risk they took with the first investment.

2. **Split acquisitions, or, you buy the land, we'll buy the business.** Splitting assets and simultaneously selling them to another buyer not only adds to your purchasing power but prevents later squabbles over management control: You each have marbles you can pick up and take to another game.

Daniel T. wanted to buy the upscale barber shop where he was manager. The owner was getting ready to retire. The business simply consisted of renting chair space to barbers and beauticians. The chair space rentals were sufficient to provide the owner with a $30,000 per year profit. Each operator provided his own hair dryers, razors, scissors, and other equipment. The owner provided only the mirrors on the wall, the chairs, the decor, and a receptionist. The value of the equipment, all rather new, was $20,000. The value of the building, which the owner also wanted to sell, was $80,000. Daniel T. had about $5,000 cash. The owner was not overly anxious to make a profit on the sale, so he offered the business to Daniel T. at the value of the equipment, $20,000, payable over five years, $5,000 down. He wanted 30 percent down on the building, and was willing to finance the balance over twenty years at a market rate of interest.

Daniel T. was good friends with a husband and wife beautician and hair stylist team, also tenants of the shop. Sal and Sol had managed to save up about $20,000, but they were not anxious to ruin a good friendship by becoming partners. So the simple deal they styled was for Sal and Sol to buy the building and lease it to Daniel T. Their cut paid their payments, and put a little tax-sheltered cash in their pockets each year. Daniel T. was willing to take the risk of some empty chairs, and the other risks of running the business.

Daniel T., Sal, and Sol had preserved their friendship, having confined their business relationship to a strictly business level, where everything was black and white (either the rent was paid or it wasn't) and there were few mutual decisions. Daniel T. picked up a $30,000 income, with which he was able to replenish his $5,000 savings account.

A prospect for financing your business acquisition may be someone associated with the business. Keep your eyes and ears open, and question everything you see on the balance sheet. There are assets on (and off) many balance sheets you could sell to finance your purchase.

3. **Joint venturing.** Similar to split acquisitions, here you split the enterprise into different products or other arenas and each take a different part. Another approach would be to split it up into different functions. You buy the sales part of the company, somebody else buys the real estate, a third group buys the manufacturing, and still another provides the management. You remember divide and conquer, don't you?

4. **Sale-leaseback.** This technique is an old one for financing acquisitions of hard assets, and is closely related to split acquisitions. You could use an outside lender (doctors like these deals), but it might also work with a seller. In short, you only buy part of the assets from the seller, and the seller or other lender (lawyers, accountants, and architects like them, too) leases you the rest. If you set up the lease with gradually increasing rents, you will not only be able to get your financing but simultaneously strengthen your cash flow.

5. **Broker's commission paid over time.** It happens more often than the brokers want to admit. But if you're only an inch away from closing, close enough for the broker to smell the aroma of the commission already sizzling on the grill, the broker might be willing to take half a hamburger today and another half tomorrow. Just remember the broker lives off those commission checks, so don't expect to work this deal with the whole commission. Don't expect a long-term note, either.

6. **The Small Business Administration.** This government agency has an undeserved black eye for runaway paperwork and bureaucratic slackness. Don't you believe it! Paperwork is little more than for a normal bank loan, and under the Preferred Lenders Program, a bank in your area can write an SBA-guaranteed loan for between $100,000 and $1 million, without prior SBA approval. See Appendix C and *Mancuso's Small Business Resource Guide.*

Some Tips For Getting SBA Loans

You've probably heard horror stories about SBA loan paperwork and delays. Don't get too concerned. There really isn't that much paperwork. There are only three or four forms and the SBA promises to turn the request around in a few weeks. In fact, in every community there is an SBA Preferred Lender Program (PLP) lender. The PLP bank itself acts for the SBA in approving or rejecting a loan, which also results in a quicker turnaround. There is also a certified lender status, which is a notch lower, and you'll find more of these than PLPs. Certified is slower—but only by days—and gives the bank a higher guarantee.

Don't pay consultants and most of all don't check the box on the SBA form that says you paid consultants. If you check this box, it may actually hold up your loan while the SBA investigates the broker/consultant! Accountants and attorneys are not considered consultants for this purpose. A consultant, for instance, is someone who claims to be able to broker a loan with the SBA.

Typically, the SBA loan is for seven years. Just remember that you are dealing with bureaucrats. Bureaucrats eat, sleep, and drink paper. They want lots of documentation. If you are asking for a seven-year loan, they will want seven years' worth of projections. Don't send in a five-year projection and hope to get a seven-year loan, because in many SBA offices your request will be bounced for the two missing years.

The SBA normally likes a 3:1 debt to equity ratio. We are aware of one particular case of a 5:1 ratio, but that was unusual. In other words, if you put up $50,000, the SBA will let you borrow $150,000, assuming you will be using the funds to acquire "bankable" assets.

The SBA will bail out their own bad loans, but they will not take over somebody else's bad paper. Therefore, if you think you'd like to have an SBA loan, it's better to get it up front than later on. So, we often recommend choosing SBA first and a conventional loan second.

Don't try to get a politician involved. The SBA has hundreds of top-flight loan people. Because they are doing a large volume of transactions, everything takes a little longer than you think it should. Nevertheless, they are doing a good job, and if you bring in a senator or congressman, it actually tends to red-flag your file and slow things down.

The SBA always requires personal loan guarantees. The other side of the coin is the SBA is not particularly vicious about going after personal assets such as your home on their guarantees. You need to be on the guarantee because the government is on the guarantee. For example, Joe has a personal friend whose solar heating business went bad. It had a $150,000 SBA loan, and he managed to settle with the SBA for some

$30,000 four or five years later. Even though there was a mortgage on the home, the family wasn't evicted.

7. **State and local governments.** Many states and municipalities have gotten downright aggressive when it comes to promoting business in their boundaries. Check with your local library, and the state and local Chambers of Commerce for your area. The state Department of Commerce or a similar entity might also point you in the right direction. Or call the SBA answer desk (telephone (800) 368-5855, or (202) 653-7561). Don't just stick with the locale of your target: Would it make sense to locate closer to your major customers or sources of supply? Maybe the state or city in that location would be anxious to have you relocate.

8. **Composition agreements with creditors.** If you're targeting a business in financial difficulty, you can often relieve the strain merely by getting the larger creditors to discount their balances. If you were a creditor facing the possibility of getting only 10 percent after three years of bankruptcy, but could choose to get 50 percent over three years, and new sales, which would you choose?

9. **Industrial revenue bonds.** The heyday of these tax-exempt financings is past, but they are still available if you fit the requirements. The requirements change seemingly every few days, so you need to get good tax counsel involved. But it is a good way to obtain financing, often at below-market rates.

10. **Buying companies out of bankruptcy.** Once a company has filed, creditors are often psychologically ready to "just get it over with." Just as good terms can make up for a bad price, a good price can loosen a lender's purse strings—maybe even those of some of the same creditors.

11. **Bankruptcy purchase over time.** It is possible to buy over time from the bankruptcy court. Try a price a little above the auction "hammer" value, with a market rate of interest (or higher—at this price, you can afford it). Be sure to retain good legal help.

12. **Refinance after purchase.** Once the hard work of putting the finance package together has been accomplished, another lender may find it easy to improve the package. Remember our druggist friend who got his business and house financed this way? There is an old adage in the venture capital field: "The best time to ask for new money is right after the deal is funded." Why? Because that's when enthusiasm for your deal is at its highest, and the lenders' defenses are at their lowest.

13. **Borrowing against receivables.** Factors regularly lend against receivables, as do many banks. Since this procedure works as a revolving loan, and you'll always have receivables, this method has a semipermanent nature to it. In effect, you only pay back the initial advance when you choose. But banks like to clean up receivable loans every few years.

14. **Borrowing based on fair market value.** This is a venerable real estate

financing technique. Borrow against the actual market value, not the purchase price. This technique has particular application to bargain purchases, or cases where you'll use some of the funds to improve the value of the assets, such as through building additions.

15. **Making your loan convertible to stock.** This sweetener may help with nonconventional lenders and bank subsidiaries, but not with pure banks. Be sure to get a lawyer familiar with securities law to help you.

16. **SBICs.** Small Business Investment Companies (SBICs) and Minority Enterprise SBICs (MESBICs) in your area can help. Funded largely by long-term favorable loans from the SBA, but still privately owned, these groups in turn make long-term loans to, and equity investments in, certain types of small enterprises. Many are connected with a bank, serving as the bank's venture capital arm. If your loan officer speaks as if your loan is too risky, inquire about any venture capital companies affiliated with the bank. An internal referral can grease your path.

SBICs have been investing 50 percent in equity and 50 percent in debt on the average over the years. There are dollar limits on how much an SBIC or an MESBIC can invest in any single deal. SBICs can provide management assistance as well as money. Information about SBICs and MESBICs can be obtained by writing to

SBA Investment Division
1441 L Street, N.W.
Washington, DC 20416

and

National Association of Investment Companies
1111 14th Street, N.W., Suite 700
Washington, DC 20005
(MESBICs)

and

National Association of SBICs
618 Washington Building
Washington, DC 20005

17. **SBIR.** What's better than the best of both debt and equity? Gifts! That's just what the Small Business Innovation Research program provides. This program, initially intended to be temporary, keeps getting renewed by Congress. Federal agencies are required under the program to set aside funding for small companies for research and product development.

While not a source of emergency cash, this program might provide some midterm financing for that product development project your target has kept limping along. The program is administered separately at each federal agency, but comprehensive information is available from

Office of Innovation Research & Technology
Small Business Administration
1441 L Street, N.W., Room 500–A
Washington, DC 20416
(202) 653-6458

18. **The IRS.** If you're buying stock, a large tax refund (perhaps a tax loss carryback) might be combined with a bridge loan to bootstrap the deal. Make sure you ask your CPA to check for this possibility, when he does his part of the investigation.

19. **Leasing fixtures, equipment, and other tangibles.** Even carpeting! If some new (or previously well-cared-for) tangibles will be needed, consider leasing. Short-term leases give you a try-it-out advantage as well as limited exposure and possible off-balance-sheet financing. Longer-term leases often look like loans (witness the large deposits comparable to down payments in a purchase), and therefore will often have to be booked as such, at least in larger companies subject to Generally Accepted Accounting Principles (GAAP).

20. **Buying used equipment from dealers.** The dealer owns (and pays interest on) trade-in equipment—not so with all new equipment on the showroom floor. For instance, some equipment may be on consignment. So which is the dealer most anxious to sell? An anxious seller is a willing lender—not a shoo-in, but worth being considered.

21. **Asset-based lenders.** Included in this group are factors, commercial finance companies, and insurance companies. These lenders are usually interested in loans over (often read "well over") $1 million. While they are difficult to locate, and often more expensive than banks, they do fill a real gap in the market between pure venture capital and low-risk bank lending. They are more concerned with asset values than cash flow. (Bankers are more interested in cash flow, and don't want to own your collateral.) However, they won't ignore cash flow—they won't loan themselves into a failing company just for the fun of foreclosing. See Appendix D.

22. **Letters of credit.** These are useful where you have good credit, but don't want to give financial data to the seller (who may be a competitor) or to an outsider, and where the seller or other outsider can offer better terms than the bank but is unwilling to assume the risk of lending to you. The technique is simple: The bank or other third party guarantees to pay if you don't. You'll have to pay the bank a fee based on a

percentage of the amount it has to set aside in case it eventually funds your credit. This technique has in several instances spelled the difference between doing and not doing a deal.

23. **Surety bonds.** Widely used in the construction industry, a surety bond is a guarantee of an insurance company or other outside party that you will perform your contract or pay an obligation. The bond can be used to obtain a large piece of new business (such as from a state agency), which can then be used to support a bank loan, or to guarantee outright the loan from a bank or from some other lender. In the latter case, the surety company will likely ask for a significant equity position (25 percent to 45 percent) and large fees. Don't let the fees scare you off. For nonbankable companies, like service firms, it may be the only game in town. This area of finance is still developing (and populated by more than a few insurers who don't have the financial clout to do the deal—and who therefore waste your time) so you'll have to search out knowledgeable attorneys, CPAs, or investment bankers to help you find the proper lenders and insurers.

24. **Older assets.** Remember that they may have increased in value, giving you more loan value. An appraisal of key pieces of equipment could be worth the investment.

SELLING OR RENTING ASSETS AND RIGHTS

1. **Financiers of other acquisitions.** Look again through those back issues of business journals and newspapers. Were there any similar-sized acquisitions in your target industry or community? If so, it can be worth a visit to the new owner to get referrals to their financing sources.

2. **Selling off unneeded assets.** Just as big business sheds unwanted divisions to finance their leveraged buyouts (LBOs), so you can sell unwanted equipment, product lines, and yes, divisions, to other companies. The cash and your leaner look can do wonders for your cash flow and borrowing ability.

3. **Time-sharing of partially used assets.** Rent out excess manufacturing or computer time. Rent out the whole factory for the second or third shift to a noncompeting company. Borrow time from another company, and sell your factory or equipment. If you're renting out, give a 5 percent to 20 percent discount for payment of a whole year in advance. Rent out excess space to a complementary business during your off-season—the Christmas Tree Wonderland folks may just love to have your swimming pool showroom during off-season. Across from Joe's office in Manhattan is the famous discotheque "179 Varick." By day it's a breakfast and lunch restaurant for factory

workers but every evening they store the chairs, the lights go down, and "179 Varick" appears.

4. **Selling off excess inventory.** Remember the auto parts store buyer who let the owner keep some of the inventory to use in his car repair business? In essence, you buy less of the business (in his case, less inventory). Less price equals less financing.

If the business has more inventory than you want to carry, either the seller or you can hold an inventory reduction sale. Some inventory, such as slow-moving items, does not justify shelf space. Sell it back to the jobber. Scrap out shopworn items to scrap iron buyers. There are even buyers for used fat from french fryers!

5. **Subsidiary spinoffs.** Does your target have a subsidiary in an industry where your team has little or no experience? Or a product line that could be spun off? Would a competitor in that line like to have the subsidiary?

6. **Excess motor vehicles.** A fleet of autos or trucks can be an ego booster to a small business owner. Automobile costs can drive your business out of control quickly. Are all those vans needed? Could a different ordering system supplant one or two? A different supplier? Do all the people with company cars really need one? There is a constant market for used motor vehicles: Treat them as a cash equivalent.

7. **International marketing rights.** A product with a demand in other parts of the world could be licensed overseas, with the licensing fees providing acquisition funding. A product you consider a poor candidate for international markets might just be sorely needed in some Third World country. The Department of Commerce is anxious to increase exports, and so is the SBA. They can lead you to specific countries, and even specific companies, who are seeking your product. Contact

Market Overseas with U.S. Government Help
Small Business Administration
P.O. Box 15434
Ft. Worth, TX 76119
(800) 424-5201

or

TOP Bulletin
Trade Opportunities Program
U.S. Department of Commerce
International Trade Administration, Room 2323
Washington, DC 20230
(202) 377-3181

Many states have programs to assist with exports. Call your state capital, or

SBA Answer Desk
(800) 368-5855
(202) 653-7561

8. **Selling timber.** Like we said, stop, look, listen, and think. What's on the unused back half of the property?

9. **Leasing out the parking lot.** Maybe the theater across the street would love to have access during your off-hours.

10. **Franchising the business idea to others.** Remember Ray Kroc? He's the guy who bought a hamburger stand from two brothers named McDonald, with the crazy idea of letting other people copy it, for a fee. Could be he'll have something there, some day. You could franchise before closing to see if there is a market, or after closing to get the funds to pay off notes to the seller. Carrying it a step further, you could use the proceeds of your later public offering to buy back the franchises, much as Holiday Inn has done.

11. **Customer lists.** Selling doesn't mean you can't use them, just that the buyer can reuse them. Is there a noncompeting business that sells to the same market? You make comforters and blankets; they sell pillows. If you have a big list, you could make some regular income this way. Perhaps better in the long run would be to trade lists, improving your sales by getting new prospects.

12. **Selling or licensing patent rights.** This can be done at home or overseas.

13. **Renting advertising and display space.** Even the very walls can be profit centers—if you put billboards on them. A small display of video tapes and books about sporting and exercise techniques would complement your sporting goods store.

14. **Selling distributor territories.** Your product is a bundle of rights: The same product can be sold to different markets for different uses, and rights to each marketplace can be sold to different people. Geographic boundaries can be set up and rights to each territory can be sold separately. Rights can be sold with time restrictions (e.g., time-share condominiums). Methods of sale can be parceled out to different resellers: mail order, door-to-door, in-store sales. Different forms of the same product can be awarded to different retailers: book sales to one distributor, motion picture rights to a second, and video sales to a third.

15. **Realty and leases.** Excess realty can be sold or leased out. But don't neglect the lease. What is a lease, after all, but the right to control real estate for a period of time? Many leases restrict your right to sublet space or assign the lease, but does leasing space for a vending machine for your employees violate your factory lease? (Better get a legal opinion on such gray areas.) Your landlord might be willing to give you a waiver for certain uses.

16. **Sponsoring or creating an association.** Who says an association has to be

nonprofit? Collect dues to pay off your down-payment note. Be careful of misleading people into thinking you have a not-for-profit entity.

Sponsoring an independent nonprofit club or association might give you a way to show people your public-spirited nature, and perhaps get you a broader mailing list. You could perhaps put their logo on your products. One businesswoman recently created a charitable foundation to promote art appreciation in, and purchase art for, a local parochial school. For a few thousand dollars, she gets priceless free publicity when her name (and often, her photo) are linked regularly to the foundation.

PERSONAL SOURCES

1. **Life insurance loans.** Quick, easy, low-interest rate, and most often forgotten. Take an inventory of your policies now. What cash surrender values and loan values do they carry? Your chartered life underwriter (CLU) would be happy to inventory these facts for you.

2. **Family and friends.** Should you borrow from family and friends? Our advice is forget it. Business is, after all, only business. It is replaceable. But family relationships and friends are not. They are a more valuable asset. The easiest way to ruin a friendship or a family relationship is to bring money into the picture. It's like pouring vinegar into milk. Both the vinegar and milk will be ruined. Our advice is not to get a loan but an outright gift. It is still "father's money," but it sits better for the whole family, because nobody expects a gift to be repaid.

3. **Building your credit history.** Start while you're in the deal flow stage or before. Borrow on personal lines of credit at one or more banks, paying back on (or ahead of) time. Then go back and borrow more, gradually building a good track record with increasing amounts. When you're ready to close, and a few thousand dollars short, you'll have a personal borrowing ability to help fill your need.

4. **Borrowing from a supplier of another business you control.** If the target's suppliers want to keep its business, don't you suppose the suppliers of your other business want its business, as well? If the businesses use the same supplies, you may have financing and pricing possibilities.

5. **Borrowing against the equity or assets of your present business.** Lenders you have in place are more likely to make a loan than new people. Equity you have built up is a natural collateral for your new enterprise. Too natural. Go slow, and don't give up more collateral than you need. It's both a strong argument against an overeager lending officer, and a bank axiom, that "More collateral doesn't make a bad loan into a good one."

By making your businesses interdependent, you are constructing a house of cards. If one business should collapse, loans secured by another business could be called, causing that one, and the next, ad infinitum to tumble. You'll have a stronger financial structure if each pillar has its own separate foundation, and there are cross-braces among the pillars.

6. **Borrowing against your house.** Despite the obvious risks, this is often necessary. For reasons given previously, try to limit the amount and keep it separated from your business loans in the paperwork.

7. **Saving ahead.** Start at the earliest possible time to put your pennies away and build a war chest—a venerable method to be sure. It didn't get to be venerable without being sure.

8. **Buying an income.** Buy some income real estate or invest in some other venture to support you and underwrite the lack of salary during the early years following your acquisition.

9. **Cutting your personal expenses.** Sell your house, or move into a smaller apartment in a less expensive neighborhood. Sell your luxury car and buy a used one.

10. **Creating a holding company.** Each seller can be paid partly in stock of the holding company; each seller in one stroke retains an interest in his company and diversifies his holdings. Since you are issuing a "security" you'll need the help of a securities attorney. Because of the paperwork (offering memoranda, etc.) and the selling job needed to convince the seller to take your own stock, this option won't fit everybody. It would be most useful in a preplanned campaign to acquire several businesses.

INCREASING OPERATING CASH FLOW

1. **Reduce expenses.** Perhaps you can find ways to cut the cost of production. Your team members might donate their time. A spouse or relative could work for you for free just to see you succeed. Combine your cost cuts with a three- or six-month down-payment note to get you the keys.

2. **Improve collection policies/procedures.** If your target business regularly gets paid fifty days after invoice, a ten-day improvement could generate a permanent influx of cash equal to one-fifth of a month's sales. How closely do the target's people monitor new accounts? Is a major customer slipping further and further behind, indicating a need for COD sales terms? Could a few phone calls to the four or five largest accounts generate a substantial sum of money? Could a personal visit or two loosen up a big check that just never gets cut?

3. **Develop new lines of business.** Buying a hardware store and still a couple thousand dollars short? Give do-it-yourself classes for $25 each to 200 people over four weekends. Ask your seller to allow you to pay the last $5,000 of the down

payment five weeks after closing, or in four weekly payments. (As with a lot of good ideas, you probably don't want to lay out your plan to the seller, particularly if there are a lot of dollars involved.)

4. **Use direct mail.** You might increase business by judicial use of direct mail. You can find mailing list brokers in most telephone directories. Find a knowledgeable one, and grab hold. Ask a lot of questions and inform your broker what it is you are trying to accomplish with your mailing. By spending a few extra dollars on mailing lists, you can get a list of people who have already purchased by mail from other hardware stores, for instance. A good list broker might even nail it down to the type of screws and bolts the customers bought. Then you sell the proper tools to go with their earlier purchases.

The new buyer of a manufacturing company that made consumer products increased sales by offering the company's products and those of other manufacturers in an attractive catalog mailed directly to consumers. Our old friend Victor Kiam is aggressively leading his Remington Company in just this direction.

5. **Make up a newsletter.** If you are buying a business that has information about a newsworthy subject, you may have a natural for a newsletter. If you have a well-written newsletter (and you can get good ghost writers—contact your local high school and college English departments), you could sell subscriptions and use the proceeds as part of your down payment.

6. **Discount a large receivable for early payment.** Combine this idea with a partially delayed down payment, and you can use the cash to meet your note. Remember, there is no reason you can't begin these negotiations before closing. Just be clear to consumers that you're not the owner yet and you can't speak for the owner if your deal doesn't go through.

7. **Rent concession space.** Large department stores regularly rent out space to entrepreneurs, who then turn the space into their jewelry or furniture department. Restaurants rent space for vending machines. So do factories. Have a small extra room accessible to the public? Rent it out for a video arcade. Rent space in your parking lot for a kiosk. Would some other business meet a need of your customers or employees, or just the people who drive past your plant? Some fast-food restaurants are renting space to cookie and candy vendors.

TIMING

1. **Pay your down payment out of cash flow.** The original bootstrap technique, this time-honored method does not necessarily rely on a particularly strong cash flow: It can be a variation of increasing the accounts payable. The difference is here the

buyer increases them after closing. Just make accurate projections so you don't end up in bankruptcy court because your cash didn't flow in the right direction at the right time!

2. **Use postdated checks.** For some reason, some sellers otherwise reluctant to take a promissory note will take a postdated check. Legally, it's the same thing. If you're a few thousand dollars short, this option might save the day. Or hold closing on Saturday (assuming the banks are closed in your town) and cover the check out of weekend proceeds (assuming the business is open on the weekend).

3. **Shift closing so prorations and accruals work in your favor.** Real estate taxes, utilities, tenant rentals, vacation pay, payroll taxes, sales taxes, and many other items are accrued or prorated at closing. Determine what these items are as early as possible. A day can make a lot of difference.

IV

Negotiating Your Deal

11

Negotiating Your Best Deal

Treaties are observed as long as they are in harmony with interests.
—NAPOLEON I, *MAXIMS*

Your If is the only peacemaker. Much virtue in If.
—SHAKESPEARE, *AS YOU LIKE IT*

THE IMPORTANCE OF ATTITUDE

WE COULD REHASH here for you hundreds of techniques that will make your negotiating more effective—but we won't. Techniques, tactics, stratagems, devices, and ploys all have their place, but what is their place? How do you know when it is time to seek peace or to push for an advantage?

A proper attitude is the keystone upon which all negotiations must be built. The proper attitude has three characteristics: (1) determination, (2) trust, and (3) friendliness. Determination means that no matter what happens, you are going to make this deal happen. Whether you explain it as self-fulfilling prophecy, bullheadedness, or something else, the presence of this attitude on both sides has seen many negotiations through problems that derailed others. Promote this attitude among your team members and outside advisors. Naturally, you will temper it with a healthy dose of good judgment about the "other side" and the deal as a whole. But don't let your advisors run rampant with negatives, either. Every deal has negatives and nitpicking is a deal killer.

Second, you must project the attitude that you are trustworthy, and you must let the other side know you find them trustworthy, as well. The confidence of both parties is

155

essential to every good deal. Tell it like it is. If the truth will kill your deal, you didn't have a deal. Telling painful truths builds trust like nothing else.

Friendliness is equally critical. The television stereotype of the negotiator in a pinstripe suit pushing past the secretary to throw down an ultimatum is in real life a poor negotiator. More deals are glued together with honey than with vinegar. Do you make your best deals with a person who acts as if you're stupid? You're better off if you act like you just got off the boat. Show up initially without a battery of lawyers and accountants, and just be friendly.

Everything else flows from the right attitude. So check your attitude before you go into the negotiating room. If it's right, you'll remember what techniques to use, and you won't have to clutter your mind trying to remember all the other ones.

WHO SHOULD DO YOUR NEGOTIATING?

Clearly, you should manage your side's negotiations. The person who actually has the speaking role will vary from deal to deal, and from day to day in the same deal.

On some technical matters, the lawyers will be given the speaking parts. In some financial areas, the two accountants may do most of the wheeling and dealing. But overall, the parties at the highest level must agree on the main points of the deal. These people may be the head of the group working on the buyout and the comptroller of the subsidiary or division selling out. Advisors (lawyers, accountants, and others) are there, at least in part, to point up hazards and protect you as much as possible. They are, therefore, inclined to nitpick. Only the person who will manage the company after the buyout can ultimately make the decision about how much risk is warranted.

What if the parties get too emotionally involved? When this happens, call a time-out. If you see it happening to you, send in another team member to speak for you. If you have no one else on the team who can help, your lawyer might be a good choice, assuming she has developed a relationship with the other side. Or you might consider bringing in a business owner–friend. The business owner will likely take a practical approach to the problem.

TERMS ARE MORE IMPORTANT THAN PRICE

One of the major worries of first-time business buyers is "What price should I pay for the business?" Every buyer is concerned about overpaying. One of the best ways to make sure it doesn't happen to you is to make generous use of appraisers. There are appraisers available for land, for equipment, and for whole businesses. Appraisers do cost money, but they're one of the best investments you can make in your campaign to buy a business.

Get the hard assets of the business appraised. Get the whole business, including goodwill, appraised. The appraisals will help keep you from overpaying, but more important they will give you a feeling of confidence about the price on which you ultimately settle.

Beware of the seller who gives you a price based on a formula: "five times sales plus fixed assets," or "price-earnings multiple of six to eight." There is no such thing as a formula. Even the best appraisers will say they don't know what a company is worth. There is no comparability between publicly traded and closely held companies. Brokers say so. The IRS says so (see Appendix F). The courts say so. Don't let a seller tell you differently.

On the other hand, if the seller is hung up on a formula, maybe you could use that to your advantage. . . . No matter what price you decide on, terms will usually be more important than the actual dollar price. It is axiomatic among business brokers and investment bankers that "Price doesn't kill deals—terms do." Arthur Lipper III, one of the big-city money men and publisher of *Venture* magazine, bought his home after negotiating terms:

Lipper: "What's your price?"
Seller: "One million dollars."
Lipper: "Okay, I'll pay one million. Let's shake on it!"
Seller (shaking hands): "Gee that's great. But tell me something, Mr. Lipper. I really expected to do some horse trading on the price. You're such a big-time negotiator. How come you didn't argue with me on the price?"
Lipper: "I never negotiate on price. I always pay the asking price. But now that we know what the price is, let's talk a little about when and how you'll get your one million dollars. Let's take a long walk and discuss it."

FOCUS ON WHAT'S IMPORTANT

While we don't want to ignore the truth of the expression "The past predicts the future," you are not buying the past—only its effects. Instead you are buying the future, and only a vision of the future at that. Use the past to temper your enthusiasm.

Nonetheless, you should spend only about 5 percent of your time in any deal studying the past, and 95 percent studying the future. Here is where you can protect yourself from the seller's rosy pictures and give yourself an advantage unknown to the seller.

It is a common mistake of sellers to consider the buyer as a mirror image of themselves. But on a surface level, you will have changes you'll institute in the business, and you'll have different goals for it. Even more deeply, you should investigate the future with a view toward synergy: For instance, if your cost to establish an account with a new customer is running $1,500, and the target company has 1,500 accounts that you consider desirable, you would be ahead in money, time and effort to buy the business now for any price less than $2,250,000 (and you could consider the hard assets as a freebie). Again, if the target has a product that could round out your product line, your savings in elapsed time and design costs could make past sales results irrelevant to you.

Such synergy is often invisible to sellers. And there is no reason to reveal it. By the same token, observing how much time the seller spends explaining the past, as opposed to selling the future, is a big clue to his level of negotiating savvy.

GIVE AND TAKE

There are many excellent easy-to-understand books on negotiating. Find one or two and study not just the techniques but the reasoning behind the techniques, before you present your letter of intent. No two books have all the same techniques. There is often disagreement among the experts as to what techniques do and don't work.

However, there is one common thread. It is a point with which we firmly agree, based on years of personal negotiating experience. If one side wins and the other loses, both sides lose. If we have "put one over on you," you may not know it when you sign the papers. But you will find out, and you will find out sooner than we expect. And when you find out, you are going to look for a way to even the score. You're mad, and all of us have lost.

What follows is a list of ideas and techniques learned from real-life negotiations. Choose those that apply to you and your deal.

1. Remember that people usually have two reasons for doing anything: one that sounds good, and the real one. How do you dig out the real reason? It's not easy, particularly if you've ignored our admonitions to spend time building rapport with the seller. But if you have spent time building rapport, and if you are beginning to understand what makes the other person tick, you can sometimes make good use of a simple question: "In the back of your mind, is there another reason why you don't like

our offer?" The "in the back of your mind," or the "in addition to that" phrases tell the other person that it is all right to have another reason. Whatever the rationale, it works. Try it and see.

2. By now, you know your seller well enough to know her major needs. Make your offer so close to her acceptable range it is hard for her to reject it out of hand. If you make a "sleepless night offer," one that makes the seller nervous about rejecting it, you stand a better chance of acceptance than if you've made a ridiculously low offer. The seller can easily toss aside the ridiculous one. But a reasonable offer, close to or within the seller's range of acceptable deals, carries a high probability of success.

3. Most businesspeople consider themselves fair-to-middlin' horse traders. Entrepreneurs actually enjoy the give and take. So, although you want to get in the seller's reasonable range, you still want to be on the low side of the range, so you can ultimately congratulate the seller for driving such a hard bargain. Let him haggle you up a bit, and you both win.

4. The first person to speak after the handshaking and introductions are done sets the tone for the session. Your side should seek that role.

5. Questions can open up discussions ("What do you think of this issue?") and close them down ("How many full-time employees do you have?"). Leading questions can put you in control, unless they're abused ("Didn't you lose five of your nine dealers in the last twelve months?"). The one who's asking questions is the one who's in control.

6. A question can sometimes be viewed as argumentative, whether or not that was your intention. Prepare the ground for your questions. Explain why you are asking the question before you ask it.

7. Remember Abraham Maslow's hierarchy of human needs. Once people have fulfilled their more basic needs, they move on to higher ones. If you can pick out where the seller is on this hierarchy of needs, you can pinpoint your arguments to push the seller's hot buttons. Maslow's hierarchy is:

1. Physiological needs (food, clothing, and shelter)
2. Safety and security
3. Love and belonging
4. Esteem
5. Self-actualization (being all one can be)
6. Knowing about and understanding the world around us
7. Aesthetic needs

Maslow claimed every human being has these needs, but each person would concentrate on fulfilling the most basic ones first. The caveman thought first about getting food for his growling stomach and then about clothing and shelter to protect him from the night storms. No human being is totally on one level or another, since we each have all levels of needs. If your seller talks a lot about his wife and children, that may be a clue to highlight the extra family time he'll have available after he sells out (to you, of course). If he talks instead about goals, you may emphasize the freedom he will soon have to find new worlds to explore and conquer. In other words, first you listen. Then you think. Then you talk. Get it in the wrong order and you could end up with a bad case of hoof-in-mouth disease.

8. If the seller says something obviously emotional, or that carries emotional undertones, try saying, "I understand how you feel," and then shut up. The judicious use of silence, and particularly an approving silence, can be quite effective.

9. Avoid using threats and insults. You don't like them. Neither does the seller.

10. Get and keep the other person talking. It helps to find common ground. Try repeating her last three or four words with a question mark on the end. Ask "Why?"

11. Another way to get people to talk is to mirror their language. For instance, if they are auditory people, they will say (and you should follow their lead), "I hear what you're saying. . . ." "That sounds good to me. . . ." If they are visually oriented, they will say, "That looks good to me" or "I see what you mean." Kinesthetically oriented people will likewise talk about feelings or touching. You might try paraphrasing the other side or agreeing with them or simply saying "umm-hmmm." If all else fails, ask.

12. Give feedback. Feedback encourages further discussion, and helps you find more common ground.

13. According to an old Chinese proverb, the man who strikes the first blow admits his ideas gave out. Raising your voice is the same as striking a blow. Don't get angry. Try to keep on even ground.

14. Instead, usurp the reasonable position for yourself. Don't be heavy-handed. Try, "I realize the issues we are dealing with are important and therefore can be emotional. Perhaps if we can go on to a different point and come back to this one later, or maybe just take a break, we can make more headway."

15. When an issue does become emotionally charged, try to get the other person to talk about his emotions. "I hear you saying that my offer makes you mad—you consider it so low as to be an insult." This sort of active listening can be effective. Basically what you are doing is repeating back to the person what he has just said, without getting mad about it yourself. You have thus encouraged the person to open up to you. Open communications can only help make the deal work, giving you an opportunity to find common ground.

16. If someone gets emotional, try responding with facts and figures, not with emotions.

17. Stick to just a few major points and let the others take care of themselves. If

you're negotiating a $500,000 deal, don't let the $250 issue of who pays for the title insurance ruin the whole deal.

18. Agreements in principle are easier to get than detailed pacts. If you reach a sticking point, seek to agree to the big picture and delegate the details to others. That's why letters of intent are so useful. See the discussion about them later in this chapter.

19. Try to develop a good memory for what happens in the negotiating room. Concentrate on what you hear and see. Develop your peripheral vision. Did you notice the seller coughed when his attorney made that outrageous demand? Does it give you a clue to what the seller is thinking? File it away for later use. As Friedrick Foerster said, "If you don't use your eyes for seeing, you will need them for weeping."

Another technique is to somehow associate what you see and hear with a mental picture. You will improve your memory if you make your pictures silly and outrageous and somehow attach the important little thing you just heard to that picture visually.

20. Keep good notes. Try to become, or have someone on your team become, the secretary of the meetings. Keeping the minutes gives you an immense power over the person who cannot cite chapter and verse.

21. "A confused mind says no." Keep your ideas simple and easy to understand. Draw diagrams. Limit yourself to three or five points. Don't you just hate it when a speaker gets up and says, "There are 14 essential steps, and the failure to observe any one of them can bring disaster"? You can't recall any of his points when he is done. But if he gets up and says that there are three points, tells you what they are, explains them, and then tells you again what they were, you will probably retain them and use them. The same is true of your seller.

22. Cover the minor issues first so you get the momentum going in favor of agreement.

23. One of the national hamburger chains figures it needs to get a message to your conscious mind six times before you will buy. If repetition works for the big boys, you can make it work for you too. The more you say something, the more likely the other side is to believe it, or at least believe it is important to you. If it is important to you, and if the seller wants to make the deal work, it becomes important to him.

24. Many authors will tell you that you should sit at the right of the person you are trying to persuade, since it is the traditional seat of power. They offer all sorts of explanations, such as when kings met other kings they put the person they trusted on their right-hand side and the person they did not trust on their left-hand side. Thus, it was easier for the right-handed host to stab the distrusted guest on his left, and harder for the guest to stab the host. That theory went out the window the first time someone invited a left-handed king to dinner!

Studies have shown that our logic and reasoning abilities reside in the left hemisphere of our brains, and that the intuitive and emotional abilities reside in the right hemisphere, for most right-handed people (we still have to watch out for left-handed kings!). We also know that the right side of the brain is connected with the left side of the body and vice versa.

We are told, "Logic never sells; logic only tells." Psychologists are beginning to find out what advertisers and salespeople have known for a long time: In order to sell anybody anything, you have to appeal both to the person's logic and to the person's emotions. If you don't appeal to both sides, your chances of making a sale are slim. It is, in fact, the emotion that makes the sale.

Therefore, the theory now goes, if you want to persuade a seller to accept your terms, speak to his left ear. The new theory would have you seat your seller to your right so you can speak to his left ear. It might be worth trying.

25. Don't underestimate the power of a friendly and sincere smile. Use it again and again throughout the negotiations.

26. Maintain good eye contact, too. If the person thinks you have shifty eyes, he may not trust you.

27. Try to build goodwill. If you say you are going to do something, move heaven and earth to do it. It will help the next time around, even if it was trivial.

28. On the other hand, avoid predictability. Take a fresh, imaginative look at the whole deal after you think you have completed your preparation. Your technique in actual negotiating sessions could be merely tactical: Review the first two paragraphs of the document, jump to the last paragraph, then move to one in the middle. Reopen an agreed point once in a while. Avoiding predictability shifts control of the negotiations to you.

29. Many people feel vaguely guilty about trying to buy with limited cash, as if it somehow taints them. The fact that you're broke doesn't make you poor, or even a poor business risk. It's just present circumstances, which can change. Remember, your business ability has value. So does your ability to capture the imagination of the seller. The power you perceive in the other side is only that: a perception. Power is always limited and there is always something with which you can bargain. The single most common reason a person sells a business is boredom, and you have the power to free the seller from her business. That's often something the seller wants every bit as much as cash. So don't let a lack of cash hamper your negotiations. Always deal from a position of power. If you don't think you have power, act as if you do.

30. Where else can your power come from? You may have knowledge unavailable to the other side. Perhaps you have another deal cooking if this one sours. Maybe you can introduce some uncertainty. Perhaps you can devote more time and effort than the other side. You could have better bargaining skills. Perhaps you are able to act faster or more decisively. Sometimes there is power in irrationality. Sometimes just plain brinksmanship gives you power. These are all bargaining chips.

31. Summaries can be a strong tool in negotiations. Summarizing the position of

both parties can open up discussions. It can also serve to close discussions, as when you say "Okay, that about raps it up. Between now and our next meeting, you are going to find out the number of workmen's compensation claims you've had in the last three years, and get us an accounts receivable aging. We will prepare the next rough draft of the agreement." Summaries of what has gone on before can also organize the discussion and direct it into new areas.

32. Once you know the other person's hot buttons, try drawing word pictures of what he is seeking. If it's a trip to Hawaii, talk about the beach and use words that describe the scene and how it affects all five senses. If the seller is a subsidiary of a multinational corporation, it still works. Your negotiator is freed from managing a losing or boring business, and he can walk on the plush carpet of the executive suite without having to avoid the president's glare and apologize about the poor results of the division. He can hold his head high and experience the boss enthusiastically shaking his hand for driving such a good bargain on the deal. Get the idea?

33. Don't gang up on the other side by outnumbering them at the negotiating table. But don't let them outnumber you either. Find out who is going to be there, and come with an equal-size contingent.

34. Match the postures of the lead negotiator for the other side. This action establishes a subtle common ground. You might also consider sitting on the same side of the table to "get next to them." Or sit at the head of the table to take charge.

35. Try negotiating without a table. Furniture presents a psychological barrier as well as a physical one.

36. Always approach the negotiations from the soft side. It's easier to pick up the deal from there. Negotiations are like a tennis game. You hit the ball; the other side hits it back. Generally speaking, the shot you give is the shot you get back.

37. Watch the eyes of your opposite number. Psychologists today tell us that if the eyes dilate, you are seen as a friend. If they reduce to pinpoints, watch out!

38. Recent studies have shown that people's blink rate increases when you mention an issue they consider important. The normal rate without contact lenses is four to eight per minute, and with contacts, eight to twelve per minute. When you hit the button, the rate jumps to twenty to thirty per minute.

39. The first person to mention a price loses. It's an old rule that wins 80 percent of the time.

SIMPLICITY, SIMPLICITY, SIMPLICITY

You may recall the 1960s folk song by the Chad Mitchell Trio, "It Doesn't Pay to Be Too Hip." Well, the same holds true in negotiating a business deal.

Walter, who holds an MBA degree, fancies himself as a wheeler-dealer. Walter began pursuing a small manufacturing plant. The seller hadn't ever considered selling before Walter appeared on his doorstep. But Walter was determined. He gave the seller, Dan, a very generous but complicated offer. Dan doesn't understand fast-track techniques.

Walter has a fantastic mind, and it's always working. He is forever coming up with new ideas. As a result, Dan didn't know which end was up from week to week, because Walter kept changing his offer. True, the offer got sweeter for Dan as it went along, but it was hard to pick this out in the barrage of paperwork.

The parties finally reached agreement. Six months later Dan's attorney was threatening suit. Dan was being paid for stock over several years, and he had seen Walter do many sophisticated things with the corporation like moving assets among his various corporate enterprises. Walter was not very good at communicating the reasons for his actions. Dan got scared and threatened suit.

The root problem was Walter himself. Walter liked complicated things. But he could have made a conscientious effort to simplify things, so that other people would understand and cooperate. In short, don't be too creative. Build trust!

TIMING: MAKING THE CALENDAR WORK FOR YOU

In timing, as in other areas, the more you know about the seller and the situation, the better you will negotiate. If you know it will cost the seller an extra $440,000 in income taxes if he doesn't close by December 31, you can make that deadline work for you. Many, many businesses were sold on December 30, 1988, because of the tax law change.

If it is now November 12, you might take your time responding to her counter offer. Not so long as to be obvious, but November 29 is a nice time to make your response: not quick, but then again, not so slow as to suggest a delay. And perhaps you might include a requirement for some time-consuming step on one side or the other before a final decision can be reached. As you get closer to the deadline, the seller's positions will begin to soften. The person with the known deadline has the weaker position. If you have a deadline, don't make it known, and make it seem insignificant. You need to have time on your side. It's a great ally.

If there is one thing more important than anything else in negotiations, it is to find out as much as you possibly can about the other side. The other side's timing is one of the key facts you want to discover early. Don't be afraid to let the other side know a great deal about you generally (with the exception of your deadlines and your specific plans). The more each side knows about the other, the more likely a common ground can be found. All deals are based on trust, and trust is commonly based on a depth of mutual understanding. Don't hamper the process by holding back, and never be afraid to ask for more. Get them talking. It can make your deal.

The best way to avoid getting hung out to dry on the timing issue is to avoid unrealistic expectations as to time. Most business acquisitions take six to eighteen months from first contact to closing. Typically, about 400 hours of meetings with your counterparts and team members are involved in the process. The timing can be broken down as follows:

Deal Flow	60–90 days
Initial contact and review	30 days
Detailed evaluation	60–90 days
Business plan written, negotiations proceed simultaneously, letter of intent signed	30–60 days
Due diligence, documentation	30–90 days

According to the Geneva Company, a nationwide business brokerage firm,

50 percent of all deals fail at the letter of intent stage,
25 percent of all deals fail at the due diligence stage,
15 percent of all deals fail at the documentation stage,
10 percent of all deals make it to closing.

In view of these factors, it is wise to adopt a long-term viewpoint and let the other guy get hung up on his own deadlines.

LETTERS OF INTENT

The purpose of a letter of intent is to get on paper the major terms prior to the preparation of a formal contract. It is strictly what it says: a statement of the parties' plan to buy and sell this business, an agreement in principle.

However, in at least one case, a court has held a letter of intent to be binding on the parties. In other words, once the letter of intent was signed, neither party could back out of the deal. Nor could either party prepare a formal, detailed contract covering the other important points of the deal!

Be clear in your mind and on paper about the purpose of your letter of intent. Make sure to state in black and white whether or not it is to be binding. Is a letter of intent, then, good to have? The answer depends on your situation. An example might point the way.

Frank D. was negotiating to buy a retail store in a small town in northern Indiana. Frank had been involved in the management of a similar operation in another town, and was anxious to try his hand at running his own shop. George M., the seller, was burned out, and wanted a different kind of retail business.

Negotiations started on August 22 and culminated, Frank thought, in a twelve-page agreement presented to George M. on January 10. The length of the agreement scared George M. Next commenced a fourteen-month on-again, off-again negotiation complete with yelling and screaming. On March 15 of the following year, a two-page letter of intent was finally signed. On July 11, almost two years after negotiations started, the deal closed. The only thing that kept the deal together was George M.'s psychological commitment to sell, made in the letter of intent.

Thus, a lengthy contract can be the wrong card to play first. Instead, the letter of intent serves the useful purpose of getting a psychological commitment to the deal (remember the determination factor?), which can then be translated into a bought business.

Frank's example was not totally unusual; you can expect the seller to get cold feet some time in the last week before closing and threaten to call the whole thing off. That's normal, and every seller has to work through it. Making an irrevocable decision about a "child" is traumatic.

You, as buyer, can also expect to get cold feet about a week ahead of the seller. Again, you are making a momentous financial decision, and that, too, is difficult. Don't give up. Even though things may not look like they are moving along the way you would like, even if the deal looks like it's off, it can ultimately come together.

Frank's letter of intent was signed whereas the detailed contract was not. The seller simply was not emotionally ready to go through the details of the lengthy document.

A letter of intent can and should be drawn without a lot of legalese. It should be a nonthreatening business document. It is most frequently written in the form of a letter making generous use of first names in order to strengthen its nonthreatening nature. We have even seen a letter of intent as just an outline with no signatures. Still, you should try to get signatures, or at least initials, so you have a psychological commitment. Because there are fewer details, there is less opportunity to disagree.

Once a letter of intent has been signed, both parties will work hard, spend money, and labor into the small hours of the night to try to make the deal happen. The letter of intent is the physical act embodying the emotional decision to sell at this price and these terms.

Would it be better for the buyer if the letter of intent were binding? In most cases, no. Myriad details remain to be worked out, even after the major terms have been struck. For instance, there is always give and take on the allocation of the total price to particular assets in an asset deal. In the early stages there is seldom an agreement as to such allocations: The only thing the parties want to do is to agree on an overall price. If you already have a binding agreement in the letter of intent, you are tying your hands and preventing your advisors from coming up with a detailed contract later, which will be binding on everybody, including the IRS.

Then, too, you might not be ready to be tied down to the deal. We're not suggesting you actively look at three or four businesses at once. Looking at one business is time consuming enough, and if you persist in negotiating with three or four sellers, you will at least get a little cross-eyed.

Often you can't yet know whether the deal will definitely work out. Financing needs to be nailed down. There are partnership or corporation decisions to be made with your inside people. There is much you have yet to find out about your target business, all of it significant, and some of it capable of ruining your deal. For instance, negotiations for a local Coca-Cola bottling plant involved checking over the Coca-Cola Company contract to see whether it could be assigned to the buyer. If the contract had prevented this assignment, or if the Coca-Cola Company had said no, the whole deal would have been called off.

You may also uncover liens of which neither party was aware. You may discover lawsuits that point toward a bigger problem, in turn causing you to reevaluate this target. The list goes on and on. If you keep your options open at this early stage, you have the ability to negate a poor deal. The same is true for the seller. In most cases, neither party wants to have the letter of intent binding.

How do you make it nonbinding? Have your contract specifically state that it is not binding, and that neither party is liable even if the other changes its position or spends large amounts of money in reliance on the contract.

Look at the two examples of letters of intent. Example A is a letter of intent for a retail establishment. Example B is from a manufacturing deal. These were written for specific transactions, and are therefore not something you will want to copy for your own deal, but they give you something against which to compare the one you get from your lawyer.

You should always be given an opportunity to review contracts, letters of intent, and other significant documents before they are presented to the other side. Thus, you can suggest changes and terms that may have occurred to you after you told your attorney what you wanted in the document. It is a good idea to read the document a couple of times, make your changes, and sleep on it overnight, coming back to it fresh in the morning.

Example A

June 15, 19X1

Jones Five and Dime, Inc.
Attn: John Jones, President
PERSONAL AND CONFIDENTIAL

Dear John:

Concerning: Offer to Purchase

I hereby offer to purchase from you certain assets of the business known as Jones Five and Dime, Inc., according to the following terms and conditions:

1. The purchase price for inventory items and the following noninventory items will be a total of $200,000.00: fixtures, shelving, office equipment, leasehold improvements, all other tangible assets of the business; customer lists and telephone numbers of the business; collectable trade accounts receivable; business name, "Jones Five and Dime"; goodwill; and for your covenant not-to-compete. If the amounts in paragraphs 3 and 4 are different, the price will be adjusted accordingly, up or down.

2. The purchase price for inventory and noninventory items shall be paid as follows: $1,000 earnest money is tendered with this offer; and the balance will be paid by certified or cashier's check at closing.

3. I will also assume at closing, and agree to pay all present accounts payable, not to exceed $100,000.00.

4. The actual salable inventory at date of closing shall not be less than $160,000.00, and trade accounts receivable shall not be less than $17,000.00.

5. This agreement is contingent upon all of these:

A. My being able to negotiate a lease-purchase agreement for the premises on which the business is now being conducted, on terms agreeable to the landlord and to me;

B. A review of your books, records, and financial statements by me and by any representatives I may choose. The review shall show information and conclusions acceptable to me. You agree to make your president and your regular accountant available to me or my representatives or both at reasonable times;

C. My ability to obtain financing acceptable to me for this purchase. I will have no more than one week in which to begin an application, and no more than five weeks thereafter to get a written loan commitment; and

D. Our ability to reach a formal agreement of sale, including a covenant not to compete and allocation of purchase prices.

6. The closing of this purchase and the sale shall be on or about June 30, 19X1 at the offices of the corporation, or at such other time (sooner, or later, as agreed) or place as shall be agreed to by the parties.

If you agree to these terms and accept my offer, please indicate by signing below. The copy is for your files.

Sincerely,

Thomas Hopeful, Buyer

Enclosure: Check for $1,000.00

AGREED AND ACCEPTED:
Jones Five and Dime, Inc.

By: _____
    John Jones, President

Example B

December 27, 19X1

Mr. John Jones, President
General Manufacturing

Dear Mr. Jones:

After various discussions with Joe Greene, Don Selle, and Fred Lake, and after reviewing the information you have provided, a company will be formed to enter into an agreement with your company to purchase certain assets located at your plant in Universal City, N.I.

The assets to be purchased include inventories, equipment, land and buildings, drawings, bills of material, jigs, fixtures, dies, molds, tools, tooling, advertising material, manuals, office furniture and equipment, customer lists, trademarks, trade names, consultants' reports, and any and all records and information necessary to run the business in an orderly fashion. Accounts receivable will not be purchased and will remain the property of General Manufacturing.

The purchase price for the above assets will be $850,000 ($1,100,000 − $250,000), based on the plant balance sheet as of October 3, 19X1. Any changes from these amounts until the day of closing will be reflected in the final price.

The terms of payment will be cash at the time of closing equal to $850,000. The accounts receivable will be collected by our company and passed on to General Manufacturing as collected.

The purchase price shall be structured as follows:

Inventory — Currently Good Inventory Taxable Value at 10/31/X1 (Estimated LIFO Amount Based on $525,000 of FIFO Valuation)	$410,000
Fixed Assets	125,000
Balance—Noncompeting and Consulting	315,000
Total Cash at the Time of Closing	$850,000
Accounts Receivable (Kept by the Seller)	250,000
Total	$1,100,000

It is anticipated that the transaction will close within thirty days from the date of acceptance of this letter.

This letter is not intended as a legal document but rather a statement of our intent. It shall not be binding on either of us, even if one or both of us shall change our position or expend significant time, money, or effort in reliance on this letter. If you agree with the terms of this letter, please so indicate by your signature below. Preparation of the necessary legal documents will commence immediately upon acceptance.

Very truly yours,

Thomas Hopeful

ACCEPTABLE:
General Manufacturing

By: _____
     John Jones

The buyer usually prepares the first draft of the formal contract. This process normally carries over to the letter of intent, but not always. It's not as critical at the letter of intent stage who prepares the document. But make sure you familiarize yourself with the reasons your side should prepare the formal contract (see Chapter Twelve), and then magnanimously offer, in the letter of intent, to prepare the formal contract.

BUTTERFLIES: PRESENTING YOUR OFFER

Under normal circumstances you won't want to send your letter of intent through the mail to your seller. There is so much behind words that you cannot put on a printed page, and so many negatives that a seller could read into them. If you just send it through the mail, the seller's reactions will almost always be more negative than if you personally deliver it. In short, your mailed letter of intent has less chance of being signed than a hand-delivered one.

Not only should you hand deliver the letter but you should explain it in detail first. The best way is to present the terms orally, even before the other side knows you have a written document. If you hand somebody a document as significant as a letter of intent, he will stop listening and read through the entire document before he tunes back to your voice. Just handing him the letter of intent, or handing it to him prematurely (that is, before you have explained it), is the same as or worse than sending it through the mail.

Who on your team should write the letter of intent? Ideally, the lead manager should prepare the first draft. If that's you, and you are uncomfortable with writing, at least list the major terms of the deal, such as price, payment terms, when the deal is to be closed, and similar items. Then give your first draft to your accountant. Your accountant can make sure that you have covered all the financial terms of the deal, which at this point have precedence over the legal terms. She may have some additional terms to make the document complete.

Now you can take the document along with your accountant's suggestions to your lawyer. Your lawyer will put the document into final shape, make his own improvements, and see that provisions such as the nonbinding clause get included.

Next, take the draft and read it as if you were the seller. Are you offended? Is the tone a little too strong? Does it convey a message you don't want? Get these problems corrected.

Now re-edit the document to make sure all necessary details are covered. Analyze it based on who, what, where, when, why, and how. Give it back to your lawyer for the final draft. That draft is the one you present to the other side.

Who should present the letter of intent? The answer to this difficult question depends in part on the advisors on each side. In Frank D.'s case with George M. and the retail store, both Frank and George got along well enough, but George could not make a decision. Frank decided his lawyer should present the offer to George's accountant, because they had a good working relationship. The result was a signed letter of intent.

In another instance, the broker (whom the buyer had hired) made the presentation directly to the seller. The deal was in excess of a million dollars and involved numerous facts and figures. The seller was a large corporation, and the buyer was a wealthy individual. The broker happened to be a CPA, and the party in charge of negotiations for the seller, the controller, was also a CPA. The negotiations went smoothly because they spoke the same language.

REJECTED: WHAT NEXT?

So you have presented your offer and the seller just gave you a flat "no," or worse, laughed at it. Or the seller's attorney said, "That's not even in the ball park. It's not worth discussing further." What do you do next? Take a lesson from the sales field. Statistics reveal that most sales are made after as many as seven callbacks. Remember, "no" is easier to say than "yes." Once the seller has said "no," he can always change his mind without losing face.

Turn the situation around by saying, "Please don't make a final decision until I have had time to dig up additional facts that may shed more light." Don't wait for an answer; just act fast. Get the seller talking, maybe about side issues, like the vacation she has planned for this summer. Later you can bring the conversation back to the proposed deal and try to find out what's missing. Ask "why?" Listen carefully to the answer. Ask, "What else in the back of your mind didn't you like about the offer?" Use whatever techniques you can to get the seller talking so you can find some common ground.

Try to get the seller to feed back your offer to you: It's possible some key term was not heard or understood correctly. Get the objection on the table. It's easier to deal with a known problem.

COUNTEROFFERS AND READING BETWEEN THE LINES

So you've made an offer, and you get the standard "We'll think about it." After a couple of weeks of nervous waiting, you get a counteroffer in the mail. It is almost 180 degrees from your offer. The price is impossible. The terms just won't work in the cash flow scenarios you have prepared. And the seller has turned the deal on its head to where it is going to cost you another 30 percent, because of extra income taxes. Now what?

First, reread the offer for tone. Did the author try to downplay negative aspects? Were soft words or hard words used? Did the seller suggest or demand? Ask yourself if the changes are so big as to be ridiculous, or do they just represent good old-fashioned hard bargaining?

You will probably find both hard and soft words. It's a good bet the numbers represent hard bargaining, and not totally unrealistic proposals. After all, the seller thought enough of you and your offer to counter. If such is your case, congratulate yourself and your team. The seller is taking you seriously and wants to make the deal work.

Assuming the tone was demanding and the counter was unrealistic, you need to ask yourself whether you want this business enough to make a bad deal. The answer should ordinarily be "no." But if the answer is "yes," we leave you to your own devices to figure out ways to make it less onerous.

Assuming that the counter is in good faith, you have work to do. Take a hard look at your previous cash flow projections to see how close you can come to the counter proposal. Much of your earlier preparation will have given you a pretty good idea of where your upper limits lie. It still pays to take another look, since you have undoubtedly learned new things you didn't know when you made your initial projections.

If the counter included both hard and soft words, take another look at those hard words. They may be indications of the seller's biggest needs, maybe even the absolute-must-have-or-I'll-not-sell provisions. Take a close look, and in your counter to the seller's counter, try to include these provisions, or variations that meet both parties' needs. Make sure your attorney makes the counter-counter specific so the seller doesn't get something you didn't intend to give.

Sit back and make sure you are not making a bad deal. Take still another look at your cash flow projections. Make sure that you can afford the payments, even if things don't go as well as planned. Does the deal make sense overall? Call in a friend whose business judgment you trust and explain the deal orally. Doing so can clarify your thoughts and show you weaknesses and strengths you missed. His independent viewpoint doesn't hurt, either.

CHECKLIST OF MAJOR TERMS FOR EFFECTIVE LETTERS OF INTENT

1. How will individual items be allocated? Usually the letter of intent covers only the overall price and not the allocation of individual items. Still, if you are buying assets, you will eventually have to allocate your purchase price among the items you are buying, to get the best tax advantage. For instance, a covenant not to compete will be deductible as paid. However, equipment will be deductible over the life of the equipment (a long time), and buildings will be deductible over the life of the buildings (a much longer time). Some things (such as the business name and land) will not be deductible at all. Usually the allocation is not handled in the letter of intent; only the overall price is handled. Be sure to get professional tax advice about allocations: The above list of deductions was good when written, but Congress gets the whim to change the tax code every few months.

2. Will the seller get all cash at closing, or will it take some paper back? Generally

speaking, it's smart business to pay some of the price to the seller over time, even if you could pay all cash. It gives you a hold over the seller if something doesn't work out as expected.

3. Will there be a covenant not to compete? Will there be a consultation agreement? Sometimes these are fully decided as to time and geographic limits by the time you sign the letter of intent, and sometimes they are left for the final document.

4. Is the name of the business to be transferred? Don't just rush past this one: Keeping the name may help keep the customers. The same is true of telephone numbers.

5. When will possession change hands?

6. Will there be prorations of rents, income, utilities, and taxes? Commonly, prorations are left for the final document, but they can represent a major dollar amount. You might want to discuss them early.

7. Will part of the purchase price be held in escrow? If so, for how long? What triggers the release?

8. Is the real estate leased? If so, the seller usually needs the landlord's permission to assign the lease or sublet to the buyer. On the other hand, if the seller owns the building but is not selling it, you want to get the broad outlines of a lease into your letter of intent.

9. What important facts must be true before you will agree to buy? Is it important that all of the equipment be in good working order on the day of closing? Or that all of the customers who normally buy more than $100,000 per month have continued ordering over the last two months?

10. How will you handle inventory? Are you going to pay one price and get whatever inventory is on hand (normal with a service business)? Or will you agree to a price plus the value of the inventory at or near closing (normal with a manufacturer or a retail store, where inventory is the major item, and can vary day-to-day)? An inventory is taken (perhaps by an outside inventory service) on the weekend and the closing is held on Monday. Do you want clauses to prevent the seller from loading up on inventory or running it down to zero?

11. Will there be an earnest money deposit? Cash is the tie that binds the parties to the deal, both legally and emotionally. Under what circumstances do you get it back, and under what circumstances does the seller keep it?

12. When and where will closing be? If you have a touchy seller, it might be best to have the closing on his turf.

13. Should the deal be contingent on something? For instance, you may want to condition it upon receiving a bank loan for $675,000, at 1 percent over prime, for seven years. Or you may simply condition it upon a review of the books and a favorable recommendation by your CPA.

12

Making Contracts, Side Agreements, and Closing Work for You

It is not the oath that makes us believe the man, but the man the oath.
—AESCHYLUS, *FRAGMENTS*

Too MUCH PAPER is generated in a business acquisition. It is not uncommon for the formal documents alone to be two or three inches thick. All that loophole plugging can be deadening. On the other hand, you wouldn't want the whole deal to fall apart six months from now when it could have been cemented with the right clause in the contract today.

The trick is to document the high points and avoid the trivial ones. The clause forgotten is the one that will rise and bite you. When a problem or disagreement arises, everybody runs back to the documents to search for an "out." Take the example of the tax code: Every time Congress meets to plug a loophole, business people, tax lawyers, and accountants scurry around to find the new ones created. So it goes with every business deal. You can't cover it all.

The fewer words you use, the less room for discord, but don't be too terse. Cover the main areas of agreement, and look down the road for potential slippery spots. Salt or sand those spots lightly using your best judgment, and then forget them.

Don't tighten up your documents so nobody has room to maneuver. An agreement should express a living, breathing relationship. The documents merely give the outside boundaries of the relationship. You are going to have to live with the seller's management team at least until your note is paid off, and often longer, because you may need to call upon him to help deal with a problem with a major customer or supplier. If the acquisition gets audited on both parties' tax returns, you may want to compare notes.

Much of the typical basic acquisition agreement "survives closing" as the lawyers say: There are agreements to do things for months and perhaps years after closing. Your relationship is a dynamic one, and your agreement should be elastic enough to allow the relationship to grow and change. It should have the features of loose-fitting cotton clothing with elastic waistbands, not of iron plate armor. Ideally, as new circumstances arise, you should amend the agreement, even after closing.

The purpose of the contract is to benefit both parties over time. Thus, a contract should represent more nearly a process than an event.

WHO SHOULD WRITE THE FIRST DRAFT?

Usually, the buyer's side prepares the first draft. The buyer normally needs clauses and terms of which the seller has no advance knowledge. For instance, it might be important to the buyer to have the seller warrant all equipment to be in good running order. It might be important to the buyer that contracts with major suppliers be valid, in force, and transferable to the buyer. The buyer may want to be sure all income taxes of the business have been paid, and there are no outstanding audits. There are literally dozens of things the buyer will need or want, of which the seller will be unaware.

Well, then, wouldn't it be easier and cheaper to let the seller go to the expense of preparing the rough draft, and you can just add the paragraphs you want? Seldom does it work out that way. It has been our experience that the seller's attorney normally aims at binding the deal, covering only the barest bones. Then the buyer's attorney must either cut and paste, or start from scratch. If she cuts and pastes, she needs to review the other side's document in detail, looking for nuances of meaning that could cause you big problems down the road. And the seller could be offended by the volume of changes. Offense taken, deal shaken.

The seller's side quite naturally proceeds from the attitude that the document his side drew up represents a "done" deal. The new draft is therefore a proposal to change essential terms, which puts you in the defensive position of having to argue for what you always expected to see in the deal. You may even have to prove your good faith all over again. On the other hand, if your side prepares the first draft, you can include everything that you want and need, and the other side will likely just fine-tune your language.

Additionally, do not underestimate the effect on the other side of a well-prepared agreement. It is the mark of a careful lawyer, and should gain you a measure of respect from the sellers. So offer to have your lawyer draw up the document, and eight times out of ten the seller will accept.

THE FIRST DRAFT

When your attorney gets done with the first draft, do not just send it to the other side for review, even if you are in a rush to get the deal done. Make sure your accountant gets a copy of all drafts from both sides. Your accountant will have valuable input and must not be bypassed.

Each member of your management team should read through the document. Let it sit overnight. (Sure it's hard to do. But invest the time now to do it right, or you may have to invest infinitely more time trying to fix it by lawsuit later.) Then look at it again and make sure it contains all necessary details.

Next, sit down with your lawyer and CPA and go through the document page by page. Get your lawyer to explain things that don't make sense. Discuss strategy. Make changes and give a clean draft to the other side. (Word processors are wonderful.)

What happens next depends on the relationships of all people involved, including the attorneys. Sometimes the seller's attorney will phone the buyer's attorney to discuss possible changes. Sometimes the principals will meet to discuss the changes. Sometimes a big meeting with principals, attorneys, and CPAs is held. The latter is usually most efficient. Everybody can sit together and make needed decisions without incessant games of phone tag and repetitious discussions. Of course, it's hard to carry on private strategy conferences with the other side sitting right next to you. But the openness does lead to a feeling of mutual trust, and you can always go to another room to discuss strategy.

YOU VERSUS YOUR ATTORNEY

Your attorney has been subverted by law school. When she went away to law school she was just a normal person with a good practical mind. By the time she got out she had been trained to look for the potential disaster in every situation. If there is a risk she was told to explain it to her client. If there is a problem, no matter how insignificant, it could suddenly rise and ruin her client. The crux of the problem is law schools don't tell fledgling attorneys how to weigh the risks they uncover.

Here, then, is your job: You must get all the information you can from your professional advisors and evaluate it for yourself. If the risk seems slight, you are justified in assuming it as a normal business risk. So if your lawyer tells you she has found a potential problem in your acquisition, and you think the risk is low, your decision controls. Most lawyers will respect your judgment and write the documents accordingly.

One exception is when your lawyer says a proposal is unethical, immoral, illegal, or all three. You should seriously consider her judgment on this point. If you decide to go further, you will need to hire other counsel; your lawyer is required to withdraw.

A second exception is when she says you'll be a fool to proceed. Lawyers seldom give such advice lightly. If you hear it, don't give way to your anger. Instead, sleep on it and give it cool and quiet reflection in the morning.

In other situations, if you disagree with your attorney you prevail. If you don't, you need a different attorney.

WHY THAT CLAUSE?

Here are the whys and wherefores of what can go into the big paper. Not every agreement has each term below: there probably are none that have all. It is nevertheless a useful checklist of points to cover.

1. **Recitals.** These opening paragraphs seem at first unnecessary. They name the parties and invariably give a brief description of the transaction—sometimes too brief. This brief description is what courts first review when called on to interpret the agreement. So it can be important material years down the road. Special concerns for one or both sides should be fully explained here.

2. **Purchase and sale terms.** Here is the basic deal: what is bought and sold; the price; covenants not to compete. The closing date and place are specified. This section should detail the specific assets being purchased and what liabilities are or are not being assumed, so there can be no questions later.

Most details should be included in attachments or exhibits. If you find an extra tool that should have been included, you can add it to the end of the list, without retyping the whole agreement.

Side agreements, such as the covenant not to compete, should be attached to the main agreement in their entirety, right from the first draft. Don't leave them for a surprise at closing. Resolve all problems before closing!

3. **Seller's representations and warranties.** Normally, this is the battleground. To the uninitiated, it looks like a lot of legal mumbo jumbo. In point of fact here is where you cement your deal. For instance, there is usually a representation that the seller owns what it is selling and there are no contracts or liens that block or cloud its sale.

The purpose of this lengthy section is twofold: to gather information you need to make a final decision to buy, and to allocate risks between the parties. This second purpose is less well understood, even by attorneys who write these agreements. If a representation is untrue, then the seller has to pay whatever it costs to fix it. But if the sellers have disclosed the problem, they are more likely than not off the hook, and the buyer pays.

Often, the seller will want to qualify or limit your proposed representations with phrases like "to the best of the seller's knowledge." Consider what is at stake. Don't just give in. The request may not be as reasonable as it seems. For instance, let's say your lawyer has included a clause saying there are no outstanding product liability claims. The seller objects, saying that he can't be 100 percent sure—somebody in another state may have been injured by the product, but may not yet have filed suit. If you are seeking to limit your exposure to product liability claims to a certain date (such as the closing date), then you should press for the clause as it stands. Why? Because this language allocates the risk of those unknown claims to the seller, instead of to you. As you would expect, there is much give and take on areas of materiality and knowledge.

Doug usually includes a paragraph saying the seller doesn't have knowledge of any breach of the agreement by either party. You don't want to be stuck by a seller who has put in some innocuous-looking clause that allows her to declare you in default immediately after signing. Since the paragraph cuts both ways, it also brings to the fore any breach by the seller. It is simply a good faith clause. A parallel clause should be included in the buyer's representations.

4. **Buyer's representations.** Usually, the only concerns are that the buyer have proper corporate and other legal authority to enter into the purchase. Be sure to get an opinion letter from the seller's attorney, and possibly from the IRS (the IRS can take three to nine months to answer) stating the seller has such authority. See number 8 below.

5. **Survival of representations and warranties.** If the seller is only on the hook for representations and warranties until closing, or for only a short period after closing, you have lost their benefit.

6. **Seller's covenants.** The representations and warranties were a snapshot of the business at a point in time. But what does the seller do between now and closing, and even after closing? For instance, you want free access to the records of the business to complete your investigation. You will probably require the business continue to be run in the ordinary course (this means no unusual transactions, such as sale of major assets, without the buyer's permission). Governmental consents need to be obtained. The seller should update the schedules and disclosures to reflect new developments. Tax returns need to be consistent with the purchase agreement. You'll also want a catchall clause that any actions, even if missed in the agreement, will be taken to carry out the agreement.

As for after-closing actions by the seller, here is where you'll put earnouts, noncompetes, and consultation agreements. Remember, although the seller is motivated today and really means it when he says, "I'll stick around for six months to really help you be a success," somehow the mere act of getting a big check at closing has a marvelous way of changing his attitude. It might be a good idea to make sure you have a large percentage of the money contingent on future performance.

7. **Buyer's covenants.** In addition to covenants to mirror the seller's, there will probably be covenants providing for confidentiality of information if the deal falls through, and agreements not to raise salaries, pay dividends, or take money out of the corporation until the purchase money notes have been fully paid.

8. **Conditions prior to closing.** Here is a listing of steps each party must take before closing. If not completed, the other party can walk away. These may include written statements that all representations remain true as of closing date, and certificates from the attorneys that the corporation is in good standing, the contracts and notes are legally enforceable, and all licenses or contracts are transferable. Here's the place where you can have the seller's lawyer (who may have years of inside information on your target business) working for you at the seller's expense. Don't pass it up.

9. **Bulk sales clause.** If you sell all your assets and go out of business, your creditors cannot be left holding the bag. The law gives creditors the right to follow assets sold and repossess them from the buyer. In essence, the buyer of business assets guarantees the creditors of the business that their bills will be paid when due.

If you don't like the idea of paying your seller's debts, make sure there is a "bulk sales" provision in your asset purchase agreement. The clause requires the seller to provide a sworn list of assets (the list is probably already prepared for the sale) and a list of all creditors. Each of the creditors is notified by mail of the transaction, and a notice to creditors is published in the local newspaper.

Sellers usually object to the bulk sales clause. You might have objections, as well. For instance, if customers or suppliers discover the business is changing hands, your sales or supplier relationships could be damaged. This legitimate concern is one to deal with only after considering everything you know about the business, its customers, and its suppliers. Sometimes you will ultimately agree to waive compliance with the bulk sales act, and sometimes not.

The seller faces potential problems with customers and suppliers if the transaction does not go through. The seller may also object to the paperwork burden and the time delay: Ten days notice has to be given, at a time when everyone is anxious to close.

Stanley C. purchased a retail business and ran into trouble with the bulk sales clause. He had worked for the business before buying it, and thought he knew what bills were outstanding. He did not—to the tune of about $6,000. Stanley paid the $6,000 and had to arm wrestle the seller for partial reimbursement.

Don't waive your protections if you have any questions at all about who the creditors are or how much they are owed. Don't forget that product liability claimants are creditors. At the very least, waive the notice only before closing, but require the sworn lists of creditors and assets. Get the seller to agree to pay any claims not included on the list. Better yet, escrow a few dollars for six or seven months for undiscovered liabilities. After closing, mail and publish the notice yourself. There is a legal argument that the creditors only have six months in which to come forward or they are out of luck. Whatever the legalities, the notices may get the potential troublemakers to step forward sooner. The sooner you know about them, the better your chances of getting an adjustment from the seller.

10. **Miscellaneous provisions.** Even lawyers call these sections "boiler plate," but they do serve useful purposes. For instance, one typical clause says, "This agreement supersedes all prior written or oral negotiations." The clause applies to any letter of intent. In other words, if it isn't in writing, *in here,* you don't have it. There may be provisions about where to send notices or communications between the parties (it helps to require the other party to send a copy of all notices to your attorney as well as to you, so you have two shots at actually getting a notice), some language about successor corporations being liable (your seller doesn't want you to transfer its assets to a new corporation, and then be unable to collect), which state's law governs interpretation (so the parties can be sure it will be read the same way it was written) and similar matters. It's helpful to build in a cooling-off period of a month or two, so if one party feels wronged by the other, you can get together to resolve your differences without going to court.

SIDE AGREEMENTS

Most acquisitions, besides the formal contract to buy and sell, will have several of the following related documents:

Covenant Not to Compete
Consultation Agreement
Employment Contract
Deeds
Bills of Sale
Financing Statements
Assignment of Patents, Trademarks, and Copyrights
Closing or Settlement Statement
Promissory Notes
Security Agreements

Attachments should be circulated as early as possible. Ideally, they should be attached to the first draft shown to the other side. Some attachments, such as lists of assets and creditors, cannot be prepared by your side. Even if in your locality there is a standard form (a charming creature existing only in mythology) for a particular document, such as a deed or a security agreement, and even if it is the practice for the seller's attorney to prepare the document, insist that your counsel prepare and attach them to the first draft. Standard forms are an excuse not to think. Every standard form ever devised has in one deal or the next been doctored by writing in or crossing out. If the form can be changed, don't you want the momentum to be on the side of your changes?

Closing should be an anticlimax. Everything should be settled ahead of time. The only reason for closing is to get everybody's signature and exchange a check for the keys. It should not be a battleground. With proper effort ahead of time, it need not be.

The last two documents, the promissory note and security agreement, are commonly battlegrounds themselves. Don't let them become purely legal battlegrounds. Here is where you must allow your deal to breathe. These documents are the ones within which you must live and continue your relationship with the seller for months and years to come. Don't abdicate your business judgment to the attorney. Be creative. Think in functional terms. The seller wants to be protected in case your fortunes reverse. The seller does not want to come back in and pick up the pieces. The seller, after all, wants out. The smoothest repossession in the world only puts the seller back into problems and headaches.

On the other side, the buyer doesn't want a minor financial reversal or seasonal fluctuations to turn into a lost business. Business is not a black-and-white proposition, but a variegated rainbow of all colors.

In short, both parties have an interest in making sure the buyer has all reasonable opportunities to make the deal work.

Therefore, it is in your mutual interests to move away from the legal boiler plate and provide a series of tools (not necessarily weapons) to solve problems: a fly swatter for minor problems; a crowbar and hammer for malleable problems; a sledgehammer to "persuade" bigger discrepancies into line; and an elephant gun for cases when the business really must be put out of its misery.

Room to Breathe Clauses

As idea starters, consider the following:

1. Adequate time to cure minor problems.

2. A level of capital that can be scaled up over four or five years to account for changing needs, instead of a requirement that the buyer maintain a certain preset working capital level.

3. A grace period, or even different financial targets, to allow for seasonal fluctuations.

4. A cooling-off period.

5. A requirement that the seller's key people consult with the buyer's personnel if problems arise. This consultation might be triggered by failure to meet certain ratios for two or three months running. A variation would be to put some of the seller's people on the buyer's board of directors, perhaps giving them the power to call board meetings. If the buyer can call upon the seller's knowledge and experience, it might prevent a problem from getting out of hand.

6. A requirement that specified financial information and events be communicated to the seller within days of occurrence. However, even if you don't have such a clause, you should make it a policy to keep the seller's team informed as completely and promptly as possible. The more you keep the channels of communications open, the more likely you are to work out problems. Stonewalling the other side only accelerates the problem.

7. A once-per-year payment moratorium. Some commercial banks offered loans a few years ago in which the borrower had the option to skip a payment once a year. The only requirement was to mail a coupon informing the bank of the skip before the payment due date.

8. Some flexibility built in for yourself in the event everything goes as well as, or better than, expected. For instance, if you have been up-to-date in all of your payments, once the note is three-quarters paid down, then your key employees will be permitted a 15 percent pay raise.

The concept of all of these ideas is to provide ahead of time a mechanism to solve problems. Some potential problems are foreseeable, and probably as many are not. While it may be difficult to agree today to a six-month moratorium on principal payments if you get in trouble, it is easier by far to agree to discuss problems and try to work out solutions.

Here is where the businessperson can shine. The lawyer can bring to mind similar deals that turned sour, but may not have a solution to offer. You think about these things and come up with solutions and have your attorney put them in the documents. You think; he writes.

STRUCTURING YOUR DEAL: THE DEAL MAKER

You can choose from a half-dozen different ways to structure your purchase: (1) asset purchase, (2) stock purchase, (3) merger, (4) consolidation, (5) ESOP-assisted, (6) tax-free, (7) stock swaps, and (8) recapitalizations. There are others, even more esoteric. Here is where professional deal makers really shine. We have seen deals where the structure was worth as much as 45 percent of the entire deal (note, that's the deal, not the commissions and professional fees, which combined are usually much less than 15 percent of the deals). And, of course, there is the cheapest way to buy: (9) all cash.

You must make your choice known in the formal purchase agreement. Most of the structures listed are reserved to the $20,000,000 and over transactions, or to special situations below that range. For instance, ESOP-assisted transactions normally require a business with more than a hundred employees to be practical. A recapitalization is useful if you are buying your father's business. Stock swaps, mergers, and consolidations make sense if you can offer publicly traded stock the seller wouldn't mind having instead of his stock (the owner of General Midwest Supply Company, Inc. will be more willing to trade her stock for stock in IBM than in Sam's Body Shop, Inc.). Tax-free exchanges normally require the buyer to be a publicly held concern, and in any event they involve going to the IRS for an advance ruling on the transactions, which is too time consuming for most people.

That leaves asset and stock purchases. These are the most common. One national business broker recently estimated them at 85 percent of all midmarket deals. In the asset acquisition, in theory you are picking and choosing which assets you'll buy, and assuming only certain liabilities. In practice, the seller may not agree to the deal unless you take undesirable assets and liabilities. In the stock purchase, you buy only a stock certificate. Along with it you acquire all assets and liabilities of your target company. Here again, there are ways to let the seller keep the assets she wants, and to eliminate some liabilities.

Our advice to buyers is to buy assets. On the other hand, sellers are usually advised to sell stock. Why the difference? If you are a seller, you want to walk away from the business and be done with it. You want no creditor knocking on your door next year saying, "Where is my money?" As a buyer, you don't want any surprises. There may be liabilities of which even the seller is unaware, substantial liabilities. For instance, somebody fell in the parking lot last week and at this very moment is preparing to sue. Or the IRS is preparing for a full-scale audit. You don't want to pick up hidden liabilities.

You may be able to cover the liability issue with insurance. Make sure your liability insurance counselor checks this issue carefully. Sometimes it's hard to get coverage for prior acts or events. Some forms of insurance are nonexistent, or can't be had at sufficient levels of coverage, or are just prohibitively expensive. Check it out.

But to most people the question of taxes is more important than the liability exposure. If a seller sells stock, he pays a capital gains tax on the difference between the price paid and the price at which it was sold. However, if he sells assets and dissolves the corporation, the business pays a capital gains tax on the assets and then the stockholder pays a capital gains tax on the stock itself. In other words, the seller in an asset deal is faced with two capital gains taxes on the same money!

The buyer on the other hand gets a tax benefit from doing an asset deal. Let's say the business has a ten-year-old, well-maintained forklift truck. On the seller's books, it's been depreciated out. If you allocate $10,000 of your purchase price to the lift truck, you can depreciate it all over again. If you had bought stock, you would not get any depreciation. By buying assets you could write off significant portions of your purchase price. Buying stock usually cuts your available deductions.

The difference can be significant. Say you bought a $1 million business and were able to allocate $900,000 to depreciable assets. If your new business was in a 40 percent combined state and federal tax bracket, you would in essence reduce your tax bill by $360,000 (40 percent of $900,000). Your $1 million business actually cost you only $640,000!

Because of this strong tax advantage to asset deals, the majority of business purchases lately have been done as asset acquisitions. However, you can bet that since the seller is getting socked twice, and you are getting a tax break, there will be some fancy horsetrading over how this tax burden/benefit is to be split between buyer and seller. Nevertheless, it is generally better for the buyer to do asset deals.

So how you structure your deal will require thoughtful and knowledgeable consideration. Here's where your attorney, CPA, and perhaps an experienced deal maker, working together, can earn you hundreds of times more than the fees.

WHEN THE CLOSING IS ACTUALLY HELD

In most business deals the parties have developed a mutual respect and trust. Such is the glue that holds the deal together. In a majority of cases, the formal agreement is signed at the closing. When you arrange to buy a new home, you sign an offer and the seller accepts. Then you secure the bank financing, check the title, have termite and radon inspections done, and a month and a half later you go to closing. That's when you sign the check and get the keys.

Most business acquisition contracts are written as if there would be that same month-and-a-half interval. See the two examples in Appendix G. In actual practice all inspections and financing have been taken care of by the time the agreement to purchase is finalized. The inspections took less time than the contracts, the opposite of a real estate deal. The parties have little need or desire to wait longer for closing.

During the negotiation process the parties are developing a mutual trust. They are each spending perhaps thousands of dollars to put the deal together, arrange the financing, do the inspections, and check out the other side. If the deal did not go through, each side would be out a great deal of money. In effect, each is spending money and effort based on trust and confidence that the other side will complete the transaction. Until closing, neither party knows whether the deal has been made; until closing, nothing is binding.

Your attitude in the home-stretch negotiations is essential to maintaining and fostering that element of trust. Take a reasonable approach. Don't hold out for every nickel. Keep things in perspective and give up what is unimportant (like ego) in order to get what is important (like money). Don't give up important protections just to get the keys to your own business—that is the sure path to bankruptcy. But do not hold out for something when the alternative is reasonably adequate to meet your needs.

SIMULTANEOUS CLOSINGS

The logistical key to buying a business for very little cash is to hold simultaneous closings with the seller in one room and the financier in another, and you scurrying back and forth between the two. Without simultaneous closings, the lender won't lend you money against a business until its liens are in place, and the seller won't give you title so you can put those liens in place until the seller gets his money. In practice what happens is that in room one you sign the deal with the seller and then run all the paperwork to room two. There, the lender reviews the documentation, and when satisfied, hands you the check. Back to room one you go to hand over your own check to the seller, accepting the keys in return.

The drama may be played out with variations. In a recent large deal, the closing, which started at 2:00 P.M., was adjourned at 3:00 P.M. so the buyer and seller could hold a meeting with the employees at the 3:30 P.M. shift change to announce the sale and briefly answer questions. When they got back at 4:30 P.M., the closings continued.

THE CLOSING AGENDA CHECKLIST

The most organized person controls the meeting. When Doug was a fledgling attorney in a large law firm, he assisted another attorney in a large business transaction. Involved were bond counsel, attorneys for the the bank and the seller, counsel for the municipality, as well as real estate brokers, and two of the principal parties. Doug was no more than a spear carrier among mighty warriors. Astonishingly, none of the high-powered counsel thought to prepare an agenda for closing. Since Doug was the only one who had an agenda, everyone followed his checklist, which psychologically put Doug and his client at the head of the table every time someone asked what was next. Several sticking points in the closing, both minor and major, were resolved because of this control.

Be wise. Your team should prepare and distribute the agenda for the closing. Pass it out before closing and before anyone else does. Each agenda closing checklist is different. Here are some ideas to help you build yours:

1. Read through the final draft of the purchase agreement and all side agreements. List all documents to which reference is made. Each will be a separate line item on your agenda. Look for things that have to be done by one side or the other before closing. List those items that must be proved or examined at closing.

2. Outline a closing statement or settlement statement, showing the purchase price and all adjustments. For instance, will you need adjustments for:

Utility prorations?
Vacation pay accruals?
Personal or real property tax prorations?
Assumption of liabilities?
Inventory valuations?
Deposits with utilities, landlords, and others?
Actual receivable values at date of closing?
Payment for title insurance or abstract charges?

3. Consider who needs to attend. In your distributed agenda list by name the other side's people who need to be present. List your own team members who should be present so that schedules can be coordinated.

4. List all licenses to be obtained or transferred and what documentation needs to be present at closing.

5. Do a final day-of-closing walk-through of the business premises before closing.

6. Complete all actions necessary to perfect the buyer's incorporation.

7. Complete all corporate action to authorize the purchase.

8. Obtain any necessary proxies.

9. Prepare certified copies of corporate resolutions authorizing transactions with various parties.

10. Get properly signed bills of sale and deeds for assets purchased.

11. Obtain and deliver patent assignments.

12. Transfer alarm codes.

13. Transfer computer security devices, instructions, and codes.

14. Transfer customer lists.

15. Transfer telephone numbers. Make sure the main agreement says you are buying all telephone numbers of the business.

16. Get meter readings and take other steps to transfer utilities.

17. Transfer equipment leases.

18. Take care of continuation of insurance coverages.

19. Take care of continuation of bonding coverages.

20. Sign the lease or obtain the deed.

21. Make sure all outstanding liens and encumbrances are removed.

22. Have proof of compliance with bulk sales laws.

23. Obtain and deliver letters of credit, notes, and security agreements.

24. Prepare amortization tables for loans. Being a few pennies off on your payment can give a jittery seller reason to foreclose. Passing out the amortization schedules at closing can obviate the problem.

25. Deliver opinions of counsel.

26. Pay or provide for brokers' fees.

27. Deliver the check.

28. Get the keys.

V

After Closing

13

The Transition Stage . . . and Beyond

The births of all things are weak and tender, and therefore
we should have our eyes intent on beginnings.

—MONTAIGNE, "OF MANAGING THE WILL," *ESSAYS*

THE CLOSING IS finally over. A few minutes ago everyone stood around, all smiles, as each in turn congratulated you and wished you well. Then they packed up their briefcases and left you standing there with a mixture of exhilaration and that pit-of-the-stomach, "What did I do?" feeling. But it quickly passes only to be replaced by "What do I do now?" Unless there is some emergency to take priority, your first business concern will be your employees.

EMPLOYEES

Your employees are your business to every outsider. If customer relations are important to you and your business, if relationships with suppliers, delivery people, and anyone else outside your business is at all important to you, then your employees are as important.

You can test and screen and still not know how well any particular person is going to fit into your operation. That can only come with experience. Therefore, it is important that you have a trial time with each employee prior to committing yourself to a long-term relationship.

But how can you arrange a trial if you are buying a business with employees who have been around for twenty years? You are of course committed to any contracts you assumed from the prior employer. But for everybody else, it is essential to start from scratch.

First, have a meeting with all employees. Inform the employees you intend to keep the business going, and ask for their help. Your first job is to calm their fears. Most likely, they will have these fears:

1. They may lose their jobs.
2. Their habitual ways of doing things may be upset.
3. It may be difficult for them to handle new managers, co-workers, and equipment.
4. They may have less chance for advancement.

It will pay you to treat each of these fears seriously and spend ample time reducing them. Be honest if the fears could be realized, but don't overplay them either.

Go the extra step and find out if there are any other fears or concerns. Don't assume these are the only four. Seek cooperation and participation. Ask for ideas. Show you value the employees and their ideas. Let them know how important they are to your business.

Your second job is to keep your options open. Reiterate that you expect to keep most or all employees, and that interviewing toward that end will begin right away. Make it clear that you are interviewing for all jobs and that continuing with the new company is a matter of merit, not anything else. You need the flexibility to do what needs to be done, such as letting troublemakers go, even when prior management didn't. Make it clear that after being hired the worker is on probation for a reasonable period, say sixty or ninety days. Have each employee complete an employment application, and have team members interview each one.

In the interview you are looking for two things. First, you want to protect yourself against any potential problems with the employees—not just problem employees, but people who aren't really suited for the job they hold. Look into academic and business backgrounds. Find out what makes them tick. Ask about career goals. Ask about hobbies. Ask where they think their personal strengths and weaknesses lie. Ask about their greatest professional accomplishment and their biggest disaster. See how well they can take a sincere compliment. All these questions will unearth clues. Consult *Hiring the Best* by Martin John Yate (1988, Bob Adams, Inc., Boston), which is filled with hundreds of in-depth questions and even complete interviews.

In the second part of your interview, ask each employee for suggestions for improving operations. Many employees will have none. Check out the ideas you turn up. If they show promise, implement them. Don't pass up this opportunity to improve your business. There is much accumulated wisdom in the people who've been doing the job.

Many things done in business are done purposefully, for a historical reason. Even if they seem inefficient, they might be the most efficient way to do business. Therefore, make changes slowly. But keep your eyes open, poke your nose into all phases of your new business, and listen for complaints, problems, and situations that can be turned into opportunities. Keep asking questions, particularly "Why?" and "What better way can we do that?" Look for the big picture. Once you have found a solid way to improve, move quickly and decisively.

WHAT YOU CAN AND CANNOT ASK

Your goal is to find the best candidate for each job. Don't let petty prejudices get in your way; why should something irrelevant keep you from getting the best candidate for your employment dollars?

During the interview try to listen actively. Lean forward and show sincere interest in your applicant. Prepare your questions ahead. Try to ask every applicant for the same job the same categories of questions. Listen for attitudes. A good attitude can make up for lack of experience or speed in many jobs. A bad attitude can spoil a whole bunch of employees.

Test by asking the candidate to solve a problem. Thomas Edison is reported to have tested prospective engineers by having them determine the volume of a glass light bulb: Those who pulled out their slide rules failed; those who filled the bulb with water passed! Listen for how your candidate thinks, not for a "right" answer. Then test resolve by asking if they'd bet $1 on their answer—$10? $1,000?

Many people worry about what they can and cannot ask in an employment interview, afraid they could be sued for a miscue. It is a complicated area because so many people these days think suing is the answer to every problem.

For the most part you can protect yourself pretty well if you keep your questions to ones relating directly to what the candidate must be able to do on the job, not what he or she is. Beyond that, study the following lists more for flavor than for specifics, and you'll do fine:

STAY AWAY FROM . . .	THESE ARE OKAY . . .
Religion	Inform of required workdays; ask if there is a problem.
Race	
Gender	Gender might be appropriate for a gynecologist's assistant.
How do you prefer to be addressed? (Mrs., Miss, Ms.)	
Marital status	Inform of policy against husband and wife at same plant, and ask if this is a problem.
Spouse's job	
Birth control	Inform of frequent required moves.
Pregnancy	Inform that heavy lifting is required.
Weight and height	Do you have any physical conditions that might interfere with this kind of work? Don't inquire beyond a yes or no answer.
Disabilities	
Arrest record	Conviction record
(You're innocent until proven guilty.)	Inform that bonding is required. Ask if bondable. Can't inquire past yes or no.
Former name	Have you ever worked for this company under a different name or nickname?
Maiden name	
Age	Present and past addresses and duration of each
Citizenship	Are you a U.S. citizen?
Birthplace	Do you have legal permission to stay in U.S.?
(self, spouse, parents)	Do you intend to stay permanently in U.S.?
Derivation of name	What languages are you fluent in?
Foreign residences	
National origin	
Membership in organizations	Specific relevant memberships
Photographs	Photos *after* hiring
Specific bank reference	Can do a credit check
Credit rating	
Names and addresses of relatives	Who should be notified in case of an emergency?
Making notes on file	Educational background
Anything you wouldn't want to be asked yourself	Work experience
	Level and complexity of prior work
	Job responsibilities
	Job performance
	Questions that call for a long answer
	Questions about attitudes and motivation
	Student activities
	Reasons for leaving prior jobs
	How do you rate yourself at . . .?
	Is there anything else I should know about you?

You'll notice the areas to avoid are pretty specific, but the question areas remaining are still fairly broad. Learn to ask open-ended questions and give tests for bona-fide job skills and you'll find yourself picking stars.

Be sure to ask for and check out references. One problem you may run into is the previous employer who won't divulge more than name, rank, and serial number. Even then you can at least check out titles and pay rates, although many will ask you to produce written authorization from the employee. When you do get a supervisor who will answer your questions, treat his time with respect. You have a jewel you do not want to lose. Try to limit your questions to a half-dozen. Open-ended questions are better than the yes-or-no variety. Your questions might revolve around the specifics of what job the person did for this supervisor, strengths and weaknesses your interview uncovered, and any other strengths and weaknesses the reference will share. Always ask, "Is there anything else I should know?" And, of course, "Would you rehire this person?"

Many times, you will be surprised at what the prior supervisor will share with you. There may be new information about which you hadn't the slightest inkling. Once, Doug almost hired someone who said she had been a night supervisor at a nursing home. She interviewed very well and had the right credentials. Doug really didn't want to call the reference late at night, but did. The reference verified the applicant had indeed worked the night shift, but she wasn't a supervisor, just a nurse's aide. In fact, the applicant had lied to that employer about her qualifications, and had been a troublemaker among employees. Take a lesson from this near-miss: Check out all references. And from references get other references to check!

Remember, too, that you have a source of excellent references among your employees. Be sure to ask your employees about their colleagues. Don't pry, and don't be a spy: Just ask for strengths and weaknesses for the present job and whether they might work out better in a different job. You could discover some hidden gems.

PROTECTING YOUR FAMILY FROM YOUR PARTNERS

You haven't forgotten your family since you started your escapade into heady business wheeling and dealing, have you? They're probably one of the reasons you did all the things you've done the last few months. There are a couple of steps you should consider taking to protect their future.

One is to set up a buy-sell agreement. Here's the problem, in a real-life example: Sam F. and his two brothers owned a construction business. Sam, age sixty-three, was tired and wanted to retire. It was fine with his brothers if Sam retired—he would no longer be drawing a paycheck—but they didn't want to buy him out, nor did they have a pension plan.

When three people each own equal stock in a corporation, no one person has enough to force anything to happen. If his brothers both disagreed with him, Sam could not vote himself a salary, he could not vote himself a dividend, he could not vote himself a pension, and he certainly could not vote a purchase of his shares. If he couldn't vote his shares for salaries or dividends, neither could an outside buyer. What would you pay for an investment like that? That's the problem with a minority interest in a small corporation—it's essentially worthless.

A buy-sell agreement is simply a contract between the owners of the corporation, so if one person becomes disabled, or dies, or retires, the other owner or owners will buy that person out. The agreement benefits both the buyer and seller. First, a price is usually agreed upon ahead of time, which eliminates much wrangling at the time of the sale. Second, the seller's family is protected. They now have something spendable (cash) whereas before they had something of limited value (stock—because of the inability to vote salaries, dividends, etc.) that certainly wasn't spendable.

Third, the buyer gets a free rein to run the business. It can take valuable time away from running the business if you have to keep answering questions about financial matters from three children and fourteen grandchildren who are now your fellow shareholders. These questions can range anywhere from "Why did you pay yourself a bonus?" to "Why aren't you paying any dividends to the stockholders since you showed a profit last year?" There is a classic conflict of interest any time one shareholder dies: The heirs of the deceased shareholder want cash, and the remaining shareholder wants a free hand to run the business, to plow back profits, and to grow the business. A buy-sell agreement can head off these problems before they bring everything to a standstill.

Fourth, a buy-sell agreement can specify the payment schedule and other terms of the buyout. For instance, will payment be all cash, or will a long-term payout be necessary? If there is a long-term payout, will any liens be given as security? Will there be limits on salaries or dividends while the promissory note remains unpaid? These serious questions need to be addressed. A buy-sell agreement can prevent arguments from killing the deal at the time when it is essential to both parties that it work.

How do you agree ahead of time to a price for the corporation? It may be worth so much today, but may be worth much more (or even much less) when the buyout actually takes place. There are basically four different approaches to value in buy-sell agreements.

1. Value can be determined by a formula. For instance, it could be a simple five times average earnings. Or it could be much more complicated, with different weight

given to earnings, asset values, number of customers, asset appraisals, and similar factors.

The best way to come up with an accurate formula is for you and your partners to sit down individually to determine what you think this business is really worth. Then look at what different things you each considered in arriving at a mutually agreeable value. Work backward from there. Look at what you did to get to your number, and restate those factors in terms of a formula.

Have your accountant and attorney look over your formula. But you do the initial work. You are the only one who knows your business intimately. Only you can know what you would be willing to pay for a similar business. Your outside advisors can only give you ideas, and help you fine-tune your own. You should not rely entirely on them to give you a price, unless of course they are full-fledged business appraisers.

A formula is one method, but it is perhaps the hardest way since you and your partners may not be able to agree on all the factors to make up the formula. It'll be easier to agree now than later when a problem may surface. At least now you are still agreeing with each other. At the time a sale has to take place, you will not be as agreeable (and one of you may no longer be present), and it will be harder to reach a reasoned decision on the emotion-charged issue of price.

Remember what we told you in Chapter Eleven: There is no such thing as a formula that applies to every business or every industry, or even to a particular company at every time. At best, formulas are sloppy guesses at value. So, if you use a formula in your buy-sell agreement, make sure you review it every few years, work out an actual price from it, and see if the result is reasonable. If not, amend your formula. Amend the formula any time your underlying business has changed. For instance, you may be in the business of manufacturing wooden wagon wheels. At some point in time, the demand for wooden wagon wheels drops off, and you decide to go into the business of renting factory and warehouse space. Now you need a different formula.

2. The second method is the easiest but the most expensive. Simply provide for an appraiser or several appraisers who will determine the value.

Typically, agreements call for the accountant to determine the value. It is true that accountants can come up with a value, but most accountants are not professional appraisers. They may also be uncomfortable with the idea of arbitrating a dispute between two clients. If you want your accountant to be your appraiser, do him the favor of asking first. See if he feels comfortable making appraisals, and whether he is willing to be the final arbiter of price.

What if you can't agree on an appraiser, or the one you've chosen declines? One solution is for each party to name an appraiser. The two appraisers work together. But be careful. Business appraisals are expensive—they entail a lot of work. (The Geneva Corporation charges a flat $29,500 for an appraisal, for instance.) As a result, if both parties can agree on one appraiser, the cost is reduced.

What if the two appraisers disagree? Then the appraisers can get together and choose a third one to settle the differences. Now you have three bills for the same work. This option is also the most expensive because appraisals are not guarantees of actual value. They are only well-researched guesses by outsiders. The only way to get an actual value is to put the business on the auction block, and sell it. An appraised value that is way off is expensive to the party who drew the short straw.

3. The third option is to agree annually with your co-owners as to the current value. This method is probably the most accurate, but the disadvantage is that the parties may be too busy to get together, or may at some point reach an impasse. Because of a 1986 law and a 1989 interpretation of it (known as Internal Revenue Code sec. 2036(c)), the method has gone out of vogue. Typically, that problem is handled by requiring an appraisal in the event that the last agreed price is more than one or two years old. Obviously, you are again brought face-to-face with the cost problem.

4. A fourth method is the "shootout." Few people use it, for good reason. Here partner A sets a value, and partner B says who will be buyer and who will be seller. There is risk for both parties, but the theory, at least, is that you have come up with an accurate value. It's the old "let one boy divide the pie, and the other one choose which slice he eats" method. However, experienced negotiators know it's better to be the one who selects rather than the one who cuts.

John and Fred were brothers who'd years earlier started a wholesale business supplying the RV (recreational vehicle) and automotive repair shop industries. Over the years they'd built the business into a well-known profitable one. John brought his son into the business, and Fred brought in his two sons.

John died unexpectedly in his mid-fifties. Peggy, John's widow, didn't know how to run the business and her son felt he might be psychologically outnumbered in business decisions with his uncle and two cousins. So Peggy wanted to buy Fred out. She didn't want to overpay (because her inheritance was not large), but she didn't want to force her son to compete with the business established by his father and uncle. The buy-sell agreement was of the shootout variety, so Peggy couldn't control who'd be the buyer. She elected not to spend the money for an appraiser.

But Peggy had no idea of values, and her son wasn't much better off. Her accountant and lawyer came up with a range of values. Then all three decided on an offering price above the probable value because Peggy wanted to buy.

After the formal offer went out, it was nail-biting time. After forty-four days Fred answered: He would buy! True, Peggy got a high price, and from it had the money to set up her son in business. But the new business struggled for several years. Did John properly protect his wife and son?

*   *   *

A buy-sell agreement has a side advantage: The agreed price binds the IRS, for estate tax purposes. For a revealing look at what the IRS and most appraisers look at in valuing a business, see Appendix F.

Once you've settled on a pricing method, there is another question: How is anybody going to be able to pay for the stock all at once? Typically in a small business there is little cash available to finance the purchase of stock. Going to the bank to borrow the money is not always viable, because the company may already be in debt about as far as the bank will allow. Therefore, it is usually necessary for the seller or his family to allow some sort of long-term, easy-payment schedule.

But the seller has another problem. A $500 monthly payment does not go very far in replacing a $4,000 monthly salary. So the seller usually wants a substantial down payment. The buyer is not any better off. She has a $500 payment, plus she has to hire someone to take her partner's place, maybe at a higher salary than her partner was drawing.

The answer can be life insurance. The business or maybe the shareholders themselves buy insurance on each of the shareholders. If one dies, the proceeds can be used to make the down payment, if not the full payment. If the person simply retires, or becomes disabled, the cash value in the life policy can be used for the down payment. It is a relatively painless way to raise money. The life insurance agents call this money discounted dollars: In effect, you pay a dollar today for $100 or $1,000 sometime in the future.

Who should be the buyer? Either the agreement is a stock redemption agreement (the entity itself buys out the shareholder) or a cross-purchase agreement (the other shareholder buys the stock). There are tax and other advantages both ways. Under some states' laws, a corporation cannot legally redeem stock from a shareholder unless there is a certain amount of retained earnings. Usually a small corporation does not have enough to allow for a redemption. Therefore, in those states, the buy-sell may have to be in the cross-purchase format.

If you may eventually sell the shares you are buying, consider especially carefully the tax implications of a cross-purchase agreement. Let's say you and your partner each put in $1,000 to start the company twenty years ago and today the corporation is worth $100,000. If the corporation redeems your partner's shares for $50,000, and you then sell out for $100,000, you will pay tax on a gain of $99,000 ($100,000 less the $1,000 you paid for your stock). On the other hand, if you personally bought your partner's shares for $50,000, your basis in your shares is now $51,000. When you sell all of the shares for $100,000, you have only a $49,000 gain upon which to pay tax. That's $100,000 minus the $50,000 and the $1,000—same dollars in and out, but much less tax.

But there is another side to this cross-purchase coin. Congress has recently decreed that personal interest (as opposed to business interest and home mortgage interest) is nondeductible for your federal income taxes. Interest paid on your buy-sell is usually deemed personal interest. Consequently, you'll pay out interest to buy stock, but when you go to sell out and pay your capital gain taxes, you can only deduct the principal. The interest is "lost" money. But if the corporation made the purchase, it's business interest, which is deductible.

Most shareholders, when confronted with these facts, choose the entity purchase (stock redemption) format. They are gaining current deductions, and they'll worry about capital gains taxes later.

Since we're dealing with an uncertain future, many opt for a combination cross-purchase/entity purchase agreement. Here, the corporation has first rights to buy, then the shareholders have second rights, and eventually, the corporation must buy. This option is the best of both worlds—the shareholders can wait and see which way works out best. This format is for understandable reasons known as the wait-and-see buy-sell.

Whatever you do, get your buy-sell in writing, or it's no good. Even buying a life insurance policy is not an equivalent, although it will help. It will help in the sense that it provides the dollars. But it does not substitute for an agreement specifying what to do with the money.

PROTECTING YOUR FAMILY FROM UNCLE SAM

Not only do you need to resolve things ahead of time with your business co-owners but you need to do so with Uncle Sam. When you buy a business, you soon come to the realization that the seller's "baby" has become your "child." At this stage, many new business owners find they have much more to protect than they've ever had in their lives before; and those who don't come to this conclusion should. Although it might not seem logical, the new business owner has a strong desire not only to protect his family but also to see the business is kept "alive." Logical or not, the feeling is there, and it is strong. Just as strong a factor as it was when you were using it in your negotiations with the seller. Consequently, estate planning, wills, trusts, and protecting your estate from the tax collector is a natural concern as you complete your acquisition.

It comes as a shock to a lot of business owners that even though the IRS has been a big partner with them all their financial lives, the IRS wants a chunk of what's left over when they die. Presently the law gives Uncle Sam at least 37 percent of what you have when you die, if your estate is big enough to be taxable.

The maximum rate can go up to 55 percent. Uncle Sam won't carry you longer than your mother did: He expects to have the tax paid, *in cash,* nine months after you die. There is an exception currently available that allows a business owner to pay part of the tax over as long as fourteen years. You must plan for this exception in order to be able to use it (it sometimes forces business owners to do awkward things) so it may not be for you.

There are also state inheritance taxes that can take quite a bite out of your estate. How big does your estate have to be to be taxable? Only $600,000. Why "only"? Because your estate in Uncle Sam's book includes more than you could spend today. It includes the fair market value of your business. See Appendix F for the factors the IRS takes into account when it determines the value of your business for this tax. Rest assured that your dear old Uncle Sam will argue for the highest justifiable value, often higher. Now it may gratify your ego to have an outside party say you have built your business up to double or triple what you paid for it, but it also doubles or triples your estate taxes.

What else is included in your taxable estate? The value of your home (at the time you die, not what you paid for it twenty years earlier), any investment real estate, and any other investments you may own (again, the value on your date of death, even if the bottom drops out of the market the next day, making your stock virtually worthless).

Also included is your life insurance. Since Uncle Sam wants the highest possible value he uses the face value (the amount the insurance will pay if and when you die), not the cash or loan value. Also included is any pension plan that will survive your death. Some pension plans run out after you and your spouse have both died, but others have a value that will be transferred to your heirs. The value transferred to your heirs is taxable.

Everything else you own or have any interest in is taxable. Your stamp collection, your automobile, your household goods and personal effects, and even money you inherited from your rich old aunt the day before you died. Even things you gave away are taxable. If you made a gift of over $10,000, that amount will come back into your estate and be taxable.

Even though every possible asset you have is taxable, some people say the federal estate tax is a voluntary tax—with good reason. First, anything that you leave to your spouse is nontaxable because of the "marital deduction." Second, any amount up to $600,000 (the current amount of the "exemption equivalent") is nontaxable.

"If everything I leave to my spouse is nontaxable, doesn't that solve the problem?" No, because your spouse is going to die someday and leave everything to the kids. That's when Uncle Sam steps in and takes a big bite out of the second estate. So the marital deduction is not the whole answer.

Part of the answer is to give an amount to your spouse to get the taxable size of your estate down to $600,000 or less. In other words, you give $600,000 to the kids and

$600,000 to your spouse. The gift to your spouse bears no tax. Because the amount that is taxable (the gift to the kids) is at or below the $600,000 exemption amount, there is no tax on that either. Using this technique, you can leave $1,200,000 to your kids tax free. When your spouse dies, leaving $600,000 to the kids, there is no tax because your spouse gets a $600,000 exemption, too.

"But," you object, "I want to leave everything to my spouse and not have the kids step in and take anything away from her. Perhaps she will be ill or have other needs for all the money." There is a way around that problem, too. You can put the money for the children into what is called a "bypass trust." The trust provides these benefits to your surviving spouse:

1. She can have all of the income and interest the trust produces.
2. She can have all of the principal in the trust, if a need arises.
3. She can have the right to take $5,000 or 5 percent of the trust (whichever is larger) each year for any reason, or for no reason at all.
4. She can will the property away upon her death, or give it away during life.

Now if you have the ability to take all of the income and all of the principal, and the right to give it away upon your death or even while you are living, is that not practically the same thing as owning the property outright? Many people think so, and have set up bypass trusts. However, the IRS closes its eyes to the spouse's interest in the trust, as if it were owned solely by the children, since it goes to them when the spouse dies. In other words, the trust is not taxable in the surviving spouse's estate.

This is a simple, garden-variety estate plan that a lot of people use to get to a zero tax level. There are more sophisticated ways to avoid estate tax, where there is a complicated estate, or where there is much life insurance, or where the estate is larger than $1.2 million. The point is that you can avoid the estate tax with a little advance planning.

Remember, you don't pay the estate tax; your children do. Therefore, you shouldn't tie your hands in a lot of red tape just to save them taxes. After all, it's all "free money" to them in a sense. But on the other hand, don't you perhaps have a duty to your family to save this significant tax, if you can do so in a way that doesn't involve excess red tape? The bypass trust is such a way for most business owners.

The time when you are making plans for your business is a good time to consider your estate plan and will. It just makes sense to get everything organized at once. It is simpler for everybody, and it can save you money both in taxes and professional fees (your attorney and CPA don't have to get reacquainted with your financial picture six months or a year later). Do it now! Remember, making a will is not something you do for yourself, but for your family.

DON'T FORGET THE ROSES

Before you leave the room where you had your closing, get on the phone and order a dozen roses for your spouse (yes, men too!), as a reward for putting up with you for the last few months. Sure, it doesn't adequately make up for everything your mate has been through, but it at least says, "I know you've put up with a lot."

Then when you're getting that dozen roses, pick up one of the cloth variety for yourself. Take it along with you to work and put it someplace where you will see it often, as a reminder that you should not take yourself and your business too seriously—that you've got to remember the roses and the important things in life, such as your health and your family. Keep things in perspective. Consider the ants: They're hard workers, but they always take time to attend a picnic. Joe likes to say he never heard an entrepreneur on his death bed say, "I wish I'd have spent more time at the office."

SELLING OUT

You are now the consummate business buyer. You know what you like and don't like as a buyer. Take a few minutes to list what you did and didn't like about buying this business, and what you would do differently next time. Yes, your time is at a high premium now. Yes, you have more problems than you have time to even identify, let alone solve. But this list will be important and valuable.

Some day you are going to want to sell out. Or maybe buy another business. The list of what you liked and didn't like, and perhaps what you looked for in a business, will be valuable to you when you get ready to sell. It will help you "pitch" your business right so you'll snare a buyer early. It may also be valuable to you if you decide to expand.

You should be thinking about selling out from the very minute you first own your new business. Businesses are difficult to sell quickly at a good price. The answer is to be prepared to sell. Richard Rodnik, the founder of the world's largest M & A (Merger and Acquisition) firm, the Geneva Corporation, has built and sold eight businesses, including Geneva. He says he never gets into a business without a specific detailed plan to get out. He sold Geneva to Chemical Bank three years ago.

One way to prepare is to divide the business at the start. Businesses are hard to sell because there are not many buyers with cash equal to 100 percent of your price.

Businesses are expensive, so if there is some way for you to reduce the price for your prospective buyer, you may increase the number of candidates available to buy the business.

Splitting up a business means putting different types of assets into different entities. For instance, you can put the real estate into a partnership, the equipment into another, and the operating business into a corporation. Once you have groomed one of your managers to take over the business, she doesn't have to come up with money to buy the whole operation. She only needs to come up with enough to buy the operating company. You can keep the hard assets, lease them to the new owner's corporation, and guarantee yourself and your spouse a retirement income for many years. You've also made your manager's new company much more solid, since it has less debt. If you need to sell the whole ball of wax, you may be able to sell to several different people more easily than you could sell the whole thing to one person.

Consider selling your business to a buyer on a low-cash-down easy-payment plan. It is next to impossible to sell a business today without the owner taking back some of the paper. You must provide some of the financing, or your business will not sell.

It can make sense to sell a business on a low-cash-down basis. For one thing, you are greatly expanding the number of prospects who would consider buying your business. There may be people who could run the business, but who do not have the financial wherewithal to make a substantial down payment. For another, if you make your business available to someone who otherwise couldn't swing the deal, you should be entitled to some additional compensation for this feature. You could get a higher price, or payments for a longer time, or a higher interest rate than you could from someone who could just write you a check for 60 percent down. There are several minor benefits, too. You get the satisfaction of knowing that you have given someone a helping hand. You get a nice, steady, secure payment each month for many years. Having many buyers on the scene puts you in the enviable position of picking the strongest buyer-candidate.

Isn't it riskier if you don't get a substantial down payment? Let's turn that around: Does a down payment, however substantial, really guarantee that the next payment will be made? Obviously not. All that it guarantees is that the amount you have received is now securely in your bank account, not the buyer's. As important as that is, getting the first goal doesn't guarantee you'll win the game. In fact, a case can be made against a substantial down payment, if it will strap the buyer so much that it makes his entire operation shaky.

But, you ask, doesn't a substantial down payment help me to determine whether the buyer is highly committed to the business? Yes, undoubtedly it does. Notice what you have suggested: It's not the amount of down payment you arbitrarily choose but the amount of down payment relative to the buyer's financial situation. For a buyer with a million dollars of marketable stocks and bonds, a down payment of $100,000 might not be substantial. But for a buyer with $5,000 cash in the bank, a $100,000 down payment is impossible. For the second buyer, a $5,000 down payment might be substantial, and possibly too high.

What you as the seller need, as much as commitment capital, is a strongly worded contract. Your contract should give you the ability to step in early, before a problem becomes serious, and correct it. Perhaps you might want to have minimum required inventory levels. Perhaps you might want to require a certain working capital ratio or net working capital dollar amount. You may want to have monthly financial statements. You may want to have strongly worded default clauses that give you the ability to correct the situation before the entire business (and your security interest along with it) goes down the drain. See Chapter Twelve for ways to build flexible default provisions.

The second protection you should have is knowledge of your buyer. Know your buyer inside and out. Insist on getting a résumé. Spend long hours getting to know your buyer and what makes her tick. Check out references. Spend time with the references. If you don't spend time getting to know your buyer now, you could be spending a lot of time involuntarily learning about your buyer and why she was a bad risk later—during the lawsuit you file to try to collect your defaulted note.

For some people, there is another reason to start thinking about selling out from day one: They've discovered they like buying businesses so well they make a business out of that process. There was a man who once owned a small restaurant in the upper peninsula of Michigan. But he didn't plan to own it for long. He would find a good restaurant that was not doing well (since this may sound like a contradiction, you can see why there was a real art to what he was doing). He would buy the place, fix it up physically and operationally, and sell it a year or two later at a tidy profit. Then he'd look for another.

Whatever you do, protect yourself from becoming an anxious seller. Remember the tremendous advantage a buyer has when dealing with an anxious seller. Watch out for the nine most common mistakes made by sellers:

1. They have an unrealistic price in mind. A million dollars seems to be a magic number. Appraisals can help the seller as much as the buyer.

2. They don't understand the value of the business. Most owners of closely held businesses have suppressed profits to reduce taxes. The company's financial statements don't begin to reflect the true value of the business.

3. They assume the best buyer is local. Most sellers naturally assume that the market for their business is confined to the immediate geographic area. In fact, the best buyer may be someone seeking an entry into the marketplace from anywhere in

the country, or even offshore. The buyer may want to bring his wife home to her family.

4. They don't have proper counsel. Business owners are generally better off using an intermediary to sell their businesses, instead of doing it themselves. Without professional help, they are prone to taking advice from the wrong people: spouse, partner, golfing buddy, or perhaps a lawyer or accountant who has never been involved in a company sale. It's like being your own brain surgeon.

5. They sell to the wrong people. One of the biggest mistakes is to think that the best buyer for the business is a competitor, customer, supplier, or employee. They are frequently the worst because if the deal falls through a great deal of confidential information has been given to the wrong people.

6. They don't understand the buyer's motive. Rather than emphasizing the growth potential of the business, they dwell on past performance. Buyers are looking for return on investment (ROI), growth potential, and synergy. Beauty is in the eye of the beholder, and to the buyer that means the future, not the past.

7. The company is not positioned for sale. There can be a swing of as much as 100 percent in the selling price if the company's position is solid in terms of organization, opportunity, reputation, market conditions, and industry leadership.

8. Most inexperienced sellers provide the prospective buyer with inadequate documentation about the business. They hand the buyer the unaudited financials for the last three years and a product catalog. Buyers are evaluating the purchase based on growth potential and future return on investment, so they're looking for recast financials along with three- to five-year proformas and solid market research showing the future potential for the business. Have a business plan you can show a prospective buyer.

9. There is not a firm exit plan. Many business owners haven't thought about what they will do after selling, or even what their real financial needs will be. This neglect costs them money at the closing because the buyer is willing to pay a higher price for the business if some of the purchase can be leveraged. If a seller is willing to defer some of the money, the buyer has more flexibility in financing the purchase.

ANOTHER AND ANOTHER AND . . .

Then again, maybe you don't want to sell out. Owning half a dozen businesses might be your forte. Buying the first business is the toughest. Having more than one business can free up your time. Several businesses can give you the financial wherewithal to have full-time managers and assistants. Having employees in several locations could give you the ability to move people around where they are most needed from time to time.

Consider expanding by buying more businesses of the same kind. How about your toughest competitor? Wouldn't its top manager be a strong addition to your team? Would owning more businesses give you buying power to purchase at higher discounts? Might it make you a specialist, more knowledgeable, or more efficient?

Consider expanding to totally unrelated businesses, which will give you a broader view of management techniques and access to many effective business ideas. It will also spread your risks of a downturn in one sector of the economy.

Don't get too big too fast. Take things slowly and easily and build a strong foundation, and your foundation will see you through for years.

GROWING BY GIVING IT AWAY: A WILD IDEA?

Frank is involved in several businesses. At last count, he had a half-dozen that together were worth in excess of a million dollars. He bought all of them, but he never owned any of them!

Here's what he does: A new corporation, the stock of which is owned by an employee who will run the new enterprise, buys the operating company. Let's say Frank has chosen Ted. Ted becomes the 51 percent owner of the new corporation. The other shares in the corporation are given to other key employees, such as the vice-presidents, the controller, the secretary, and the plant manager.

A general partnership is formed in which Frank has a controlling interest. Ted and some of the other key people are the other partners. The partnership purchases the real estate, equipment, furniture, fixtures, and so on.

Immediately after the purchase, the partnership enters into an agreement to lease the hard assets to the corporation at their fair market rental value. There might also be consulting agreements between Frank and the corporation so that Frank will receive compensation for the work he does for the corporation.

What does Frank end up with? As you can see, Frank gets an income from both his services and the hard assets. But the employees receive all other income earned by the business. And therein lies the incentive: If Ted does a good job, and the corporation makes lots of money, he shares in its success. If the corporation loses money, Frank is insulated from the losses.

What is to prevent Ted from running off with the corporation? First, if Ted does a good job, he knows that there will be more transactions like this down the line. Second, Frank still has the hard assets, so Ted can't easily keep the corporation running without Frank. Obviously, Ted can walk away with the business know-how, customer lists, and employees. But if he does, then he has to negotiate a new lease or go out and buy equipment, and that can be costly. Third, Ted has contractual commitments with Frank for the lease and for consulting services, which he cannot ignore. Finally, Frank has done a good job by selecting Ted. He has pulled him out of his own employee pool, where he has been able to watch Ted's abilities, motivation, and loyalty over time. These factors all combine to reduce significantly the risk of Ted running off with the business.

Can this sort of thing work for others? It is far from an ordinary setup, but the factors are in place to reduce risks. The plus factor for Frank or anybody in his shoes is that with a motivated manager he is free to develop another business. That way, he has several Teds working for him, and he has reduced his risks even further. If he has four businesses in all, and one person runs off, he still has lost only 25 percent of his assets or income. But with four businesses, Frank has increased his profits, has multiplied his efforts by developing highly committed managers, and has increased his chances of hitting a real winner. The proof of the pudding: Frank owns two homes worth in excess of $200,000 each (real money at this writing), and other assets worth conservatively in excess of $15 million, accumulated within the last ten years!

Perhaps Frank's approach is a bit bold. Our purpose in presenting this idea is not to advocate it but to stretch your thinking. Oliver Wendell Holmes once said, "Every now and then a man's mind is stretched by a new idea and never shrinks back to its former dimensions."

So don't be afraid to come up with some new approaches to business ownership, or business, in general. You may just figure out what everybody has been looking for, and make yourself famous, as well as rich!

14

The Dreamsmith's Shop

No man who does not see visions will ever realize any high hope
or undertake any high mission.
—WOODROW WILSON

If we were to do all we are capable of doing we would literally astonish ourselves.
—THOMAS A. EDISON

EVERY YEAR, hundreds, perhaps thousands, of businesses close their doors for lack of
someone to carry on. Not because they failed, but because nobody in the family
wanted the business, or because there was no family. Closed, because someone
wanted to retire, or the owner died, or because the owners didn't know they could sell
the business. (True!) But more often closed because prospective buyers got "cold
feet," or didn't see their own potential in the business, or simply didn't persevere past
the problems that inevitably arise in every business acquisition. Thriving businesses,
or businesses that could have been made to thrive had they only had an infusion of
some new energy and ideas, close their doors.

The *Wall Street Journal* on January 27, 1989, reported a substantial rise in middle-
market leveraged buyouts (LBOs), due partly to the aging of members of the generation who started businesses shortly after World War II. This generation, now in their
sixties, is approaching the point where they'll want to cash in their chips and enjoy life.
This trend means many good businesses will be coming on the market in the next
decade or two. And many of them will close for lack of qualified buyers.

Closed businesses result in losses of jobs and job-producing entities for the community, country, and world. Bad as that might be, the real loss to our world is the loss of

the ideas and efforts of new entrepreneurs. Every time a would-be entrepreneur passes up a buyout, he withholds ideas and efforts from the world economy. Every time a seasoned business owner decides against an acquisition in favor of just playing it safe (the real kiss of death for most businesses), that business owner may be limiting the ability of some rising star within his business to push upward from the present owner's plateau in a few years. That loss is impossible to measure, but very real.

Perhaps the most profoundly sad deathbed words were Leonardo Da Vinci's: "I have offended God and mankind because my work didn't reach the quality it should have." As Oliver Wendell Holmes, Jr. said, "Most of us die with our music still in us." We hope by now we've amply demonstrated how buying a business and running a business is much more music than dollars. Don't shrink from your own greatness.

Is buying a business difficult? No. Is it hard work? Yes. By now none of this should be news to you. There is no magic formula that will drop the keys to a business into your lap. We hope, however, you have picked up a few techniques and approaches to make your acquisition more effective, techniques and approaches to help you spend less time on unimportant details and more time on the big picture.

Think of yourself as a dreamsmith and not just as someone who dreams pipe dreams and never accomplishes anything. Instead, you will dream big dreams, and hitch them to the team of horses called hard work. Together, dreaming and smithing have accomplished all the goodness and greatness the world has ever seen. Become a dreamsmith.

Appendixes

Appendix A: Locking in on a Target

Target is probably the key word for the person or company looking to buy a business. By targeting, you make your search more efficient and more likely to succeed. It is the most important thing you can do in a business acquisition.

The biggest mistake companies and individuals make when on the prowl to acquire an established business is to look at every profitable business they encounter. Typically they'll contact a broker and say, "I understand you know of some businesses for sale. Can you send me a copy of your list?" The answer is usually, "No, we don't give out a list because it is of little value. But we'll be glad to talk with you about what you're looking for and try to point you in the right direction." There is experience behind this answer.

Jim Kowalski is a case in point. He came to Doug for help in reviewing financial statements for a small grocery store. After a half-hour of probing, it became clear what Jim wanted most was out: out of his corporate environment, out from under a boss who would not let him show what he could do, out where he could be himself. In fact, what Jim really wanted to do was run a specialty gun shop. Now that's about as far away from a grocery store as you can get. If he had bought the grocery store, in six months he'd have felt as trapped by it as he did by his big company job. Take a lesson from Jim Kowalski. Target the right kind of business for yourself, because your business always takes a big slice out of your life.

TARGETING FOR THE COMPANY SEEKING TO BUY

Here are some criteria to help your team focus on what kind of company you should target. Targeting is always a highly specific process.

1. What size company would be best? Should it be larger or smaller than yours?
2. How much sales volume should the new company have?
3. How many employees should the company have?
4. Should the company be labor intensive?

5. What stage of development should the target be in: start-up, growth, maturity, stagnation, or revitalization?
6. Should the product involve high or low technology?
7. Should the product be compatible with your own, or should you expand into an entirely different area?
8. Should the product fill a hole in your current product mix and give you a product "system" to offer to the marketplace?
9. Should the product be capable of being run on your present production line?
10. What goes into manufacturing your present product line and the target's product? How should the product fit within your current production system?
11. Should the target company be with or without a union? Some buyers do seek unionized settings.
12. Should the target company be in a skilled or unskilled labor market?
13. Should the labor market for the target industry be a buyer's or seller's market?
14. Should labor costs in the target industry be high or low? Compared to what?
15. Should materials be readily available?
16. Should the target industry be one with high or low insurance costs? High costs could keep competition down and margins wide.
17. Should the target company be located close to its customers?
18. Should the target company be located close to its suppliers?
19. Should the target company be located in a geographic area that key management likes?
20. Should the cost of living in the target company's locale be a factor?
21. Should the quality of life in the target company's locale be a factor?
22. Should the target company have assets your present company does not possess? What assets?
23. Should the real estate of the target company be leased or owned? Do you want to lease or buy?
24. What industry should the target company be in?
25. What industry characteristics should the target company have? Should it be an industry dominated by one company or one where the industry is fragmented with no acknowledged leaders?
26. Should the industry be in a stage of start-up, growth, maturity, decline, or revitalization?
27. Can your management people manage in an environment of rapid growth if they have previously worked only in mature industries?
28. Should the industry be subject to relatively heavy government regulation? Again, there can be advantages both ways.
29. Should the target company be in an industry that has a busy season to complement your own?

30. Should the customer base of the target be similar to your own? Should there be overlap?
31. Do you want to expand horizontally or vertically?
32. What knowledge and skills does your present work force possess?
33. What knowledge and skills does your present management possess?
34. What are the likes and dislikes of your key managers?
35. What is the philosophy of your current management? Do you prefer to go for high-quality, high-end marketplaces or price-sensitive marketplaces?
36. What environment and management style does your company have? If the target industry has different ones, will you be able to handle the differences?
37. Do you want your target's management to stay or leave?
38. What return on investment do you expect?
39. What price range do you want to target?
40. What financing possibilities do you have in place?
41. To what extent can you absorb additional debt burden?
42. Are you willing to pay for goodwill? Do you seek goodwill?
43. Should you try to acquire a particular large customer by buying a company servicing that customer?
44. Should the size of any particular customer's business relative to the target's total sales be a factor?
45. What are your company's weaknesses? What are your strengths? Ideally, you want to bring synergy to the melding of the two companies.
46. Do you seek economy of scale?
47. Do you seek to increase the effectiveness of your management?
48. Do you seek to share services and functions with your target company, consequently saving costs?
49. Do you have the ability to bring additional capital to a new industry to better serve the customers?
50. Do you seek a new product distribution system?
51. Do you seek a target with a nationwide, regional, or purely local market?
52. What kind of sales force should the target have: salaried, commissioned, in-house, manufacturer's representatives, company-owned stores or distributors, franchise outlets?
53. What market share should the target company have?
54. Do you seek a company that is primarily a job shop or one with a proprietary product?
55. Do you seek a target company with strong or weak competitors? Look behind the obvious.
56. What deadlines do you have? Are the deadlines real, or only perceived? What are the consequences if you don't meet them?

57. What business are you really in? What business do you want to be in twenty-five or fifty years from now? Take the long view and see if your proposed acquisition campaign fits within your future.

58. Ideally, once you have targeted a particular company, both companies should contribute personnel for a joint task force to study the proposed acquisition. Not only does the communication help solidify the acquisition once it's made but it helps you determine, early enough to disengage, whether it is a good match.

TARGETING FOR INDIVIDUALS

This section is designed to help the Jim Kowalskis of the world determine what industry they would be happiest in and whether they should go into business for themselves. Happiness is not necessarily being your own boss. There is much to be said for the security in private industry and government—the lesser responsibilities, and the steady paycheck, too. The frustrations of business might not be for you. An excellent tool to help you decide if you and business ownership are cut out for one another is Joe's classic Entrepreneur's Quiz. We have reproduced it for you in Appendix H.

What follows is a list of questions individuals and managers in the corporate setting can profitably use to increase the likelihood of a successful business acquisition. After all, if five years from now you're managing a company you'd just as soon not be managing, it was not a successful acquisition, even if you're putting a million dollars a day into your pocket.

1. In what businesses, if any, do you have experience?

2. What types of work or tasks have you performed? (Throughout this list, volunteer activities count as much as paid work.) In particular, have you had experience in any of the following:

Physical labor
Management
Financial management
Accounting
Production
Technical work
Customer/client contact
People management

3. Now go back to the list in the prior question and to the left of each of the categories put an L next to each one you liked doing. Then go through the list a second time and put a G next to each one you are good at.

4. What is it about business in general that excites you? Be as specific and as honest as you can. Remember that nobody but you needs to see your answers. Is it the money? Perhaps you like working with figures and accounting. Maybe you like building the product or designing new ones. Go through your mind and conjure up a typical day in the life of a business. Start with the first person to unlock the doors in the morning through the customer who comes in to place an order, the customer who calls to complain, the employees who need to be directed, the ordering of inventory and supplies, the design of new products, the sales work, the accounting for money in and out, the writing of checks, the bank deposits, the sweeping of floors, the shoveling of snow from the walks, and everything else you can picture happening, until the last person locks the doors at night. For each one of these tasks, which ones would you like doing the most, and which ones the least?

5. How do you get along with secretaries, bosses, underlings, agreeable customers, nasty customers? What things do people do that make you mad? Are you able to calm angry people? Are you able to make yourself understood when you give directions? Do you get angry often?

6. What training do you have? Be sure to include college, trade school, continuing education, and on-the-job training.

7. How are you at disciplining yourself? Can you concentrate on a project without getting distracted?

8. In what areas are you more up-to-date than the general populace? Than businesspeople in general? Than businesspeople in the field?

9. What publications do you read? Which ones do you subscribe to personally (and pay for out of your own pocket)? Which ones do you read cover-to-cover?

10. What new business ideas have you tested with customers and buyers?

11. List your proudest accomplishments. List the most important awards you have received. What do they say about your abilities and likes?

12. List all your strengths in each of these areas:

Age
Height
Weight
Gender
Appearance
Personality
Interests

Prejudices
Virtues/faults
Education
Occupation
Hobbies

You might consider your youthfulness a plus in a video game company, or your maturity useful to a fledgling concern. Weight in a larger-sizes clothing manufacturer may be good (if you weigh 180 pounds) or bad (93 pounds). Many seemingly irrelevant factors may turn out to be relevant.

13. Now list all of your weaknesses in each of the areas in the prior question.

14. How could you get each weakness you listed under control? Which weakness could you turn into a strength? How? Which weaknesses will it be better to bring in someone else to help you overcome?

15. Rank in order of importance to your spouse these factors in your life:

Family
God
Business
Self

16. Now rank each of the items in the prior question in order of importance to you.

17. Now rerank each of these items based on your real, heart-of-hearts order of importance, irrespective of how you think it would make you look, or how you should rank it.

18. What do you do better than anything else you do? What do you most like to do?

19. Dig out your high school yearbook and read every comment written in it. What skills and abilities did people recognize in you at that time in your life?

20. If you had unlimited cash and ample free time for your continuing education, what courses would you most like to take?

21. In your three favorite industries or businesses where will the new competition come from in the next five years? Ten years? For instance, office supply stores in mid-size towns are currently facing competition not from the other local office supply stores but from the big mail-order outfits. Also, life insurance companies are competing with stockbrokers, who are competing with bankers, yet ten years ago these were separate and distinct industries. Just where is each of your favorite industries headed?

22. What dangers does the future hold for each of your three favorite industries or businesses?

23. Which tasks do you most dislike in your present job? Which tasks do you regularly try to get others to do? Which tasks do you put off as long as possible? Take a sheet of paper and put it nearby at work and every time you find yourself disliking a task, or avoiding it, or trying to get others to do it for you, put it on the list. In a week, see what things are on your list.

24. What are your standards for product quality and service? Do you want high quality, or do you prefer middle-of-the-road quality at a good price? Do you want a lot of service when you go shopping, or do you prefer to look around and make your decisions, needing a clerk only to take your money? Approached from a different angle, would you be happy selling low-quality goods for a low price, or would that eat at your self-esteem? There is nothing good or bad either way. Just consider what your values are.

25. How much physical and emotional energy do you have for each of your three favorite businesses? Which one would you really love doing? Which one would you be the most excited about?

26. Are you both optimistic and realistic? Both are necessary, and they are not opposite sides of the same coin. Realism involves a healthy dose of optimism and an "I can do it" attitude. If there is anything somebody is doing, you can do it. If there is anything you can imagine anybody doing, you can do it. The fact is that pessimism is not realistic. Realism is simply figuring out ahead of time what problems and obstacles you will likely meet and then devising solutions. Then it is merely a matter of deciding whether the solutions involve a price in terms of effort and resources you are willing to pay.

27. How is your self-confidence? Would you say you usually succeed at what you attempt, or do you usually fail? Or are you somewhere in the middle?

28. How is your health?

29. How important is it to you, on a scale of 1 to 10, to get into each of your three favorite businesses?

30. On the same scale of 1 to 10, how important is it to you to make each of those businesses a success? What do you mean by success?

31. On the same scale, how important is your family to you? God? (Religion is of utmost importance to many business owners.)

32. How good are you at delegating jobs? What are your three biggest strengths in delegating? Your three biggest weaknesses?

33. What do you know how to do better than is currently being done? Why is your idea better? Who will be the quickest to realize it is better? Who cares if it is better? Who will be willing to go out of their way to have it done your way? How much out of their way? How much better is what you have than what someone else has?

34. What are your hobbies? Are there any aspects that others enjoy? Are there any

aspects that could have commercial application? Would anybody pay to see you do your hobby or buy the results or products of your hobby? Would anybody pay for the privilege of doing it themselves? Can you improve the lives or effectiveness of other hobbyists?

35. What special training have you had? Be sure to include on-the-job training, training for a job or task with your church, club, or charity, training for volunteer work, and training for fun.

36. How much time each week are you willing to devote to your business? For how long? How much time do you want to devote once the business is running smoothly?

A few months ago, a professional fisherman was looking for a marina or small bait and tackle store to buy. He actually looked at several, and met with realtors, brokers, and business owners. Finally, George decided not to buy any business.

In the process, George had learned he did not want to be putting in eighty-hour weeks during the height of the fishing season when he would much rather be competing in a contest or making one of those how-to-catch-fish videos. How about you? Will long hours get in the way of what you really want to do? Or will you love the chance to spend ten to twelve hours a day at it?

37. How long do you normally stay with a job before you look for another? How long do you normally stay with a particular task within a job before you look for another?

38. What recurring daydreams do you have? Do these dreams hint at any likes or skills or opportunities in your life?

39. Ideally, how much time would you like to be able to devote each week to these areas of your life (don't worry about it exceeding twenty-four hours times seven days):

Spouse
Children
God
Community
Business
Personal needs (sleep, eating, exercise, hobbies, rest, recreation)

40. If you were independently wealthy, what would you most like to spend your days doing? Write up a three-week itinerary, starting with what you would do immediately upon waking on Monday morning.

HOW TO EVALUATE YOUR RESULTS

Working through both lists was hard work and probably took quite a bit of time. Let your answers cook for two or three days and just go about your everyday life as usual. When you come back to the lists, do so when you are relaxed and fresh. Run through the lists quickly and prompt yourself for new ideas or anything you would like to add to your answers.

Then, go through your answers and take notes on a separate sheet of paper. You are looking for recurring themes. You will see that the questions approach each factor from several different directions and try to help you discover your company and individual experiences, education, training, likes, people skills, technical skills, business knowledge, industry knowledge, strengths, weaknesses, commitment, energy, values, self-confidence, and faith. Each is an important area.

You will discover some things about your company and yourself you never knew. Now you need to ask your team and yourself what those recurring ideas and themes say about you, your company, and where you should be headed.

What happens if you discover many negatives? Does this mean you should not or cannot acquire a business? Absolutely not! What it means is you need to recognize your weaknesses, and do things to overcome them. For instance, if you are weak in sales, you could either take courses in sales, hire full-time salespeople, hire a sales representative company to sell to their own contacts on a commission basis, or hire many individual salespeople on a part-time, commission-only basis. There are solutions to most problems, and not all of them involve paying money before seeing results. But you need to recognize the problem and do something to solve it.

Many people think just because they know how to build a better computer or valve or whatever, they can go into business and capture the whole marketplace, or at least make a living at it. Time and again, we all see businesses close their doors forever. Many times, they were run by people who knew how to do the job. The problem is they failed to get financing, or keep accurate books, or make sales. All of these things are important in business, and if you have one or two weak links, the whole thing can go down hill very fast. Find your weak links and fix them, or put stronger ones in their place.

Appendix B: Financial Statement Analysis

The following two examples are provided to give you a feel for acquisition financial statement analysis. Those readers with experience in statement reviews might still pick up one or two tidbits.

THE RETAILER

In April 1986, a long-time client, whom we will call Larry, came to Doug to discuss buying a package liquor store. Larry wanted an analysis of the financials of this large retail operation. Larry had obtained the prior four years' income tax returns, and the broker promised to get the balance sheets. So while they waited for balance sheets, Doug prepared the report shown in Exhibit A. The numbers shown have been altered from the original.

Larry's liquor store was located near a large factory that employed several hundred blue-collar workers. The community had, within the past couple of years, gotten the bad news that this employer was phasing out local operations to move elsewhere. As you can see from the tax return information, the drop in sales over a period of a few years tended to reflect this bad economic news.

In addition, during the mid-1980s, there was an important sociological event. Until that time it was socially fashionable to drink: afterward there was a push to cut down on drunk driving and various alcohol and drug-related activities. Entrepreneurs sensed the shift in attitudes, and began offering free nonalcoholic beverages to designated drivers in groups of customers at their restaurants and bars. By early 1986, this shift away from alcoholic beverages pointed to a concern that package liquor sales would decline.

Over a number of years, this particular liquor store had grown because it was the only sizable one in its area of town. The more it grew, the less willing smaller operators were to compete with it. However, within the prior six months, a new competitor, part of a discount chain, had opened nearby. Although it was not clear what impact the new store was having on sales, it was a factor with which Larry had to contend.

Comparing this information to the financials we were at once struck with a 25 percent sales decline in four years! This statistic certainly raised red flags, but by itself did not tell us we had a bad deal. Perhaps if sales could have been leveled and expenses appropriately reduced, the deal would still have been a good one for Larry. In fact, the steadily increasing gross profits appeared to bear this out. The bottom-line profit on the tax return was also increasing.

EXHIBIT A

PACKAGE LIQUOR STORE ANALYSIS PREPARED FOR LARRY

Assumed Interest Rates:
. . . Building   .09
. . . Other   .12

LINE # ITEM	1982	%	1983	%	1984	%	1985	%	AVG %	LINE #
1 Sales	1,110,000	100.00	1,095,800	100.00	955,000	100.00	840,500	100.00	100	1
2 Less Cost of Sales	937,000	84.41	944,000	86.15	770,000	80.63	655,600	78.00	82	2
3 Gross Profit on Sales	173,000	15.59	151,800	13.85	185,000	19.37	184,900	22.00	18	3
4 Sign Rental	0	.00	0	.00	0	.00	1,800	.21	0	4
5 GROSS PROFIT	173,000	15.59	151,800	13.85	185,000	19.37	186,700	22.21	18	5
EXPENSES										
6 Advertising	26,000	2.34	14,000	1.28	7,600	.80	6,000	.71	1	6
7 Bank service charges	1,300	.12	1,200	.11	1,000	.10	1,100	.13	0	7
8 Car and truck expenses	1,000	.09	1,000	.09	1,000	.10	500	.06	0	8
9 Depr. & Sec 179 deduct.	4,500	.41	4,400	.40	4,400	.46	4,000	.48	0	9
10 Dues & publications	800	.07	900	.08	1,200	.13	200	.02	0	10
11 Insurance	2,300	.21	3,000	.27	3,300	.35	5,000	.59	0	11
12 Interest on bus. indebtedness	14,600	1.32	13,800	1.26	20,500	2.15		.00	1	12
13 Legal & prof. services	3,100	.28	2,700	.25	4,100	.43	2,700	.32	0	13
14 Other interest		.00		.00		.00	8,600	1.02	0	14
15 Rent on bus. property		.00		.00		.00	1,700	.20	0	15
16 Repairs	4,000	.36	4,100	.37	6,000	.63	3,300	.39	0	16
17 Supplies	3,300	.30	1,700	.16	1,300	.14	1,700	.20	0	17
18 Taxes	5,900	.53	4,000	.37	5,300	.55	5,700	.68	1	18
19 Utilities & telephone	8,400	.76	10,600	.97	11,800	1.24	9,000	1.07	1	19
20 Wages	37,000	3.33	36,700	3.35	35,600	3.73	39,200	4.66	4	20
21 UCI	500	.05	600	.05	300	.03	200	.02	0	21
22 Miscellaneous	600	.05	900	.08	900	.09	2,500	.30	0	22
23 Alarm System	1,100	.10	1,100	.10	600	.06	800	.10	0	23
24 FICA Expense	2,200	.20	1,900	.17	1,300	.14	1,700	.20	0	24
25 Licenses	500	.05	100	.01	700	.07	500	.06	0	25

Exhibit A (*cont'd*)

LINE # ITEM	1982	%	1983	%	1984	%	1985	%	AVG %	LINE #
26 Sign Rental	1,700	.15	1,600	.15	1,900	.20		.00	0	26
27 Federal UCI	300	.03	200	.02	200	.02	100	.01	0	27
28 Sales Promotion	1,200	.11	2,900	.26	3,700	.39		.00	0	28
29 Convention Expense	400	.04	300	.03	600	.06	200	.02	0	29
30 Total Expenses	120,700	10.87	107,700	9.83	113,300	11.86	94,700	11.27	11	30
31 TAX RETURN PROFIT (LOSS)	52,300	4.71	44,100	4.02	71,700	7.51	92,000	10.95	7	31

					AVG $	
32 Ending inventory	105,000	91,000	133,000	103,000	108,000	32
CONVERT TO CASH FLOW:						
Add back noncash:						
33 Depreciation	4,500	4,400	4,400	4,000	4,325	33
Add back seller's exp.:						
34 Interest	14,600	13,800	20,500	8,600	14,375	34
35 Rent	1,700	1,600	1,900	1,700	1,725	35
36 Wages	37,000	36,700	35,600	39,200	37,125	36
Deduct buyer's exp:						
37 Wages	(25,000)	(25,000)	(25,000)	(25,000)	(25,000)	37
38 Debt service—bldg.	(20,521)	(20,521)	(20,521)	(20,521)	(20,521)	38
39 Debt service—other	(80,582)	(76,157)	(89,430)	(79,950)	(81,530)	39
40 Buyer's cash flow	(16,003)	(21,078)	(851)	20,029	(4,476)	40

However, we need to be careful, since the broker, in a letter, told us much of the labor for the business is provided by the seller's family. It is possible they have fired people and are doing the work themselves. Since Larry's family is not as large as the seller's, it may be necessary to hire people for some of the work.

But looking at the wages, we see no drastic drop-off in the amount paid for help. In fact, the number took a jump in the past tax year. We will need to ask the seller why.

Examining the remainder of the statement, from top to bottom, the next thing we notice is that gross profit on sales (line 3) has jumped in the last two years. It was a large jump, which is somewhat unusual in retailing. The gross profit percentage in retailing normally does not vary a great deal from year to year. Does this mean that wholesalers have reduced their prices in order to stimulate sales? Or does it mean that the seller has increased his prices in order to help declining sales? If so, and if it is also true (as we were guessing) that a good deal of the sales have been to blue-collar workers, it may be only a short time before the sales drop off even more—particularly with the discount chain store now in the picture. Therefore, we need to make a note to ask the seller what is going on.

Out of the blue in the last year a new item of income appears: sign rental (line 4). It looks like the seller is looking for new forms of income, which is probably not a bad idea. But who is he renting to? And does the simultaneous appearance of the item rent on business property (line 15) have anything to do with the sign?

Advertising (line 6) is going down, as are several other expenses. This decrease might be seen as a good move to cut expenses. However, the drop is quite drastic, from $26,000 to only $6,000 in four years. Is this decrease going to hurt sales?

Bank service charges (line 7) have dropped, probably a sign that the seller has shopped for a better deal among the banks. It might also be a sign that the seller was using a line of credit or similar form of financing that drove up bank service charges in the past. Interest went up this year in one category (line 14): Might that be the answer?

Car and truck expenses (line 8) went down, which might also be a sign of expense cuts. Depreciation is pretty steady, so apparently no new equipment has been purchased recently. Therefore, Larry made a note to check the age of the equipment and see if replacements will be necessary soon. The repairs, except for an increase in 1984, seem to be fairly level, so there may not be much of a problem.

Dues and publications (line 10) went down, perhaps another economy move. Insurance (line 11) jumped about 50 percent in the last year! Although it is possible that the jump is due to a claim against the business, it is more likely that it reflects a general increase in liability insurance rates for package liquor stores generally. Larry made a note to ask the seller what was happening. Larry also made a note to check with his own insurance agent to see whether or not insurance is still available, and if so, what rate he can expect to pay in the next couple of years.

What's going on with loans that the business has taken out? They have had interest every year in the category interest on business indebtedness (line 12). It even increased in 1984, but then it disappeared entirely in 1985! In 1985, a new category appears, other interest (line 14), which picks up the increase from 1983 to 1984 in the account interest on business indebtedness, but not the original amount. Larry made a note to question the seller.

Legal and professional services (line 13) have been pretty steady, except that in 1984 there was a large increase. Was there a lawsuit? Repairs (line 16) have been level, with the exception of the increase in 1984. However, there was a large decrease in 1985. Did the seller put off doing necessary repairs?

Supplies (line 17) are all over the place. What categories of expenses are going into this account? Taxes (line 18) have been steady, and probably represent real estate property taxes and taxes on the value of inventory.

Utilities and telephone (line 19) are roughly constant. It looks like it was a cold winter in 1984, and perhaps a mild one in 1985. We can check this out with the weather bureau.

Unemployment compensation insurance (line 21) is a minor amount, but it gives us a major clue. Unemployment compensation was not required for family members in the state where the liquor store was located. Therefore, this figure (which should bear a steady ratio to the wages figure from year to year), because it is dropping in the face of slightly increasing wages, confirms that family members are being used increasingly. Does that use account for the increased profits? It could mean family members are underpaid and that Larry will have to pay more for the same work when he takes over.

Larry made a note to ask the seller why the miscellaneous expense account (line 22) jumped so drastically. The alarm system expense (line 23) is more or less level, and may even represent a reduction. This amount should be of no concern, assuming that we have adequate protection. The FICA expense (line 24) tells us the same thing that the unemployment compensation does.

Licenses (line 25) appear steady, although it looks like the 1983 license was not paid until 1984. Is it possible that someone with a potential lawsuit against the business could have additional rights because a license was not obtained? It might pay to ask the seller about licenses paid late.

Sign rental (line 26) disappeared in 1985. Instead, we have sign rental income (line 4). This item is another one to investigate with the seller. Sales promotion (line 28) disappeared as an expense. This might be a good sign, were it not for the fact that it may lead to lower sales in 1986 and later.

Convention expense (line 29) has dropped, but fortunately it has not been cut out entirely. It is necessary in some businesses to go to conventions to stay up-to-date on new techniques and products. Eliminating this expense could be entirely the wrong thing to do.

After letting the information alone for a day or two, Doug and Larry came up with this list of information to request:

1. A list of all equipment on hand, showing what year the equipment was purchased. (They needed to see how old the equipment was and what needed to be replaced or repaired soon.)
2. A copy of the depreciation schedule for the business. This would also help determine the age of equipment as well as what Larry might be able to redepreciate when he took over.
3. A breakdown of the professional services by year, by type of professional, and the amount spent for each. This might help Larry see whether there are any major lawsuits pending.

4. An explanation of rent on business property item.
5. A list of officer and family compensation by person by year.
6. The balance sheets.
7. An explanation of what was done to improve profits despite the lower sales.
8. Information on what basis the employees are paid. Hourly? Commission? How many are necessary to run the business? What are their respective duties?
9. Statistics on break-ins and robberies during the last three years. (Larry didn't want to get into a business where he risked getting shot.)
10. An explanation of sales promotion. Why did it go down?
11. Information on the importance of conventions.

Having examined the income statements for questions to ask and things they needed to know, Doug and Larry were still not done. The next step was to convert the numbers to a cash flow basis.

The only noncash expenditure here was depreciation. That would be an add-back. Next, they added back expenses that the seller had, but that the buyer would not incur. For instance, the seller's outstanding loans would be paid off before closing, but the buyer would have new loans to acquire the business. Therefore, the seller's interest expenses would come out, but Larry would have to add back the buyer's debt service payments. It also appears that the rent was paid to the seller himself, so this item would drop off if Larry bought the real estate, which he planned to do.

Wages paid to the seller's family had to come off, but the wages Larry expected to pay himself needed to be added. They decided that Larry could get by on $25,000 a year, and maybe less, since his wife was employed elsewhere. But what if it took more than one person to run the place? It's probably better not to cut this one too close, just in case. They therefore left it at $25,000. This produced the cash flow shown at the bottom of the statement. If Larry had owned the business in each of those years, there would have been a large loss in the first couple of years, and a cash profit in the last few years, for an average negative cash flow of about $4,500 per year.

Larry either had to improve the profit picture, or this store would not be worth buying. Note that the insurance is probably going to continue to rise, and sales may continue to drop, unless Larry is able to make big changes.

So Larry needed to ask himself a few questions revolving around whether or not he knew enough about liquor stores to turn this one around quickly enough on a limited budget. (Larry didn't have other cash to put in to bail out the store.)

THE MANUFACTURER

Tom B. had run across a small manufacturer of mobile homes and recreational vehicles. The business manufactured high-quality products to an almost nationwide marketplace. The products were well received and had a good reputation.

The current owner had started the business from scratch, and had developed a good network of dealers and manufacturers' representatives. He went annually to the large mobile home and recreational vehicle shows to display his products, and quite often came back with good leads and orders for his products.

The business balance sheet (in abbreviated form) was approximately as follows:

Line		
1	Cash	$132,000
2	Accounts Receivable	100,000
3	Equipment Net of Depreciation	30,000
4	Truck Net of Depreciation	5,000
5	Two Automobiles	10,000
6	Other Assets	40,000
7	Real Estate	50,000
	Total	$367,000
8	Liabilities	$160,000
	Net Worth	
9	Retained Earnings	187,000
10	Stock	20,000
	Total	$367,000

Before you go any further in this appendix, take a look at the facts and numbers above and see what you can discover and what questions you'd ask. Here's what Tom B. came up with:

1. There was cash (line 1) of $132,000. Why should Tom pay cash for cash? Tom can let the seller keep his own cash, thereby reducing the amount Tom has to finance.

2. The accounts receivable (line 2) was large: 27 percent of the assets. How old are the receivables? How much is owed by each of the largest five customers? In fact, is this all owed by customers, or by the major shareholder, or does it perhaps represent a note for the sale of a large asset? What is the usual payment practice in this industry: 30 days? 90 days? 180 days?

3. How old is the equipment (line 3)? The vehicles (lines 4 and 5)? Are they in good

repair? Are there hidden assets—that is, valuable equipment still in use, having a market value, but that was long ago depreciated off the books? If so, Tom might be able to deduct more of the purchase price by redepreciating these assets.

4. What is the value of the real estate (line 7) today? If it was purchased long ago (likely, here) the value today could be far greater than shown on the balance sheet. For preliminary purposes, Tom had a real estate broker guess that the buildings (other assets —line 6) and land were probably worth $140,000. This is good news since we can use the higher figure to help do away with the dreaded goodwill. It is dreaded because the IRS won't let you deduct goodwill, or depreciate it. Taxwise, goodwill is just a lost expenditure. You only get it back when and if you sell out twenty years down the road.

What is goodwill? It may help you in analyzing the price a seller is putting on this intangible asset if you think of it as the value of excess earnings. In other words, if the assets at fair market value will produce an income of $175,000, and this company produces $195,000, you have $20,000 of excess earnings. If you can quantify the goodwill, it is easier to justify paying for it. Where does goodwill come from? The owner, location, efficiency, good employee relations, good customer relations, good supplier relations, management, advertising, good credit standing—the list is endless.

There is no goodwill listed here because this business was started from scratch by the owner. Goodwill usually arises upon the purchase of a business. (In many financials, it's called excess of cost over net assets acquired.) So, if you run into it, it's a sign that the present owner also bought the business. It may be possible to get statements from near the purchase date to help you deduce what the owner paid. If it's recent enough, you may have ammunition for price negotiations. Since Tom's seller wants a price above the $207,000 net worth, by allocating more to the land, we can justify some of the higher price.

5. We can see that the owner originally invested (line 10) only $20,000 in the business, although he may also have loaned money to the company, which is classified as liabilities (line 8). We make a note to ask for a breakdown of liabilities, and especially for any amounts owed the owner. But the $20,000 figure might give us a bargaining chip and insight into the seller's thinking, since we know the business is only twelve years old. Why? Because if he asks $1 million for the business on a $20,000 investment (assuming no loans), we can argue that he is demanding too high a return on his investment.

(Note how the questions that follow are less directly related to particular numbers on the statement, and turn more to areas of inquiry suggested by the numbers.)

6. One of the first things that Tom wanted to know was whether the company was experiencing any warranty claim troubles. Products liability should be a concern for every manufacturer. If the business is producing a defective product that could injure or kill people, one of the first places problems are going to show up is in a high rate of warranty claims. Most manufacturers are going to be careful about such problems, and

take immediate steps to correct them. Thus, it is a good area to investigate, so you can head off later problems.

The warranty claims themselves can be expensive, even without product liability suits. If the company is spending time and money fixing things that didn't get done right the first time, profits will suffer.

7. Tom wanted to know whether the floor planning was full recourse or non-recourse. Floor planning is simply a method of financing inventories in the automotive and recreational vehicle industries. Full recourse means that if an RV is sold, the seller has to stand behind the note the customer gives. If the customer doesn't pay in full and on time, the bank will expect the seller to make it good. Nonrecourse means the bank will stand the loss if the customer fails to pay as agreed. Obviously, if this company's standard financing involves full-recourse notes, the buyer needs to know what will be expected of him, and what risks he'll face.

8. There was a brother-in-law in the business, but Tom did not know what position he held. Tom needed to find out whether he was pulling his own weight, whether he was management or hourly, and whether he was a plus or a minus to the business.

9. How is the dealer network set up? Tom was not so much concerned with how it was originally arranged, but more specifically whether the dealers were friends of the owner (who would disappear as soon as the owner left), or were in place for some other reason. Tom also needed to know whether or not the dealers all sold about the same number of units, or whether there was a particular area of the country or even one particular dealer who sold the lion's share of the units.

10. Were there any particular problems with dealers' floor plans? How were the dealers financed for their cash needs beyond the floor plans? Did the seller provide some of that financing? Would Tom as the buyer be expected to continue the practice in order to keep the dealers?

11. Who are the officers of the corporation? Do they all work, or are there some who are officers in title only?

12. What compensation and other amounts is the owner taking out of the business? For tax purposes, this figure is often buried in several places on the financial statements. Normally the corporation won't be paying dividends, but it always pays to ask. The owner could be getting a company-paid automobile, mileage and expense allowances, and a myriad of other benefits. The owner might also own the real estate personally and be charging the corporation rent. The same might be true of equipment and fixtures. In some businesses, you need to be alert for off-the-books income and funds: money that is skimmed out of the business, but not reported to the IRS. This money is not as likely to appear in a manufacturing business as it is in a cash-oriented business (such as a laundry or a liquor store), but it does happen. What do you do when an owner says that there is more money to be made than shows on the books? First, find out what the owner means. If the reference is to normal benefits (such as the

company-paid car, etc.) then it is important for you to find out exactly what these items are. You will need to know so that you can determine how much cash you will have available to feed your family and pay your debt service.

But if the owner is telling you about skimming or other illegal arrangements, he is digging himself a hole. It is possible the IRS in comparing your figures and his (since your figures will be accurate) will want to audit his returns. In any case, you should not pay the owner for something he cannot prove actually came in the door. You should make this clear early in your negotiations. In Tom's case, he didn't have any hint of skimming, but Tom did want to find out about compensation so he could see what cash flow he'd have available to cover his own needs.

13. When are the dealer rebates payable? In the automotive industry and some others it is commonplace to pay the dealers additional commissions, in the form of rebates, if they sell a certain level of units during the year. Rebates are normally paid only once a year. Again, you are exploring the cash flow.

14. How many company-employed salespeople are there? How are they paid? How many independent manufacturer's reps are used? How are they paid?

15. How many units must be produced before each product line breaks even? This is not just a budgeting question: The answer can be a good measure of how well the owner knows his own business. Not having the information could indicate sloppy accounting policies, which could lead you to question other numbers, too.

16. Where is the business getting its chassis? Is there a chassis pool (that is, are the suppliers in effect warehousing the chassis for the company, and selling them to the company only when needed)? Or, does the company have to order a minimum number of chassis on speculation, and hope that the sales are enough to cover the orders, and also hope that the sales are not so large that the supplier cannot provide additional chassis?

17. Is the business up-to-date on its withholding taxes and its workers compensation insurance premiums?

18. Are there any insurance plans for the employees? What are the costs? What benefits do the employees get? Do the employees think these plans are valuable to them? Or could we drop them and everybody would be just as happy?

19. What fire and building insurance is being maintained? What products liability insurance? What is the cost of each?

20. Are the production employees paid hourly or piece rate?

21. How long has the purchasing agent been with this company? What is the purchasing agent's pay? Tom was of the opinion that a purchasing agent should not stay in any particular job for more than a few years. In his opinion, to have a purchasing agent stay beyond two or three years makes it too easy for the purchasing agent to get lazy in pricing, and to rely on cronies to provide the prices, even when the market may have changed.

Appendix C: Small Business Administration Offices

The Small Business Answer Desk is a recorded message most quickly and easily accessed by touch-tone telephone, although rotary phones do work:

Office of Chief Counsel for Advocacy
Small Business Administration
1441 L Street, NW
Washington, DC 20416
(202) 653-7561
(800) 368-5855
Hours are 9:00 A.M. to 5:00 P.M., EST.

The following district offices and field offices can be helpful, and if they don't know an answer, they are helpful in guiding you to the specific office and often to the person who can assist you:

CITY	STATE	ZIP	ADDRESS		PUBLIC PHONE
Augusta	ME	04330	40 Western Avenue	Room 512	(207) 622-8378
Boston	MA	02114	10 Causeway Street	Room 265	(617) 565-5590
Concord	NH	03301	55 Pleasant Street	Room 210	(603) 225-1400
Hartford	CT	06106	330 Main Street	2nd Floor	(203) 240-4700
Montpelier	VT	05602	87 State Street	Room 205	(802) 828-4474
Providence	RI	02903	380 Westminister Mall	5th Floor	(401) 528-4586
Springfield	MA	01103	1550 Main Street	Room 212	(413) 785-0268
Hato Rey	PR	00918	Carlos Chardon Avenue	Room 691	(809) 753-4002
New York	NY	10278	26 Federal Plaza	Room 3100	(212) 264-4355
Newark	NJ	07102	60 Park Place	4th Floor	(201) 645-2434
Syracuse	NY	13260	100 S. Clinton Street	Room 1071	(315) 423-5383
Buffalo	NY	14202	111 W. Huron Street	Room 1311	(716) 846-4301
Elmira	NY	14901	333 E. Water Street	4th Floor	(607) 734-8130
Melville	NY	11747	35 Pinelawn Road	Room 102E	(516) 454-0750
Baltimore	MD	21202	10 N. Calvert Steet	3rd Floor	(301) 962-4392
Clarksburg	WV	26301	168 W. Main Street	5th Floor	(304) 623-5631
King Prussia	PA	19406	475 Allendale Road	Suite 201	(215) 962-3846
Pittsburgh	PA	15222	960 Penn Avenue	5th Floor	(412) 644-2780

CITY	STATE	ZIP	ADDRESS		PUBLIC PHONE
Richmond	VA	23240	400 N. 8th Street	Room 3015	(804) 771-2617
Washington	DC	20036	1111 18th Street, NW	6th Floor	(202) 634-4950
Charleston	WV	25301	550 Eagan Street	Suite 309	(304) 347-5220
Harrisburg	PA	17101	100 Chestnut Street	Suite 309	(717) 782-3840
Wilkes-Barre	PA	18701	20 N. Pennsylvania Avenue	Room 2327	(717) 826-6497
Wilmington	DE	19801	844 King Street	Room 5207	(302) 573-6294
Atlanta	GA	30309	1720 Peachtree Road, NW	6th Floor	(404) 347-2441
Birmingham	AL	35203	2121 8th Avenue N	Suite 200	(205) 731-1344
Charlotte	NC	28202	222 S. Church Street	Room 300	(704) 371-6563
Columbia	SC	29202	1835 Assembly Street	Room 358	(803) 765-5376
Coral Gables	FL	33146	1320 S. Dixie Highway	Suite 501	(305) 536-5521
Jackson	MS	39269	100 W. Capitol Street	Suite 322	(601) 965-4378
Jacksonville	FL	32202	400 W. Bay Street	Room 261	(904) 791-3782
Louisville	KY	40202	600 Federal Place	Room 188	(502) 582-5976
Nashville	TN	37219	404 James Robertson Parkway	Suite 1012	(615) 736-5881
Gulfport	MS	39501	One Hancock Plaza	Suite 1001	(601) 863-4449
Chicago	IL	60604	219 S. Dearborn Street	Room 437	(312) 353-4528
Cleveland	OH	44199	1240 E. 9th Street	Room 317	(216) 522-4180
Columbus	OH	43215	85 Marconi Boulevard	Room 512	(614) 469-6860
Detroit	MI	48226	477 Michigan Avenue	Room 515	(313) 226-6075
Indianapolis	IN	46204	575 Pennsylvania Street	Room 578	(317) 226-7272
Madison	WI	53703	212 E. Washington Avenue	Room 213	(608) 264-5261
Minneapolis	MN	55403	100 N. 6th Street	Suite 610	(612) 370-2324
Cincinnati	OH	45202	550 Main Street	Room 5028	(513) 684-2814
Marquette	MI	49885	300 S. Front Street		(906) 225-1108
Milwaukee	WI	53203	310 W. Wisconsin Avenue	Suite 400	(414) 291-3941
Springfield	IL	62704	511 W. Capitol Street	Suite 302	(217) 492-4416
Albuquerque	NM	87100	5000 Marble Avenue, NE	Room 320	(505) 262-6171
Dallas	TX	75242	1100 Commerce Street	Room 3C-36	(214) 767-0605
El Paso	TX	79902	10737 Gateway W.	Suite 320	(915) 541-7586
Harlingen	TX	78550	222 E. Van Buren Street	Room 500	(512) 427-8533
Houston	TX	77054	2525 Murworth	Suite 112	(713) 660-4401
Little Rock	AR	72201	320 W. Capitol Avenue	Room 601	(501) 378-5871
Lubbock	TX	79401	1611 Tenth Street	Suite 200	(806) 743-7462
New Orleans	LA	70112	1661 Canal Street	Suite 2000	(504) 589-6685
Oklahoma City	OK	73102	200 N W 5th Street	Suite 670	(405) 231-4301
San Antonio	TX	78216	7400 Blanco Road	Suite 200	(512) 229-4535
Corpus Christi	TX	78401	400 Mann Street	Suite 403	(512) 888-3331
Ft. Worth	TX	76102	819 Taylor Street	Room 10A27	(817) 334-3613
Cedar Rapids	IA	52402	373 Collins Road NE	Room 100	(319) 399-2571

CITY	STATE	ZIP	ADDRESS		PUBLIC PHONE
Des Moines	IA	50309	210 Walnut Street	Room 749	(515) 284-4422
Kansas City	MO	64106	1103 Grand Avenue	6th Floor	(816) 374-3419
Omaha	NE	68154	11145 Mill Valley Road		(402) 221-4691
St. Louis	MO	63101	815 Olive Street	Room 242	(314) 425-6600
Wichita	KS	67202	110 E. Waterman Street	1st Floor	(316) 269-6571
Springfield	MO	65802	620 S. Glenstone Street	Suite 110	(417) 864-7670
Casper	WY	82602	100 East B. Street	Room 4001	(307) 261-5761
Denver	CO	80202	721 19th Street	Room 407	(303) 844-2607
Fargo	ND	58108	657 2nd Avenue N	Room 218	(701) 239-5131
Helena	MT	59626	301 S. Park	Room 528	(406) 449-5381
Salt Lake City	UT	84138	125 S. State Street	Room 2237	(801) 524-5800
Sioux Falls	SD	57102	101 S. Main Avenue	Suite 101	(605) 336-2980
Fresno	CA	93721	2202 Monterey Street	Suite 108	(209) 487-5189
Honolulu	HI	96850	300 Ala Moana	Room 2213	(808) 541-2990
Las Vegas	NV	89125	301 E. Stewart Street	Room 301	(702) 388-6611
Los Angeles	CA	90071	350 E. Figueroa Street	6th Floor	(213) 894-2956
Phoenix	AZ	85004	2005 N. Central Avenue	5th Floor	(602) 261-3732
San Diego	CA	92188	880 Front Street	Room 4-S-29	(619) 557-5440
San Francisco	CA	94105	211 Main Street	4th Floor	(415) 974-0642
Agana	GM	96910	Pacific Daily News Building	Room 508	(671) 472-7277
Sacramento	CA	95814	660 J Street	Room 215	(916) 551-1445
Santa Ana	CA	92703	901 W. Civic Center Drive	Room 160	(714) 836-2494
Anchorage	AK	99501	8th and C Streets	Room 1068	(907) 271-4022
Boise	ID	83702	1020 Main Street	Suite 290	(208) 334-1696
Portland	OR	97204	1220 S W Third Avenue	Room 676	(503) 221-2682
Seattle	WA	98174	915 Second Avenue	Room 1792	(206) 442-5534
Spokane	WA	99210	W. 920 Riverside Avenue	Room 651	(509) 456-3783

For the entire Small Business Answer Desk Directory, showing state agencies, names of contacts at many agencies, state and federal, and a description of various SBA loan programs, see also *Mancuso's Small Business Resource Guide,* Prentice Hall Press (1988), pages 253–367.

Appendix D: Asset-Based Lenders

WHAT THEY ARE

Asset-Based Lenders (ABLs) are a group of commercial lenders who originally were willing to take on more risk than commercial banks, often by lending against accounts receivable and inventory. In recent years, they have taken the lead in leveraged buyout financing, particularly in the middle market from about $1 million to $50 million.

Loans may be the staple, but these companies are aggressive in equity and quasi-equity funding. They are interested, for instance, in providing so-called "mezzanine financing," a level halfway between debt and equity, usually in the form of an individually designed security that is an unsecured debt, convertible to stock. Because of the higher risk involved, expect a higher cost to acquire funds here than at a bank. In addition, there may be fees for valuing assets, managing receivables, and maybe even for sitting on your board of directors. The advantages are that you are financed in a situation outside normal finance parameters, and you get valuable help.

HOW TO FIND THEM

ABLs come from several industries: Some banks have ABL subsidiaries; there are true commercial finance companies; Small Business Investment Companies (SBICs) and Minority Enterprise Small Business Investment Companies (MESBICs) actively engage in asset-based lending; venture capital firms are interested; and insurance companies are actively involved. As a result, the industry is somewhat invisible, often reserving advertising to professional journals (say, to CPAs and attorneys) and primarily directing their efforts to the investment banking community. Even the *Wall Street Journal* carries only a few such ads. Some directories exist, but they are difficult for a one-time user to obtain, and often found in specialized libraries not regularly visited by the general populace. A good source is a university library, particularly if it has a specialized business collection separate from the general library. Another source to try would be your business broker or intermediary. Despite the extra effort, it is an effort worth making.

Directories

Zehring, *The Corporate Finance Sourcebook,* updated annually, National Register Publishing Company, Wilmette, IL. Has a section on commercial finance and factoring running fifteen to twenty pages, covering about fifty companies, classified by type of financing. Lists size of portfolio; minimum size of loan; types of loans; years in business; and key contacts, with telephone numbers.

Galante and Chiappinelli, *Buyouts: Directory of Financing Sources,* updated annually, Venture Economics, Inc. Needham, MA, 461 pages. Has sections divided by U.S. Senior Lenders and U.S. Mezzanine and Equity Providers, types of financing, geographic areas covered, key contacts with telephone numbers.

Membership Directory, *National Venture Capital Association,* updated annually, Arlington, VA, 124 pages. Lists companies and contact people, with telephone numbers.

Membership Directory, *National Association of Investment Companies,* 1111 14th Street NW, Suite 700, Washington, DC 20005. Lists MESBICs by state, with information on investment policy, preferred limit on loans and industry preference, contact names, with telephone numbers.

Association

National Commercial Finance Association, 225 W. 34th Street, New York, NY 10001; (212) 594-3490. Has 240 members, 70 percent of which are banks. Although at this writing a list of their members is restricted and not available for publication, the association promises to answer individual queries as to members located geographically close to you who might be interested in your deal.

Periodical

The Secured Lender, published bimonthly by the National Commercial Finance Association (cost: about $36 annually for nonmembers; see address above). Has numerous ads by lenders, which are useful sources of information about ABLs. The February issue each year lists the board of directors by name and company, giving you a starting point to find many ABLs. Even then, the company names must be searched through general business directories (such as Dunn & Bradstreet, *The Million Dollar Directory, The Directory of Corporate Affiliations,* etc.) and data bases. Another problem is that about one-third of the companies are not listed in these national directories.

Appendix E: Financing Analysis

The two examples in this appendix were chosen to give you experience with real-life financials. The goal is to help you improve your ability to spot hidden financing clues in the financials.

Example A is the balance sheet of a wholesale auto parts store. We obtained this balance sheet by answering a Sunday classified ad under "Businesses for Sale." We've changed the numbers enough to hide the identity of the business, but not enough to destroy the insights you can gain from a real-life example.

This dealer has been in business about forty-five years, and is the oldest of its type in its town. One or more of the partners own the building, leasing it to the business. Sales are 80 percent from dealer trade, and 20 percent off-the-street retail trade. The asking price is $155,000, which includes an inventory of $79,000 (according to the letter that accompanied it, although the balance sheet showed only $73,000). The sellers are asking for 20 percent down and a balloon payment in three years, with 10 percent interest. There is another loan on which the sellers pay $12,000 per year. The building includes a couple of apartments and a machine shop, all of which are rented to others to produce some of the profit.

We have numbered the lines on the balance sheet to refer to them more easily.

1. *Cash.* Normally as a buyer assume at the start you will buy assets, not stock. You ordinarily won't buy cash. If the cash is relatively small, the seller does not even consider it when setting the price. So let the seller keep his $5,000 cash and reduce the sales price (and the financing you need to find) by $5,000.

2. *Accounts receivable.* Perhaps you could have the seller keep his receivables on the theory that he knows his customers and the collectibility of particular receivables. You don't have to take the risk of collecting, and he doesn't have to take the risk that you won't be good for so much purchase price. Another approach would be for you to borrow against these with a factor (a lender who loans against such assets). However, these numbers are probably too small to interest most factors. Perhaps your banker might be interested in a loan, but probably only to the tune of 60 percent or 80 percent of the up-to-thirty-day-old receivables.

3. *Inventory.* Here is something the bank might finance as part of the purchase, but you need to prove there are few obsolete or shop-worn items included.

237

EXAMPLE A
AUTO PARTS STORE

Balance Sheet
December 31, 19XX
000 Omitted

Current Assets

1.	Cash	5
2.	Accounts receivable—trade	14
3.	Inventory	73
4.	Prepaid insurance	(1)
5.	No compete expense	0
	Total Current Assets	91

Property and Equipment

6.	Leasehold improvements	0
7.	Furniture and fixtures	4
8.	Autos	7
	Total Cost	11
9.	Less accumulated depreciation	11
	Net Property and Equipment	0

Other Assets

10.	Deposits	0
	Total Assets	91

Liabilities and Partners' Equity

Current Liabilities

11.	Accounts payable—trade	13
12.	Accrued interest	0
13.	Accrued payroll taxes	1
14.	Accrued sales tax	0
15.	Accrued property tax	2
	Total Current Liabilities	16
16.	*Long-term Debt*	42
17.	*Partners' Equity*	33
	Total Liabilities and Partners' Equity	91

4. ***Prepaid insurance.*** Since this is in parentheses, indicating a negative, it represents a liability. You might assume this liability and knock down your purchase price an equal amount.

5. ***No compete expense.*** Since this rounds to less than a thousand dollars on a $155,000 purchase, it is not worth examining in detail for financing sources. But you should check it out before you commit to the purchase. Who have they agreed not to compete against? Why?

6–10. ***Leasehold improvements to deposits.*** All these numbers show low values, meaning low finance possibilities. Most of the equipment is fully depreciated, but there may be some bankable value in autos or equipment if it is still in good shape. You should ask to see the lease. You can let the sellers collect their own deposits.

11. ***Accounts payable—trade.*** Here is $13,000 you could probably assume. The real question is whether the seller has already been operating under the presumption that you will assume these debts.

12–15. ***Accruals.*** Has the seller planned on the buyer assuming these? If not, and you do assume them, you may have a part of your down payment.

16. ***Long-term debt.*** A big item, at last. If you take over this $42,000 debt, the outside money you have to find is reduced. Again, you need to know whether the stated price includes your assumption of this debt.

17. ***Partners' equity.*** This line item does not give direct clues to financing. Indirectly, if you can use it to lower your price, your financing need is also reduced. Here, with the books showing an equity of only $33,000, you could ask why the sellers think it's worth $155,000.

One factor you don't have any feel for is the real estate value. However, the seller did provide an address, so you can have a realtor friend drive past and give a "windshield appraisal"—a range of values within which the real estate probably would sell.

Let's add up the financing possibilities:

1.	Cash seller keeps	$ 5,000
2.	Bank loan against receivables (60% value)	8,400
3.	Bank loan against inventory (60% value)	47,400
4.	Prepaid insurance liability assumed	1,000
8.	Auto loans	1,500
11–16.	Debt assumed ($42,000 + $16,000)	58,000
	Total	$121,300
	Balance to come from seller and	
	other sources	33,700
	Asking price	$155,000

Now the seller's letter says he wants a 20 percent downstroke, meaning he is prepared to finance $124,000, so there should be ample room to come up with the $33,700 you need. If you push things, you might get the seller to take back a $91,000 note for three or five years, so you don't have to go to the bank at all (the balance would be provided by $58,000 debts assumed, $1,000 insurance debt assumed, and $5,000 cash retained by the seller).

Since the seller actually advertised a willingness to take an 80 percent note, your antennae should pick up. Most sellers advertise deals as if they were cash only. They only grudgingly take back notes. So what gives? Is this a "dog" that's been on the market forever? Is it overpriced? Or is there a problem with the long term-payable—perhaps it cannot be assumed. Perhaps it's in default and the lender is suing. Whatever the case, it looks like financing may be relatively easy. Now, can the cash flow support the debt service?

Next let's switch to Example B. Example B is a larger company that does light manufacturing and is in the distribution/warehouse business, as well. The purchase price is $1,000,000. Again, the numbers have been changed to protect the identities of people involved.

EXAMPLE B
WAREHOUSE, MANUFACTURING AND DISTRIBUTION CO., INC.

Balance Sheet
July 31, 19XX
000 Omitted

ASSETS

Current Assets

1. Cash		$ 0
2. Receivables		
Accounts receivable—trade (Note B)	$188	
Advances to employees and others	1	
	189	
Less allowance for doubtful accounts	(10)	179
3. Claims for refund of income taxes		17
4. Inventory, at lower of cost (primarily first-in, first-out) or market (Notes A and B)		501
5. Prepaid insurance		7
Total Current Assets		704

EXAMPLE B (*cont'd*)

6. Investment in subsidiaries and advances to subsidiaries
   (Notes A and F)

Balance, August 1, 19XX	43	
Increase during the current year	103	
	146	
Less share of net losses of subsidiaries for the current year accounted for by the equity method	(146)	0

7. Land, building, and equipment, at cost (Notes A and B)

Land	6	
Building	33	
Molds	207	
Automotive equipment	46	
Office equipment	14	
Other equipment	95	
	401	
Less accumulated depreciation	(316)	85

8. Other assets

Leasehold improvements	6	
Less accumulated amortization	(2)	4
Total Assets		$793

LIABILITIES

Current Liabilities

9. Notes and contracts payable (Notes C, G, and H)		$279

10. Accounts payable

Trade (Note I)		$235	
Bank checks outstanding	$32		
Less balance in bank acct.	(31)	1	
Credit balances in accounts receivable		4	
Employee payroll deductions		2	242

11. Accrued liabilities

Salaries	1	
Commissions and outside services	5	
Interest	5	
Payroll taxes	0	

EXAMPLE B (*cont'd*)

Personal property taxes	12	
State income taxes	1	24
Total Current Liabilities		545
12. Long-term liabilities		
Notes and contracts payable (Notes C, G, and H)		102

STOCKHOLDERS' EQUITY

13. Capital stock		
Common, no par value—1,000 shares authorized,		
750 shares issued, of which 250 are in the treasury	1	
14. Retained earnings	157	
	158	
Less costs of 250 shares held in treasury	12	146
Total Liabilities and Stockholders' Equity		$793

(The accompanying notes are an integral part of the financial statements.)

1. **Cash.** Cash is often useful in an asset deal, because you can show the seller how much cash the seller gets to keep. Here, there is an overdraft (see number 10 below); you can take advantage of that by showing a debt you can remove from the seller's shoulders.

2. **Accounts receivable—trade.** In a note to the financial statements you learn that the accounts receivable, inventory, and equipment are pledged as collateral for a $265,000 bank loan. You might at first view the bank loan as tying your hands so you can't get new financing; however, if the bank is already loaning money against equipment, it might be interested in increasing the loan, which could have been paid down substantially since it was taken out. You will also want to check to see if UCC (Uniform Commercial Code) filings exist, indicating a lien against the receivables. The advances to employees may not be collectible. At least you probably won't see this cash any time soon.

3. **Claims for refund of income taxes.** Here is $17,000 that will probably be received soon. You could let the sellers keep it, particularly if you think there might be a dispute with the taxing authorities. Indeed, it may be cash by the time you reach closing. But think what this item means: Businesses don't often get tax refunds unless they are losing money. If experienced owners can't make money here, why do you want to spend good money to acquire the business? This is a red flag to the informed buyer.

4. **Inventory.** This is a large figure, particularly when added to the receivables. Since you know it is subject to a bank loan of only about half the total value pledged,

you might bootstrap this acquisition by increasing the loan. But the bank may not be your best resource. Banks don't want to be in the business of selling receivables or inventory. Perhaps a commercial lender would loan a higher percentage. The trade-off for more cash would be a higher interest rate.

5. **Prepaid insurance.** There is little cash you can raise from this item. It does point toward a high insurance cost. A quick review of the income statement shows insurance costs of $21,000 per year. You can perhaps cut your costs by shopping around. An aggressive new agent might find ways to add more benefits for your employees in the bargain. He might extend payment terms on premiums, or even loan you a portion of his commission to get that last few dollars of financing you need.

6. **Investment in subsidiaries and advances to subsidiaries.** With some further investigation, you may find bankable assets in the subsidiary.

7. **Land, building, and equipment.** The note to the financial statements tells you the real estate has a book value of $35,000, against which there is a mortgage of $28,000. If the building has increased in value since it was originally purchased there could be room for additional borrowings. The molds may or may not be worth $207,000. Even so, if they are custom molds, they would have little resale (and therefore loan) value. The equipment, particularly the $95,000 worth of "other" equipment, is probably bankable. In fact, some manufacturing equipment today appreciates in value over time, and therefore represents a good place to look for hidden loan value.

8. **Leasehold improvements.** Why are there leasehold improvements if the company owns the building? Is there some leased equipment you could refinance for additional cash?

9. **Notes and contracts payable.** The notes to the financial statements indicate these payables vary from 11.5 percent to 17 percent interest, and some of the loans come due within one year. Perhaps by consolidating these debts with a new lender you will not only improve some interest rates but reduce your monthly payment as well, thereby justifying further loans. Or, these notes might be assumable.

10. **Trade payables.** Here is a large item you could assume. Overdrafts in banking account and accounts receivable: Could it be that the bank would be happy to see a fresh face come in with new ideas to turn this company around? Or will it be so turned off to this business it will just want out? You need to discuss banking relationships with the seller.

Employee payroll deductions: Here is something owed to the taxing authorities you could no doubt assume.

11. **Accrued liabilities.** Again, you can attempt to assume.

12. **Notes and contracts payable—long-term.** You could perhaps assume these, as well.

13 and 14. **Stockholders' equity.** The cost of 250 shares of treasury stock shows that one of the three original equal shareholders was bought out for $12,000. If it was recent, this buyout will help you negotiate price. You can find out by asking in an offhand manner: "Did you buy out a partner some time ago? Can I expect this partner to come back at me to pay him something? How long ago did that buyout take place?"

Adding up the possibilities:

1. Accounts receivable (loan value 80%)	$ 143,200
2. Cash from tax refunds retained by seller	17,000
3. Inventory (loan value 60%)	300,600
Less outstanding bank loan	(265,000)
4. Assets in subsidiary	?
5. Land and building (assume fair market	
value = $50,000; loan value 80%)	40,000
Less outstanding mortgage	(28,000)
6. Equipment (loan value 40%)	18,400 +/−
Total Financing	$ 226,200
Additional Financing Needed	773,800
Asking Price	$1,000,000

Why not add in all those assumable loans and payables as you did for the auto parts wholesaler? You had been told that the price was $1,000,000 on a stock deal. In other words, the seller expects the buyer to assume all debts. There is a tremendous amount of blue sky here. It'll have to be a super company for you to pay that much.

Both examples have been taken out of context, but our purpose was not to analyze particular balance sheets. Our purpose was to lead you through some everyday statements to give clues on how to spot financing opportunities that exist in the balance sheet. Now you know why getting the balance sheet is perhaps more important than getting the income statement.

Appendix F: Valuing a Company

Many people who have never bought or sold a company are surprised to learn valuation of a company is not an exact science, and there is no such thing as a formula that can apply to all companies, or all companies in a single industry, or even to a single company at two different times.

Valuing the hard (fixed) assets is easy: Equipment and real estate appraisers can give you a fairly accurate range of values. But intangibles are different: Just how much is a distribution network or a customer list worth?

Intangible values are usually listed under "goodwill" or "going concern value." Goodwill can be a result of location, reputation, the quality of the product or service, an established customer base, proprietary technology, and so on. Or it can come from the owner's or principal's personal relationships with customers, unique skills, or even his last name. Goodwill value (when it exists) is frequently measured or estimated on the basis of the company's ability to earn profits above and beyond a reasonable return on all the other tangible assets associated with the business.

The common approaches to valuing a closely held (nonpublicly traded) company are legion. The more common ones are (the first three being the most-used approaches):

1. Market approach: Prices actually paid for similar companies are gathered and adjusted for differences between the company sold and the company being appraised.
2. Replacement cost approach: The cost of replacing each asset and liability in its current condition is estimated.
3. Investment value approach: Capitalization ("cap") rates for comparable investments are applied to historical income of the company being appraised, to back into an asset value.
4. Liquidation value approach.
5. Discounted future earnings approach.
6. Excess earnings approach.
7. Price/earnings multiples approach.
8. Book value approach: This is based on the fictions of accounting conventions. Only rank amateurs use it.

245

In sum, there is more art than science to valuation. Therefore, there cannot be a computer program to give you an accurate value. There is all the sense in the world in getting an expert appraisal, but remember, even your expert doesn't know what the company is worth.

What follows are excerpts from the classic Internal Revenue Service ruling (Rev. Rul. 59–60) on valuing a company, and two (Rev. Rul. 65–193 and 68–609) that modify it (the first by allowing separate valuations of tangibles and intangibles, and the second by "outlawing" the formula approach for all but unusual cases). Note that even the IRS says there is no such thing as a formula that applies to all companies. And, though studying these rulings will give you the tools to critically analyze the appraisal you get, it won't turn you into a valuation expert.

EXCERPTS FROM REV. RUL. 59–60

Sec. 1. Purpose

The purpose of this Revenue Ruling is to outline and review in general the approach, methods and factors to be considered in valuing shares of the capital stock of closely held corporations for estate tax and gift tax purposes. . . .

Sec. 3. Approach to Valuation

.01 . . . . No formula can be devised that will be generally applicable to the multitude of different valuation issues arising in estate and gift tax cases . . . . [V]aluation is not an exact science. A sound valuation will be based upon all the relevant facts, but the elements of common sense, informed judgment and reasonableness must enter into the process of weighing those facts and determining their aggregate significance.

.02 The fair market value of specific shares of stock will vary as general economic conditions change from "normal" to "boom" or "depression," that is, according to the degree of optimism or pessimism with which the investing public regards the future at the required date of appraisal. Uncertainty as to the stability or continuity of the future income from a property decreases its value by increasing the risk of loss of earnings and value in the future. The value of shares of stock of a company with very uncertain future prospects is highly speculative. The appraiser must exercise his judgment as to the degree of risk attaching to the business of the corporation which issued the stock, but that judgment must be related to all of the other factors affecting value.

.03 Valuation of securities is, in essence, a prophesy as to the future and must be based on facts available at the required date of appraisal. As a generalization, the prices of stocks which are traded in volume in a free and active market by informed persons best reflect the consensus of the investing public as to what the future holds for the corporations and industries represented. When a stock is closely held, is traded infrequently, or is traded in an erratic market, some other measure of value must be used. In many instances, the next best measure may be found in the prices at which the stocks of companies engaged in the same or a similar line of business are selling in a free and open market.

Sec. 4. Factors to Consider

.01 . . . . The following factors, although not all-inclusive are fundamental and require careful analysis in each case:

(a) The nature of the business and the history of the enterprise from its inception.

(b) The economic outlook in general and the condition and outlook of the specific industry in particular.

(c) The book value of the stock and the financial condition of the business.

(d) The earning capacity of the company.

(e) The dividend-paying capacity.

(f) Whether or not the enterprise has goodwill or other intangible value.

(g) Sales of the stock and the size of the block of stock to be valued.

(h) The market price of stocks of corporations engaged in the same or a similar line of business having their stocks actively traded in a free and open market, either on an exchange or over-the-counter.

.02 The following is a brief discussion of each of the foregoing factors:

(a) The history of a corporate enterprise will show its past stability or instability, its growth or lack of growth, the diversity or lack of diversity of its operations, and other facts needed to form an opinion of the degree of risk involved in the business. For an enterprise which changed its form of organization but carried on the same or closely similar operations of its predecessor, the history of the former enterprise should be considered. The detail to be considered should increase with approach to the required date of appraisal, since recent events are of greatest help in predicting the future; but a study of gross and net income, and of dividends covering a long prior period, is highly desirable. The history to be studied should include, but need not be limited to, the nature of the business, its products or services, its operating and investment assets, capital structure, plant facilities, sales records and management, all of which should be considered as of the date of the appraisal, with due regard for recent significant changes. Events of the past that are unlikely to recur in the future should be discounted, since value has a close relation to future expectancy.

(b) A sound appraisal of a closely held stock must consider current and prospective economic conditions as of the date of appraisal, both in the national economy and in the industry or industries with which the corporation is allied. It is important to know that the company is more or less successful than its competitors in the same industry, or that it is maintaining a stable position with respect to competitors. Equal or even greater significance may attach to the ability of the industry with which the company is allied to compete with other industries. Prospective competition which has not been a factor in prior years should be given careful attention. For example, high profits due to the novelty of its product and the lack of competition often lead to increasing competition. The public's appraisal of the future prospects of competitive industries or of competitors within an industry may be indicated by price trends in the markets for commodities and for securities. The loss of the manager of a so-called "one-man" business may have a depressing effect upon the value of the stock of such business, particularly if there is a lack of trained personnel capable of succeeding to the management of the enterprise. In valuing the stock of this type of business, therefore, the effect of the loss of the manager on the future expectancy of the business, and the absence of management-succession potentialities are pertinent factors to be taken into consideration. On the other hand, there may be factors which offset, in whole or in part, the loss of the manager's services. For instance, the nature of the business and of its assets may be such that they will not be impaired by the loss of the manager. Furthermore, the loss may be adequately covered by life insurance, or competent management might be employed on the basis of the consideration paid for the former manager's services. These, or other offsetting factors, if found to exist, should be carefully weighed against the loss of the manager's services in valuing the stock of the enterprise.

(c) Balance sheets should be obtained, preferably in the form of comparative annual statements for two or more years immediately preceding the date of appraisal, together with a balance sheet at the end of the month preceding that date, if corporate accounting will permit. Any balance sheet descriptions that are not self-explanatory, and balance sheet items comprehending diverse assets or liabilities, should be clarified in essential detail by supporting supplemental schedules. These statements usually will disclose to the appraiser (1) liquid position (ratio of current assets to current liabilities); (2) gross and net book value of principal classes of fixed assets; (3) working capital; (4) long-term indebtedness; (5) capital structure; and (6) net worth. Consideration also should be given to any assets not essential to the operation of the business, such as investments in securities, real estate, etc. In general, such nonoperating assets will command a lower rate of return than do the operating assets, although in exceptional cases the reverse may be true. In computing the book value per share of stock, assets of the investment type should be revalued on the basis of their market price and the book value adjusted accordingly. Comparison of the company's balance sheets over several years may reveal, among other facts, such developments as the acquisition of additional production facilities or subsidiary companies, improvement in financial position, and details as to recapitalizations and other changes in the capital structure of the corporation. If the corporation has more than one class of stock outstanding, the charter or certificate of incorporation should be examined to ascertain the explicit rights and privileges of the various stock issues including: (1) voting powers, (2) preference as to dividends, and (3) preference as to assets in the event of liquidation.

(d) Detailed profit-and-loss statements should be obtained and considered for a representative period immediately prior to the required date of appraisal, preferably five or more years. Such statements should show (1) gross income by principal items; (2) principal deductions from gross income including major prior items of operating expenses, interest and other expense on each item of long-term debt, depreciation and depletion if such deductions are made, officers' salaries, in total if they appear to be reasonable or in detail if they seem to be excessive, contributions (whether or not deductible for tax purposes) that the nature of its business and its community position require the corporation to make, and taxes by principal items, including income and excess profits taxes; (3) net income available for dividends; (4) rates and amounts of dividends paid on each class of stock; (5) remaining amount carried to surplus; and (6) adjustments to, and reconciliation with, surplus as stated on the balance sheet. With profit and loss statements of this character available, the appraiser should be able to separate recurrent from nonrecurrent items of income and expense, to distinguish between operating income and investment income, and to ascertain whether or not any line of business in which the company is engaged is operated consistently at a loss and might be abandoned with benefit to the company. The percentage of earnings retained for business expansion should be noted when dividend-paying capacity is considered. Potential future income is a major factor in many valuations of closely-held stocks, and all information concerning past income which will be helpful in predicting the future should be secured. Prior earnings records usually are the most reliable guide as to the future expectancy, but resort to arbitrary five-or-ten-year averages without regard to current trends or future prospects will not produce a realistic valuation. If, for instance, a record of progressively increasing or decreasing net income is found, then greater weight may be accorded the most recent years' profits in estimating earning power. It will be helpful, in judging risk and the extent to which a business is a marginal operator, to consider deductions from income and net income in terms of percentage of sales. Major categories of cost and expense to be so analyzed include the consumption of raw materials and supplies in the case of manufacturers, processors and fabricators; the cost of purchased merchandise in the case of merchants; utility services; insurance; taxes; depletion or depreciation; and interest.

(e) Primary consideration should be given to the dividend-paying capacity of the company rather than to dividends actually paid in the past. Recognition must be given to the necessity of retaining a reasonable portion of profits in a company to meet competition. Dividend-paying capacity is a factor that must be considered in an appraisal, but dividends actually paid in the past may not have any relation to dividend-paying capacity. Specifically, the dividends paid by a closely held family company may be measured by the income needs of the stockholders or by their desire to avoid taxes on dividend receipts, instead of by the ability of the company to pay dividends. Where an actual or effective controlling interest in a corporation is to be valued, the dividend factor is not a material element, since the payment of such dividends is discretionary with the controlling stockholders. The individual or group in control can substitute salaries and bonuses for dividends, thus reducing net income and understating the dividend-paying capacity of the company. It follows, therefore, that dividends are less reliable criteria of fair market value than other applicable factors.

(f) In the final analysis, goodwill is based upon earning capacity. The presence of goodwill and its value, therefore, rests upon the excess of net earnings over and above a fair return on the net tangible assets. While the element of goodwill may be based primarily on earnings, such factors as the prestige and renown of the business, the ownership of a trade or brand name, and a record of successful operation over a prolonged period in a particular locality, also may furnish support for the inclusion of intangible value. In some instances it may not be possible to make a separate appraisal of the tangible and intangible assets of the business. The enterprise has a value as an entity. Whatever intangible value there is, which is supportable by the facts, may be measured by the amount by which the appraised value of the tangible assets exceeds the net book value of such assets.

(g) Sales of stock of a closely held corporation should be carefully investigated to determine whether they represent transactions at arm's length. Forced or distress sales do not ordinarily reflect fair market value nor do isolated sales in small amounts necessarily control as the measure of value. This is especially true in the valuation of a controlling interest in a corporation. Since, in the case of closely held stocks, no prevailing market prices are available, there is no basis for making an adjustment for blockage. It follows, therefore, that such stocks should be valued upon a consideration of all the evidence affecting the fair market value. The size of the block of stock itself is a relevant factor to be considered. Although it is true that a minority interest in an unlisted corporation's stock is more difficult to sell than a similar block of listed stock, it is equally true that control of a corporation, either actual or in effect, representing as it does an added element of value, may justify a higher value for a specific block of stock.

(h) Section 2031(b) of the Code states, in effect, that in valuing unlisted securities the value of stock or securities of corporations engaged in the same or a similar line of business which are listed on an exchange should be taken into consideration along with all other factors. An important consideration is that the corporations to be used for comparisons have capital stocks which are actively traded by the public. In accordance with section 2031(b) of the Code, stocks listed on an exchange are to be considered first. However, if sufficient comparable companies whose stocks are listed on an exchange cannot be found, other comparable companies which have stocks actively traded in on [sic] the over-the-counter market also may be used. The essential factor is that whether the stocks are sold on an exchange or over-the-counter there is evidence of an active, free public market for the stock as of the valuation date. In selecting corporations for comparative purposes, care should be taken to use only comparable companies. Although the only restrictive requirement as to comparable corporations specified in the statute is that their lines of business be the same or similar, yet it is obvious that consideration must be given to other relevant factors in order that the most valid comparison possible will be obtained. For illustration, a corporation having one or more issues of preferred stock, bonds or debentures in addition to its common stock should not be considered to be directly comparable to one having only common stock outstanding. In like manner, a company with a declining business and decreasing markets is not comparable to one with a record of current progress and market expansion.

Sec. 5. Weight to be Accorded Various Factors

The valuation of closely held corporate stock entails the consideration of all relevant factors as stated in section 4. Depending upon the circumstances in each case, certain factors may carry more weight than others because of the nature of the company's business. To illustrate:

(a) Earnings may be the most important criterion of value in some cases whereas asset value will receive primary consideration in others. In general, the appraiser will accord primary consideration to earnings when valuing stocks of companies which sell products or services to the public; conversely, in the investment or holding type of company, the appraiser may accord the greatest weight to the assets underlying the security to be valued.

(b) The value of the stock of a closely held investment or real estate holding company, whether or not family owned, is closely related to the value of the assets underlying the stock. For companies of this type the appraiser should determine the fair market values of the assets of the company. Operating expenses of such a company and the cost of liquidating it, if any, merit consideration when appraising the relative values of the stock and the underlying assets. The market values of the underlying assets give due weight to potential earnings and dividends of the particular items of property underlying the stock, capitalized at rates deemed proper by the investing public at the date of appraisal. A current appraisal by the investing public should be superior to the retrospective opinion of an individual. For these reasons, adjusted net worth should be accorded greater weight in valuing the stock of a closely held investment or real estate holding company, whether or not family owned, than any of the other customary yardsticks of appraisal, such as earnings and dividend paying capacity.

Sec. 6. *Capitalization Rates*

In the application of certain fundamental valuation factors, such as earnings and dividends, it is necessary to capitalize the average or current results at some appropriate rate. A determination of the proper capitalization rate presents one of the most difficult problems in valuation. That there is no ready or simple solution will become apparent by a cursory check of the rates of return and dividend yields in terms of the selling prices of corporate shares listed on the major exchanges of the country. Wide variations will be found even for companies in the same industry. Moreover, the ratio will fluctuate from year to year depending upon economic conditions. Thus, no standard tables of capitalization rates applicable to closely held corporations can be formulated. Among the more important factors to be taken into consideration in deciding upon a capitalization rate in a particular case are: (1) the nature of the business; (2) the risk involved; and (3) the stability or irregularity of earnings.

Sec. 7. *Average of Factors*

Because valuations cannot be made on the basis of a prescribed formula, there is no means whereby the various applicable factors in a particular case can be assigned mathematical weights in deriving the fair market value. For this reason, no useful purpose is served by taking an average of several factors (for example, book value, capitalized earnings and capitalized dividends) and basing the valuation on the result. Such a process excludes active consideration of other pertinent factors, and the end result cannot be supported by a realistic application of the significant facts in the case except by mere chance.

Sec. 8. Restrictive Agreements

Frequently, in the valuation of closely held stock for estate and gift tax purposes, it will be found that the stock is subject to an agreement restricting its sale or transfer. Where shares of stock were acquired by a decedent subject to an option reserved by the issuing corporation to repurchase at a certain price, the option price is usually accepted as the fair market value for estate tax purposes. See Rev. Rul. 54–76, C.B. 1954–1, 194. However, in such case the option price is not determinative of fair market value for gift tax purposes. Where the option, or buy and sell agreement, is the result of voluntary action by the stockholders and is binding during the life as well as at the death of the stockholders, such agreement may, or may not, depending upon the circumstances of each case, fix the value for estate tax purposes. However, such agreement is a factor to be considered, with other relevant factors, in determining fair market value. Where the stockholder is free to dispose of his shares during life and the option is to become effective only upon his death, the fair market value is not limited to the option price. It is always necessary to consider the relationship of the parties, the relative number of shares held by the decedent, and other material facts, to determine whether the agreement represents a bonafide business arrangement or is a device to pass the decedent's shares to the natural objects of his bounty for less than an adequate and full consideration in money or money's worth. . . .

EXCERPTS FROM REV. RUL. 65–193

Revenue Ruling 59–60 . . . is hereby modified to delete the statements, contained therein at section 4.02(f), that "In some instances it may not be possible to make a separate appraisal of the tangible and intangible assets of the business. The enterprise has a value as an entity. Whatever intangible value there is, which is supportable by the facts, may be measured by the amount by which the appraised value of the tangible assets exceeds the net book value of such assets."

The instances where it is not possible to make a separate appraisal of the tangible and intangible assets of a business are rare and each case varies from the other. No rule can be devised which will be generally applicable to such cases. . . .

EXCERPTS FROM REV. RUL. 68–609

. . . . The question presented is whether the "formula" approach, the capitalization of earnings in excess of a fair rate of return on net tangible assets, may be used to determine the fair market value of the intangible assets of a business.

The "formula" approach may be stated as follows:

A percentage return on the average annual value of the tangible assets used in a business is determined, using a period of years (preferably not less than five) immediately prior to the valuation date. The amount of the percentage return on tangible assets, thus determined, is deducted from the average earnings of the business for such period and the remainder, if any, is considered to be the amount of the average annual earnings from the intangible assets of the business for the period. This amount (considered as the average annual earnings from intangibles), capitalized at a percentage of, say, 15 to 20 percent, is the value of the intangible assets of the business determined under the "formula" approach.

The percentage of return on the average annual value of the tangible assets used should be the percentage prevailing in the industry involved at the date of valuation, or (when the industry percentage is not available) a percentage of 8 to 10 percent may be used.

The 8 percent rate of return and the 15 percent rate of capitalization are applied to tangibles and intangibles, respectively, of businesses with a small risk factor and stable and regular earnings; the 10 percent rate of return and 20 percent rate of capitalization are applied to businesses in which the hazards of business are relatively high.

The above rates are used as examples and are not appropriate in all cases. In applying the "formula" approach, the average earnings period and the capitalization rates are dependent upon the facts pertinent thereto in each case.

The past earnings to which the formula is applied should fairly reflect the probable future earnings. Ordinarily, the period should not be less than five years, and abnormal years, whether above or below the average, should be eliminated. If the business is a sole proprietorship or partnership, there should be deducted from the earnings of the business a reasonable amount for services performed by the owner or partners engaged in the business. . . . Further, only the tangible assets entering into net worth, including accounts and bills receivable in excess of accounts and bills payable, are used for determining earnings on the tangible assets. Factors that influence the capitalization rate include (1) the nature of the business, (2) the risk involved, and (3) the stability or irregularity of earnings.

The "formula" approach should not be used if there is better evidence available from which the value of intangibles can be determined. If the assets of a going business are sold upon the basis of a rate of capitalization that can be substantiated as being realistic, though it is not within the range of figures indicated here as the ones ordinarily to be adopted, the same rate of capitalization should be used in determining the value of intangibles.

Accordingly, the "formula" approach may be used for determining the fair market value of intangible assets of a business only if there is no better basis therefore available. . . .

Problems of the Revenue Rulings

There are several continuing problems with these revenue rulings. Here is what Scott A. Jessup, President of Business Resource Network, Inc. (a South Bend, Indiana–based mergers, acquisitions, and valuations firm) says are concerns expressed by valuation experts. The following are general considerations:

Tendency to interpret individual portions of Revenue Ruling 59–60 et. al. literally, without regard to complete text of ruling.

Excessive dwelling on financial history of the business being valued at the expense of meaningful "prophecy as to the future."

Use of averages as substitute for "informed judgment."

Application of sophisticated or very simple mathematical analyses or formulas without regard to whether or not these approaches are justified by available information—or provide "reasonable" results.

The following are market data considerations:

Failure of the rulings to consider whether shares in a publicly held company actually reflect an "equally desirable substitute" for ownership of a major portion (or all) of a closely held business. There is a growing body of evidence to indicate that investors in publicly traded companies have entirely different motivations than those investing in ownership positions in privately held companies. In essence, fifty shares of IBM is not comparable to 100 percent ownership in Mini-Chip Computer Co.

Tendency to consider "comparable" as merely meaning "the same industry" without regard for the other similarities/differences that exist between companies.

Use of published price-earnings ratios on listed companies without regard to nature of information entering into calculation of the ratio as published.

Use of unsubstantiated "adjustments" in effort to compensate for differences between "comparable" companies and businesses being valued.

Appendix G: The Big Paper—
Examples of Purchase Agreements

These examples of first, an asset purchase agreement, and second, a stock purchase agreement are presented here to acquaint you with what you can expect in the first draft from your lawyer. (Don't try to just copy these "as is"—they may not apply in your state or to your situation. Always get a lawyer to do the drafting.) They may also serve as a checklist of terms to include in your own agreement.

EXAMPLE A: ASSETS PURCHASE AGREEMENT

Business Purchase Agreement

THIS AGREEMENT is made effective the 1st day of February, 19XX, between BUYCO, INC., an Indiana corporation (herein sometimes called "BUYCO" and sometimes "BUYER") and SELLCO, INC., an Indiana corporation, with its principal office in Big Town, Indiana, (herein sometimes called "SELLCO" and sometimes "SELLER"), in multiple copies, each of which constitutes an original, and is based on these circumstances:

SELLCO has for several years conducted at Big Town, Indiana, a business known as Manufacturing Supplies Company (herein, the "BUSINESS"), all of which SELLER now desires to sell, and all of which BUYER desires to buy.

In consideration of the mutual agreements below, the parties agree to these terms and conditions:

1. SELLCO agrees to sell and BUYCO agrees to buy the BUSINESS and its assets, at the following prices:

Item	Price
Inventory (Physical Inventory at *2/1/XX*)	To be determined
All patents, drawings, records, furniture listed in Exhibit A	$_____
The Business Name "Manufacturing Supplies Company," and all telephone numbers	$_____

The noninventory purchase price shall be paid in full at closing.

255

2. A physical inventory has been taken on or about February 1, 19XX, at which a representative of the BUYER has been present. The inventory shall include only salable merchandise or usable materials, and shall be valued on a last in-first out method. BUYER shall purchase only the inventory agreed between the parties to meet the requirements of the previous sentence.

At closing, an inventory value of $_____ shall be paid from BUYER to SELLER, based on the physical inventory taken on February 1, 19XX. The final inventory listing and value (worked forward from the 2/1/XX physical) shall be submitted in writing to BUYER no later than 2/15/XX, and BUYER shall notify SELLER in writing no later than 2/28/XX, of any disputed items. The difference between the final value and the amount paid at closing shall be paid by BUYER to SELLER if the adjusted actual amount is larger, or by the SELLER to the BUYER if the closing amount is larger. Such sum shall be paid no later than 2/28/XX.

3. In addition, BUYER will pay to SELLER $_____ for its consulting agreement, a copy of which is attached as Exhibit B and made a part hereof by this reference. This compensation shall be paid: $_____ at the date of closing; $_____ on the 1st day of each month thereafter until paid in full.

4. In addition, BUYER will pay to SELLER $_____ for its covenant not to compete, a copy of which is attached as Exhibit C, and made a part hereof by this reference. This amount will be paid as follows: $_____ at the date of closing; $_____ on the 1st day of February in each year beginning on February 1, 19X1, until paid in full.

5. Payments due from BUYER to SELLER at the closing shall be in the form of a Certified or Cashier's check. Payments under paragraphs 3 and 4 will by made by BUYER to SELLER in accordance with the payment schedule indicated therein. Payments under paragraphs 3 and 4 will be secured by the security agreement, Exhibit D.

6. From the date of closing, BUYER will have the right to use the business name "Manufacturing Supplies Company" or any variation of it, or any combination of it with other names. This use shall be exclusive to BUYER in perpetuity. SELLER agrees not to use the name or any variation or any combination of it, after closing, except as it relates to the collection of accounts receivable balances as of the date of closing.

7. At closing, SELLER will be responsible for the computation and payment of all vacation pay earned by employees of the SELLER prior to the closing and will make such payment on the date of closing. SELLER agrees to accept the responsibility for payment of 19XX personal property taxes payable in 19X1 on the personal property being sold under this Agreement and will provide BUYER with proof of such payments having been made. When the 19X1 tax statements are received on such property, SELLER will pay BUYER one-twelfth of the total as its portion of the 19X1

taxes payable in 19X2 upon receipt of a copy of the tax bills. SELLER also assumes all liability for: pension and profit-sharing contributions under any plan it is or may be obligated to make on behalf of employees of the BUSINESS; and water, heat, light, and power charges incurred up through and including the date of closing. BUYER assumes charges for water, heat, light, and power incurred after date of closing and shall have billing switched over to BUYER effective at the time of reading.

8. At closing, and as required thereafter, SELLER will make available to BUYER, on request, originals or copies of all correspondence, accounting, or other documents necessary to conduct the BUSINESS in a normal manner.

9. This purchase and sale does not include accounts receivable. Each party shall collect its own accounts receivable and shall assume all risk of loss in the event any account is not collectible. In the event either party collects a receivable belonging to the other, it shall remit an amount equal to all amounts received (or the actual checks received) from customers to the other party on a weekly basis or at such other times as mutually agreed between the parties.

10. This purchase does not include the cash of the BUSINESS, or any liability of the BUSINESS. SELLER assumes and agrees to pay the liability for all trade accounts payable, other accounts payable, accrued expenses, payroll taxes, sales taxes, property taxes, interest, pensions, or profit-sharing amounts payable and any other liability of any kind by the BUSINESS incurred prior to the time of closing.

11. Since it is impossible to determine whether or not merchandise was produced before or after the closing, any defective merchandise returned by customers of the BUSINESS for which they receive credit during the first six (6) months after closing will be prorated between the parties on an equal basis up to a maximum total of $_____. SELLER will remit to BUYER within fourteen (14) days after receiving an invoice and proof of credits issued 50 percent of the credits up to the maximum total. BUYER shall bear all costs for all returns after payments from SELLER totaling above the maximum or after six (6) months, whichever occurs first.

12. SELLER will pay its broker's commissions outside closing, and hold BUYER harmless from such commissions. BUYER represents it has employed no brokers. Each party will pay its respective attorney and accountant fees outside closing.

13. Closing shall be held 2/1/19XX, or on such other date and at such time and place as is agreeable to the parties. Possession of the assets purchased shall be delivered on the date of closing.

14. In order to comply with the Bulk Transfer Article of the Uniform Commercial Code, the parties hereby agree to do the following:

(a) Within five (5) days hereof, SELLER shall furnish a list of all the existing creditors of the BUSINESS, in the form described in U.C.C. Section 6-104(2), signed and sworn to personally by Fred Sellck. The list shall contain the name and business addresses of all the creditors of the BUSINESS, the amount due, and the names and business addresses of all persons known to SELLER, its agents, attorneys, employees, or representatives, who assert any claim against it or said BUSINESS arising out of said BUSINESS, even though such claims are disputed.

(b) In addition, within five (5) days hereof, SELLER shall furnish a schedule of the property to be transferred hereunder, sufficient to identify it, as described in U.C.C. Section 6-104(1)(b), including serial numbers, if any.

(c) BUYER shall, if this purchase is completed, preserve the list and schedule above for six (6) months following Closing and shall permit inspection of either or both and copying therefrom at all reasonable hours by any creditor of SELLER at the principal office of the BUSINESS.

(d) At least ten (10) days before Closing (Closing shall not be held earlier than ten (10) days after this paragraph is complied with), BUYER shall give the notice described in U.C.C. Section 6-106 to all creditors of the BUSINESS, and further publish such notice in the manner prescribed in U.C.C. Section 6-103(7), at SELLER's expense.

15. The following are representations and warranties that SELLER makes with respect to this purchase as an inducement to BUYER to enter into this Agreement, which shall be deemed to be continuing representations and warranties, and which shall survive the closing hereof:

A. SELLER is the sole owner of all property and assets described in this agreement with full right to sell or dispose of the same as it may choose, and no other person or persons whatsoever have any claim, right, title, interest or lien in, to, or on said property and assets;

B. SELLER owes no obligation and has contracted no liabilities affecting said property and assets described in this contract that might affect consummation of the purchase and sale, nor will such purchase and sale conflict with or violate any agreement or instrument or law or regulation to which SELLER is subject;

C. SELLER has complied with all laws, rules, and regulations (including personal property and other tax laws, rules, and regulations) relating to the property to be sold to BUYER pursuant to this contract;

D. SELLER has paid in full, or will arrange for such payment, all taxes owed by the BUSINESS on property subject to this contract, or that may arise as a result of this contract;

E. There is no contract with any employee or labor organization or independent contractor of the BUSINESS that extends beyond 30 days from the date of closing nor any such contract that would in any case be binding on BUYER;

F. There are not now, to the best of the SELLER'S knowledge, any uncorrected violations of any law, regulation, code, ordinance, administrative order, or ruling, concerning the BUSINESS or the premises on which it is conducted, nor outstanding notices of violations thereof;

G. There are not now, and at the closing date there will not be, any claims, encumbrances, or liens of any kind or description against any of the subject matter hereinabove agreed to be sold by SELLER to BUYER; and no judgments and no suits at law or in equity and no attachments, proceedings, or litigation or claims of any kind or nature or in any forum (legal, equitable, administrative, through arbitration, or otherwise) are pending against or with SELLER; and SELLER has taken no action and knows of no action or thing that SELLER has done or failed to do or that any other person, firm, or corporation has done or failed to do that is or may ripen into a lien against the said subject matter agreed to be sold by SELLER to BUYER or against any part thereof;

H. SELLER is not insolvent, nor will it be rendered insolvent by this transaction or the consummation thereof;

I. All necessary corporate action on the part of SELLER required by law has been or will be taken to authorize and approve the execution and delivery of this Agreement and any documents required herein to be delivered on the closing date. Also, the making of this Agreement and the consummation of the transactions contemplated herein do not and will not conflict with any provision of SELLER'S Articles of Incorporation or By-Laws;

J. The BUSINESS of the SELLER will be conducted up to the Closing Date in the ordinary course, in compliance with all contracts connected to the BUSINESS and SELLER shall not add or remove any stock-in-trade prior to closing except as it may be added or consumed in the ordinary course of business;

K. Neither the SELLER, nor any of its agents, representatives, employees, or attorneys directly taking part in this transaction, have any knowledge of any breach of this agreement or the warranties hereunder by either party existing on the date of closing, of which SELLER has not in writing notified BUYER prior to closing, nor of any reason that this Agreement cannot be performed in all material respects;

L. Neither SELLER, nor any of its agents, representatives, employees, or attorneys have any knowledge or information that SELLER is contemplating bankruptcy, receivership, or an assignment for the benefit of its creditors, nor that any such bankruptcy, receivership, or assignment is threatened by anyone against them, nor knowledge or information that SELLER is not currently paying its debts and obligations when due;

M. SELLER is duly organized, and is in good standing in Indiana;

N. All tangible property transferred hereunder is, to the best of SELLER'S knowledge, in proper working order on the date of closing;

O. No pension, or profit sharing, or similar liability will accrue against BUYER as a result of BUYER purchasing this BUSINESS nor as a result of BUYER hiring persons who were at any time employees of SELLER or the BUSINESS; and

P. SELLER does not own, nor has it within the last 36 months owned, nor will it between now and the date of closing own, 5 percent or more of any customer or supplier of the BUSINESS, nor during that time has any customer or supplier of the BUSINESS owned 5 percent or more of the SELLER or the BUSINESS.

16. The following are representations and warranties that the BUYER makes with respect to this purchase as an inducement to SELLER to enter into this Agreement, which shall be deemed to be continuing representations and warranties, and which shall survive the closing hereof:

A. All necessary corporate action on the part of BUYER required by law has been or will be taken to authorize and approve the execution and delivery of this agreement and any documents required herein to be delivered on the closing date. Also, the making of this agreement and the consummation of the transactions contemplated hereby do not and will not conflict with any provision of BUYER'S Articles of Incorporation or By-Laws, or result in a breach of any provision of, or constitute a default under, any agreement or instrument to which BUYER is a party or by which BUYER is bound;

B. Neither the BUYER, nor any of its agents, representatives, employees, or attorneys directly taking part in this transaction, have any knowledge of any breach of this agreement or the warranties hereunder by either party existing on the date of closing, of which BUYER has not in writing notified SELLER prior to closing, nor of any reason that this agreement cannot be performed in all material respects; and

C. BUYER is duly organized and is in good standing in Indiana.

17. Each party hereby indemnifies and agrees to hold the other harmless of and from any and all loss or liability or both (including attorney fees and costs) arising out of any failure of any representation or warranty made by such party in this agreement. This paragraph shall be continuing, and the agreements in it shall survive closing, and be applicable to any other document arising out of this agreement.

18. Each party shall deliver at closing a written opinion of its respective counsel, dated the closing date, to the effect that:

A. Such party and any person guaranteeing its obligations under this agreement is a corporation duly organized and existing and in good standing under the laws of the State of Indiana;

B. All corporate and other proceedings required to be taken on the part of such party and any person guaranteeing its obligations under this agreement to authorize each to enter into this agreement and perform all of its obligations hereunder, as well as the execution and delivery of such party's other agreements contemplated by this agreement, have been duly and properly taken; and

C. This agreement and any other required by it to be delivered at closing have each been duly executed and delivered by such party and any person guaranteeing its obligations under this agreement and each constitutes a valid and binding obligation of such party and person enforceable in accordance with its terms.

19. The following conditions shall exist until the time of closing and, thereafter until the purchase price is paid in full, which conditions are precedent to closing and conditions subsequent to closing as follows:

A. The employee, Fred Sellck, shall cease to be an employee on January 31, 19XX, but will continue to enjoy all rights he might have in current profit-sharing contributions;

B. The parties shall indemnify and hold harmless the other against and in respect of any and all loss or liability or both arising out of any and all conditions herein expressed, and in the event of a dispute the prevailing party in that dispute shall be entitled to all reasonable costs, including reasonable attorney's fees to be paid it. This clause shall survive closing and be continuing, and shall apply to any other documents arising out of this agreement;

C. The BUYER agrees to maintain an average annual working capital of $_____ and maintain a fiscal year end current ratio of _____ as those terms are defined by Generally Accepted Accounting Principles. The BUYER agrees to cause the person responsible for preparation of its financial statements to immediately advise the SELLER or its representative when either of these requirements are no longer being met;

D. BUYER shall maintain fire and casualty insurance at a level equivalent to the present replacement cost coverages during the term of the payout with an assignment to the SELLER of an amount of that insurance at least equal to the then unpaid balance existing on the Promissory Notes being given hereunder. Similarly, life and disability insurance policies shall be maintained by the BUYER on Vickie M. Buye in an amount equal to the unpaid balance existing on the Promissory Notes being given hereunder and which policy shall be payable to the SELLER to the extent of SELLER'S unpaid balance, and shall also provide that the beneficiary may not be changed except upon 30 days advance written notice to SELLER. Copies of the foregoing policies shall be delivered to the SELLER as well as periodic notices of payment of premiums involved with each of those policies, with the SELLER having the right to pay those premiums in the event of default by the BUYER;

E. BUYER shall submit unaudited monthly financial statements and aging reports of the condition of the BUSINESS being purchased herein to the SELLER, together with the annual financial statements, which shall be reviewed by a Certified Public Accountant during the time any balance of the purchase price is payable to SELLER;

F. All franchises, including that with Bigco Corporation, licenses, and other permits for the doing of business by the SELLER shall be assigned to the BUYER at closing. Any ad valorem taxes, transfer taxes, income taxes, adjusted gross income taxes, gross income taxes, supplemental income taxes, or similar taxes associated with the transfer of any of the assets being transferred herein shall be paid by the SELLER. Any other tax dealing with the doing of business incurred after the effective date of sale shall be paid by the BUYER. This clause shall be continuing and survive closing, and shall *not* terminate when the purchase price is paid;

G. SELLER shall at all times have a security interest in the assets being transferred herein and right to file financing statements with the Indiana Secretary of State or the Big County Recorder, or any other county recorder in which the assets may be located; and

H. The stock interest of Vickie M. Buye in the BUYER may not be assigned except upon the written agreement of the SELLER or its successor in interest throughout the term of the payout of this Agreement.

20. The SELLER assumes all risk of destruction, loss, or damage due to fire or other casualty prior to the closing date. If there is any such destruction, loss or damage, the purchase price shall be adjusted at the closing to reflect such destruction, loss or damage.

21. All notices to be given hereunder shall be in writing and shall be deemed to be duly received or made if mailed by United States Registered or Certified Mail—

if to SELLER, to: Fred Sellck, President, Sellco, Inc.
78901 Park Avenue, Retirement Village, FL

with a copy to: F. Faithful, Attorney at Law,
2345 Indiana Avenue, Big Town, IN

if to BUYER, to: Vickie M. Buye, President, Buyco, Inc.
123 Main Street, Big Town, IN

with a copy to: Melvin Scrivener, Attorney at Law,
456 Lincoln Way, Big Town, IN

or the last address provided in a notice to the other party.

22. Indiana law shall govern this agreement. The parties agree to do any and all things, and sign any and all documents, necessary or appropriate to carry out the purposes of this agreement. This agreement shall be specifically enforceable in any court of general jurisdiction in Big County, Indiana. The masculine, feminine, and neuter, as well as the singular and plural, have been used interchangeably herein. This agreement shall be binding upon, and shall run to the benefit of, the parties hereto, their successors, and assigns.

The provisions of this Agreement or any other agreement contemplated by it or both are severable, and if any paragraph, sentence, or portion of any such agreement is found to be illegal or unenforceable, the remainder shall remain in full force and effect.

All costs to enforce this agreement, whether by litigation or otherwise, including reasonable attorney fees, shall be payable to the prevailing party, whether litigation has been instituted or not.

Both parties agree not to sue the other for any breach or alleged breach of this agreement, until the aggrieved party shall have notified the other party in writing, specifying in detail the breach alleged to have occurred. The aggrieved party shall make at least one representative, fully authorized to settle in all respects, available to the other party for at least one (1) full hour at a reasonable time within two (2) weeks of the date of the notice, at the request of the other party. If the parties shall not have settled their differences within forty-five (45) days after the notice is given, the aggrieved party may then, and only then, bring an action in a proper court. This paragraph shall be continuing and the agreements in it shall survive closing, and be applicable to any other document arising out of this agreement.

The parties have signed this Agreement effective the date shown on the first page.

SELLCO, INC., Seller   BUYCO, INC., Buyer
By: _____   By: _____
    Fred Sellck, President   Vickie M. Buye, President
Attest: Attest:
By: _____   By: _____
                 Secretary   Secretary

Continuing Guarantee

To induce SELLER to enter into the above agreement with BUYER, and in consideration thereof, the undersigned hereby guarantees the performance by the said BUYER of all the terms and conditions of the said agreement to be performed by the said BUYER thereunder, and the undersigned hereby agrees to indemnify and hold SELLER and SELLER'S successors and assigns harmless from and against any and all loss, liability, and expense, including reasonable attorney fees sustained by SELLER by reason of the failure of the said BUYER fully to perform and comply with the terms and obligations of the said agreement.

It is understood that this is a continuing, absolute and unconditional guaranty, co-extensive with said agreement between the BUYER and the SELLER, and the undersigned hereby expressly waives notice of acceptance of this guaranty and of all defaults by the BUYER and of nonpayment and nonfulfillment of any and all of said indebtedness, liabilities, and obligations.

_____

Vickie M. Buye, Individually

To induce BUYER to enter into the above agreement with SELLER, and in consideration thereof, the undersigned hereby guarantees the performance by the said SELLER of all the terms and conditions of the said agreement to be performed by the said SELLER thereunder, and the undersigned hereby agrees to indemnify and hold BUYER and BUYER'S successors and assigns harmless from and against any and all loss, liability, and expense, including reasonable attorney fees sustained by BUYER by reason of the failure of the said SELLER fully to perform and comply with the terms and obligations of the said agreement.

It is understood that this is a continuing, absolute, and unconditional guaranty, co-extensive with said agreement between the SELLER and the BUYER, and the undersigned hereby expressly waives notice of acceptance of this guaranty and of all defaults by the SELLER and of nonpayment and nonfulfillment of any and all of said indebtedness, liabilities, and obligations.

_____

Fred Sellck, Individually

Consulting Agreement

THIS AGREEMENT is dated effective February 1, 19XX, and is between Buyco, Inc. ("BUYER") and Fred Sellck residing at 78901 Park Avenue, Retirement Village, Florida ("SELLER").

WHEREAS, Sellco, Inc. is now contemporaneously selling its assets to BUYER, and

WHEREAS, BUYER wishes to have certain services of the SELLER after the sale.
THEREFORE, IT IS AGREED:

1. BUYER shall pay as compensation through June 30, 19XX, consulting fees of $_____ per month, without any contribution toward any deferred compensation or profit sharing plan.

2. BUYER shall carry health insurance on SELLER, his spouse, and family equal to that currently being carried, whether it be through the current health insurance carrier or some other carrier until the SELLER reaches the age of sixty-five (65) years.

3. SELLER shall be reimbursed for the usual business expenses reasonably required to carry out his consulting duties.

4. SELLER shall make himself available to consult with BUYER about the management of the business at times mutually agreeable to the parties.

5. This agreement contains the entire understanding of the parties and may not be amended unless mutually agreed to between the parties in writing.

6. This agreement shall be binding upon and inure to the benefit of the parties and their successors and is not assignable by any party without the prior written consent of the other party.

7. This agreement shall be governed by the laws of the State of Indiana without giving effect to the principles of conflicts of laws, including but not limited to, matters of construction, validity, and performance.

8. All costs to enforce this agreement, whether by litigation or otherwise, including reasonable attorney fees, shall be payable to the prevailing party, whether litigation has been instituted or not.

IN WITNESS WHEREOF, the parties hereto have executed this Agreement on the day and year first written above.

BUYCO, INC., BUYER

By: _____

Vickie M. Buye, President

_____

Fred Sellck, SELLER

Noncompetition Agreement

THIS AGREEMENT is made effective the 1st day of February, 19XX, by and between BUYCO, INC., an Indiana corporation (herein sometimes called "BUYCO" and sometimes "BUYER") and SELLCO, INC., an Indiana corporation (herein sometimes called "SELLCO"), and the sole shareholder thereof (herein sometimes collectively and individually referred to as "SELLER"), in multiple copies, each of which constitutes an original, and is based on these circumstances:

The BUYER has purchased from SELLER certain assets of the business known as "Manufacturing Supplies Company" (herein, the "BUSINESS"), and as part of the purchase SELLER has agreed not to compete with BUYER in certain areas for a period of five (5) years from the date of closing.

In consideration of Five dollars ($5.00), other good and valuable consideration, and the mutual promises below, the parties agree to these terms and conditions:

1. SELLER covenants that, during the period beginning this date and ending 1,826 days later, it will not without the prior written approval of BUYER, directly or indirectly finance, become an investor in, own, manage, operate, join, control, lease property to, or participate in the ownership, management, operation, or control of, or in any manner be connected with any firm, company, partnership, or corporation that is:

A. engaged in providing manufacturing supplies or any other product or service sold or offered by the BUSINESS now or from time to time in

B. any geographic market area that is now or from time to time served by the BUSINESS.

2. The parties mutually agree that in the event of a breach of SELLER'S covenant expressed by this agreement, BUYER is entitled to injunctive relief. SELLER acknowledges that any remedy at law for breach of this agreement would be inadequate and that BUYER shall be entitled to injunctive relief to enforce this agreement, in addition to any other legal remedies available to BUYER for such breach of this agreement. SELLER acknowledges and agrees that the area covered by the agreement not to compete set forth above, and the nature and duration of such restrictions, are reasonable and necessary for the proper protection of BUYER. In the event that anyone shall successfully contest the validity or enforceability of said agreement not to compete in its present form predicated upon the duration or area of coverage thereof, such provision shall not thereby be deemed invalid or unenforceable, but shall instead be deemed modified, so as to be valid and enforceable, to provide coverage for the maximum area and the maximum term of duration that any Court of competent jurisdiction shall deem reasonable, necessary and equitable.

3. The person signing below as sole shareholder is the only shareholder of SELLCO, Inc., and all those who have an option to acquire shares of SELLCO, Inc., and all those who have any interest in such shares (whether legal, equitable, or both), and agrees to be personally and individually bound by this Noncompetition Agreement.

4. The persons signing below on behalf of a corporation represent and warrant that they are authorized by the board of directors of their respective corporation, that they

have the authority to sign on behalf of such corporation, and that they have the authority to bind such corporation to the terms of this agreement.

5. Indiana law shall govern this agreement. The parties agree to do any and all things, and sign any and all documents, necessary or appropriate to carry out the purposes of this agreement. This agreement shall be specifically enforceable in any court of general jurisdiction in Big County, Indiana. The masculine, feminine, and neuter, as well as the singular and plural, have been used interchangeably herein. This agreement shall be binding upon, and shall run to the benefit of the parties hereto, their successors, and assigns.

The provisions of this agreement or any other agreement contemplated by it or both are severable, and if any paragraph, sentence, or portion of any such agreement is found to be illegal or unenforceable, the remainder shall remain in full force and effect.

All costs to enforce this agreement, whether by litigation or otherwise, including reasonable attorney fees, shall be payable to the prevailing party, whether litigation has been instituted or not.

The parties have signed this Agreement effective the date shown on the first page.

SELLCO, INC., SELLER   BUYCO, INC., BUYER
By:_____   By: _____
                Fred Sellck, President   Vickie M. Buye, President

Attest: Attest:
By:_____   By:_____
                        Secretary   Secretary

_____
Fred Sellck, Shareholder, Individually

EXAMPLE B: STOCK PURCHASE AGREEMENT

Buye and Sellck Agreement

THIS AGREEMENT is made effective the 1st day of January, 19XX, and between Vickie M. Buye, (herein sometimes called "BUYE" and sometimes "BUYER") and Fred Sellck of Big Town, Indiana, (herein sometimes called "SELLCK" or "SELLER"), in multiple copies, each of which constitutes an original, and is based on these circumstances:

Fred Sellck is the sole shareholder of SELLCO, INC., an Indiana corporation, (herein, "SELLCO"). SELLCO has for several years conducted at Big Town, Indiana, a business known as Manufacturing Supplies Company (herein, the "BUSINESS"). SELLCK now desires to sell all of his stock in SELLCO, all of which BUYER desires to buy.

In consideration of the mutual agreements below, the parties agree to these terms and conditions:

1. SELLER agrees to sell and BUYER agrees to buy all the outstanding stock of SELLCO, for an aggregate price of $_____.

2. In addition, BUYER will pay to SELLER $_____ for his Noncompetition Agreement, a copy of which is attached and made a part hereof by this reference.

3. Payments due at closing shall be in Certified or Cashier's check form.

4. From the date of closing, BUYER will have the right to use the business name "Manufacturing Supplies Company" or any variation of it, or any combination of it with other names. SELLER agrees not to use the name or any variation or any combination of it, after closing.

5. At closing, and as required thereafter, SELLER will make available to BUYER, on request, originals or copies of all correspondence, accounting, or other documents necessary to conduct the BUSINESS in a normal manner.

6. Each party will pay its respective attorney and accountant fees outside closing.

7. Closing shall be held at 1:30 P.M., February 1, 19XX, at the office of Melvin Scrivener, Attorney at Law, 456 Lincoln Way, Big Town, Indiana, or on such other date and at such time and place as is agreeable to the parties. Possession of the assets purchased shall be delivered on the date of closing. If closing does not take place by the date and time specified above, this agreement shall, at BUYER'S sole option terminate and any earnest money deposit shall be promptly returned to BUYER and thereupon neither party shall have any further obligation or liability to the other.

8. SELLER agrees to furnish a complete list of all the existing creditors of the BUSINESS sworn to by an officer of the SELLER, by January 15, 19XX. The list will contain the names, business addresses and the amounts due as of January 1, 19XX. SELLER agrees to provide an updated list as of the date of closing no later than closing. SELLER agrees to cause the BUSINESS to pay all these obligations prior to closing, and to furnish BUYER with written proof satisfactory to BUYER that all payments have been made. SELLER hereby indemnifies and agrees to hold BUYER harmless of and from any and all loss or liability or both (including attorney fees and costs) arising out of any obligations owed by SELLER as of the date of closing. The prior sentence shall be continuing and shall survive closing.

9. The following are representations and warranties that with the sole exception of the items shown on the Disclosure Schedule, attached, SELLER makes with respect to this purchase as an inducement to BUYER to enter into this Agreement, which shall

be deemed to be continuing representations and warranties, and which shall survive the closing hereof:

A. SELLER is the sole owner of all stock and ownership interests in SELLCO with full right to sell or dispose of the same as he may choose, and no other person or persons whatsoever have any claim, right, title, interest, or lien in, to, or on said stock and ownership interests, and all shares of SELLCO are fully paid and nonassessable;

B. SELLER and SELLCO owes no obligation and has contracted no liabilities affecting said property and assets described in this contract that might affect consummation of the purchase and sale, nor will such purchase and sale conflict with or violate any agreement or law or regulation to which SELLER or SELLCO or any combination of them is subject;

C. SELLER and SELLCO each has complied with all laws, rules, and regulations (including personal property and other tax laws, rules and regulations) relating to the BUSINESS and the stock to be sold to BUYER pursuant to this contract;

D. SELLER or SELLCO has paid in full, or will arrange for such payment, all taxes owed by the BUSINESS on property, or that may arise as a result of this contract;

E. There is no contract with any employee or labor organization or independent contractor of the BUSINESS, that extends beyond 30 days from the date of closing nor any such contract that would in any case be binding on BUYER;

F. There are not now any uncorrected violations of any law, regulation, code, ordinance, administrative order, or ruling, concerning the BUSINESS or the premises on which it is conducted, nor outstanding notices of violations thereof;

G. There are not now, and at the closing date there will not be, any claims, encumbrances, or liens of any kind or description against the BUSINESS, any of its assets, nor against the stock hereinabove agreed to be sold by SELLER to BUYER and no judgments and no suits at law or in equity and no attachments, proceedings, or litigation or claims of any kind or nature or in any forum (legal, equitable, administrative, through arbitration, or otherwise) are pending against or with the BUSINESS the SELLER or both the BUSINESS and SELLER; and SELLER and the BUSINESS have taken no action and knows of no action or thing that SELLER or the BUSINESS or both have done or failed to do or that any other person, firm, or corporation has done or failed to do that is or may ripen into a lien against the BUSINESS, any of its assets, or the stock agreed to be sold by SELLER to BUYER or against any part thereof;

H. The making of this Agreement and the consummation of the transactions contemplated herein do not and will not conflict with any provision of SELLCO'S Articles of Incorporation or By-Laws, or result in a breach of any provision of, or constitute a default under, any agreement or instrument to which SELLER or the BUSINESS or both is a party or by which it is bound;

I. The BUSINESS will be conducted up to the closing in the ordinary course, and in compliance with all contracts connected to the BUSINESS;

J. Neither SELLER, nor any of his nor SELLCO'S agents, representatives, employees, or attorneys directly taking part in this transaction, have any knowledge of any breach of this agreement or the warranties hereunder by any party existing on the date of closing, of which such SELLER has not in writing notified BUYER prior to closing, nor of any reason that this Agreement cannot be performed in all material respects;

K. Neither SELLER, nor any of his nor SELLCO's agents, representatives, employees, or attorneys have any knowledge or information that either SELLER or SELLCO or both are contemplating bankruptcy, receivership, or an assignment for the benefit of its creditors, nor that any such bankruptcy, receivership, or assignment is threatened by anyone against them, nor knowledge or information that either SELLER or the BUSINESS or both are not currently paying its debts and obligations when due;

L. SELLCO is duly organized, and is in good standing in Indiana;

M. No representations are made with respect to the condition of the tangible property of the BUSINESS that is being retained in the BUSINESS "as is";

N. No pension, or profit sharing, or similar liability will accrue against SELLCO nor against BUYER as a result of BUYER purchasing this stock nor as a result of the BUSINESS hiring persons who were at any time employees of SELLER or the BUSINESS;

O. All financial statements provided by SELLER to BUYER or any of her representatives are true, accurate, and complete, and pending the Closing the BUSINESS will be conducted only in the ordinary course, and there has not been since June 30, 19X-1: (1) any material adverse change in the business, prospects, financial condition or operations of the BUSINESS; (2) any material adverse change in the quality, collectibility, composition, or maturity of the receivables being retained by the BUSINESS hereunder; (3) any damage, destruction or loss, whether covered by insurance or not, materially and adversely affecting the properties and businesses of SELLCO; (4) any strike or other labor dispute; (5) any declaration, setting aside or payment of any dividend or distribution (whether in cash, securities or property) in respect of the capital stock of SELLCO, or any redemption or other acquisition of its capital stock by SELLCO, other than as required by this agreement; (6) any recapitalization, amendment to SELLCO'S articles of incorporation or by-laws, issue or sale by SELLCO of its capital stock or any securities convertible into, or options, warrants to purchase or rights to subscribe to, any shares of its capital stock; (7) any increase in the compensation payable or to become payable by SELLCO to its officers or key employees, or any adoption of or increase in any bonus, insurance, pension, or other employee benefit plan, payment, or arrangement made to, for or with any such officers or key employees; (8) any entry into any material commitment or transaction, including without limitation any material borrowing or capital expenditure; nor (9) any change by SELLCO in accounting methods or principles; and no such actions will occur prior to the Closing, except as permitted herein or authorized in writing by the BUYER;

P. Neither SELLER nor SELLCO nor both are engaged in or overtly threatened with any legal action or other legal proceeding before any court or administrative agency. SELLCO is in substantial compliance with all federal, state, and local statutes, rules and regulations, and there is no governmental charge or governmental investigation as to the possible violation or any federal, state or local statutes, rules, or regulations;

Q. Except for liabilities and obligations incurred in the ordinary course of business since the financial statements dated June 30, 19X-1, (the "Statement of Condition") SELLCO has no material (that is, over $500) liabilities or obligations of a nature required by Generally Accepted Accounting Principles to be reflected in a financial statement, which are not fully reflected in the Statement of Condition. The Statement of Condition fairly and accurately presents the financial condition of SELLCO;

R. The Disclosure Schedule contains a list of every contract (including leases) to which SELLCO is a party that is material to SELLCO, or that involves the future payment by or to SELLCO of an amount in excess of $500, or that constitutes a written employment contract, or a contract with any labor organization or independent contractor of SELLCO, and that are not terminable by SELLCO on less than 31 days notice. True and correct copies of every such contract have heretofore been given to BUYER;

S. SELLCO has good and marketable title to all of its operating properties and assets, including those reflected in the Statement of Condition and those acquired after the date thereof (except minor properties or assets sold or otherwise disposed of since the date thereof in the ordinary course of business), free and clear of all mortgages, liens, pledges, material charges or material encumbrances of any kind or character, except as reflected in the Statement of Condition, or as otherwise set forth in the Disclosure Schedule. All properties used in the present operations of SELLCO are reflected in the Statement of Condition in the manner and to the extent required by Generally Accepted Accounting Principles;

T. All tax returns required to be filed with respect to SELLCO have been properly filed; there are no pending reviews or audits or both by the Internal Revenue Service of Federal income tax returns nor by any state department of revenue of state income tax returns of SELLCO and no extensions or waivers have been executed by SELLCO for any such review; Federal, state, and local taxes of SELLCO for its 19X-1 year and all prior years have been paid in full or duly provided for; and Federal, state, and local taxes for that portion of the calendar year 19XX up to the Closing will be paid in full or duly provided for;

U. All accounts receivable are fully collectible; and

V. SELLCO does not own, nor has it within the last 36 months owned, nor will it between now and the date of Closing own, 5 percent of more of any customer or supplier of SELLCO, nor during that time has any customer or supplier of SELLCO owned 5 percent or more of SELLCO.

10. The following are representations and warranties that the BUYER makes with respect to this purchase as an inducement to SELLER to enter into this Agreement, which shall be deemed to be continuing representations and warranties, and shall survive the closing hereof:

A. The making of this agreement and the consummation of the transactions contemplated hereby do not and will not conflict with, or result in a breach of any provision of, or constitute a default under, any agreement or instrument to which BUYER is a party or by which BUYER is bound; and

B. Neither the BUYER, nor any of its agents, representatives, employees, or attorneys directly taking part in this transaction, have any knowledge of any breach of this agreement or the warranties hereunder by any party existing on the date of Closing, of which BUYER has not in writing notified SELLER prior to closing, nor of any reason that this agreement cannot be performed in all material respects.

11. Each party hereby indemnifies and agrees to hold the other harmless of and from any and all loss or liability or both (including attorney fees and costs) arising out of any failure of any representation or warranty made by such party in this agreement. In addition, the SELLER hereby indemnifies and agrees to hold the BUYER harmless of and from any and all loss or liability or both (including attorney fees and costs) arising out of:

A. any liability (against SELLCO) arising prior to Closing of any nature not fully disclosed in the Disclosure Schedule;

B. any error or omission occurring prior to Closing (whether the nature is negligence, intentional damage, tort, contract, or otherwise) of any agent, employee, or independent contractor of SELLCO, or of the SELLER.

This paragraph 11 shall be continuing, and the agreements in it shall survive Closing, and be applicable to any other document arising out of this agreement.

12. The SELLER assumes all risk of destruction, loss, or damage due to fire or

other casualty to the assets of the BUSINESS prior to the closing date. If there is any such destruction, loss, or damage, the purchase price shall be adjusted at the Closing to reflect such destruction, loss, or damage.

13. The parties to this Agreement do hereby mutually represent and warrant that all negotiations relevant to this Agreement and the transactions contemplated hereunder have been carried on directly by the SELLER and BUYER and without the intervention of any other person in any such manner as to give rise to any valid claim against any of the parties hereto or SELLCO for a brokerage commission, finders fee, or other like payment.

14. Prior to Closing, SELLER will terminate all Stock Purchase Agreements, Buy-Sell Agreements, and any other restrictions on the sale of any stock of SELLCO.

15. The obligations of BUYER to perform hereunder are conditional upon all of the following:

A. The performance by SELLER of all his obligations hereunder, and all the representations and warranties of SELLER being true;

B. BUYER obtaining an unsecured loan for $ _____, at _____ percent interest, payable over not less than _____ years; and

C. The approval by BUYER and BUYER'S Attorney of a final lease from James K. Landlord to the BUYER for the building currently used in the BUSINESS.

16. All notices to be given hereunder shall be in writing and shall be deemed to be duly received or made if mailed by United States Registered or Certified Mail—

if to SELLER, to: Fred Sellck, President, Sellco, Inc.
78901 Park Avenue, Retirement Village, FL
with a copy to: F. Faithful, Attorney at Law,
2345 Indiana Avenue, Big Town, IN
if to BUYER, to: Vickie M. Buye, President, Buyco, Inc.
123 Main Street, Big Town, IN
with a copy to: Melvin Scrivener, Attorney at Law,
456 Lincoln Way, Big Town, IN

or the last address provided in a notice to the other party.

17. BUYER may assign this agreement to a corporation of which she is at least a 50 percent shareholder.

18. Indiana law shall govern this agreement. The parties agree to do any and all things, and sign any and all documents necessary or appropriate to carry out the

purposes of this agreement. This agreement shall be specifically enforceable in any court of general jurisdiction in Big County, Indiana. The masculine, feminine, and neuter, as well as the singular and plural, have been used interchangeably herein. This agreement shall be binding upon, and shall run to the benefit of, the parties hereto, their heirs, personal representatives, successors, and assigns.

The provisions of this Agreement or any other agreement contemplated by it or both are severable, and if any paragraph, sentence, or portion of any such agreement is found to be illegal or unenforceable, the remainder shall remain in full force and effect.

All costs to enforce this agreement, whether by litigation or otherwise, including reasonable attorney fees, shall be payable to the prevailing party, whether litigation has been instituted or not.

All parties agree not to sue any other for any breach or alleged breach of this agreement, until the aggrieved party shall have notified the other party in writing, specifying in detail the breach alleged to have occurred. The aggrieved party shall make at least one representative, fully authorized to settle in all respects, available to the other party for at least one (1) full hour at a reasonable time within two (2) weeks of the date of the notice, at the request of the other party. If the parties shall not have settled their differences within forty-five (45) days after the notice is given, the aggrieved party may then, and only then, bring an action in a proper court. This paragraph shall be continuing and the agreements in it shall survive closing, and be applicable to any other document arising out of this agreement.

The parties have signed this Agreement effective the date shown on the first page.

_____   _____
Fred Sellck, Seller   Vickie M. Buye, Buyer

Appendix H: The Entrepreneur's Quiz

Who is the entrepreneur? What molds him and what motivates him? How does he differ from the nine-to-fiver, and where are those differences most telling? Why will one brother set out to build a business, while another aspires to promotions and perks? Why does one stay up nights working on a business plan, while the other brags about his pension plan? Is it brains? Or luck? Is it hard work? Or does it just happen?

When most people think of entrepreneurs, names like Henry Ford, or Edwin Land, or even Wally (Famous) Amos automatically come to mind. But in fact, American entrepreneurs number in the millions. Of the fifteen million businesses in this country, more than eleven million are operated as sole proprietorships. And while not all of these businesses can be labelled "entrepreneurial ventures," the dictionary definition of an entrepreneur is "one who manages, organizes, and assumes the risk of a business or enterprise."

Why then do we think of the entrepreneur in almost mythical terms? The answer is easy. Like the cowboys of the old American West, the entrepreneur represents freedom: freedom from the boss, freedom from the time clock, and, with a lot of hard work and more than a little luck, freedom from the bank.

More importantly, entrepreneurs are the backbone of the free enterprise system. When an entrepreneur gambles on his skills and abilities, everyone stands to win. New and innovative products and services created by entrepreneurs constantly revitalize the marketplace and create thousands of new jobs in the process. One need look no further than the light bulb, the automobile, or most recently, the personal computer to see how entrepreneurs can change the country's way of life. What's more, nothing keeps a big corporation on its toes like an entrepreneur nipping at its heels—and its markets.

So who is the entrepreneur? Anyone who's ever looked at a problem and seen an opportunity, as well as a solution, is a likely prospect. The same goes for anyone who feels his ambition is being held in check by corporate red tape. But then it takes more than just cleverness and frustration to get an entrepreneurial venture off the ground. It takes guts, an indefatigable personality, and nothing short of a total dedication to a dream. On top of that, it takes the kind of person who can call working ninety hours a week fun.

While there is no single entrepreneurial archetype, there are certain character traits which indicate an entrepreneurial personality. In this quiz we've tried to concentrate on those indicators. So if you've ever wondered if you have what it takes to be an entrepreneur, here is your chance to find out.

(This entrepreneurial profile was developed from a series of questionnaire analyses performed by The Center for Entrepreneurial Management, Inc. Founded in 1978, the Center is the world's largest nonprofit association of entrepreneurial managers with more than 2,500 members.)

Quiz

1. How were your parents employed?
    a. Both worked and were self-employed for most of their working lives.
    b. Both worked and were self-employed for some part of their working lives.
    c. One parent was self-employed for most of his or her working life.
    d. One parent was self-employed at some point in his or her working life.
    e. Neither parent was ever self-employed.
2. Have you ever been fired from a job?
    a. Yes, more than once.
    b. Yes, once.
    c. No.
3. Are you an immigrant, or were your parents or grandparents immigrants?
    a. I was born outside of the United States.
    b. One or both of my parents were born outside of the United States.
    c. At least one of my grandparents was born outside of the United States.
    d. Does not apply.
4. Your work career has been:
    a. Primarily in small business (under 100 employees).
    b. Primarily in medium-sized business (100–500 employees).
    c. Primarily in big business (over 500 employees).
5. Did you operate any businesses before you were twenty?
    a. Many.
    b. A few.
    c. None.
6. What is your present age?
    a. 21–30.
    b. 31–40.
    c. 41–50.
    d. 51 or over.

7. You are the _____ child in the family.
   - a. Oldest.
   - b. Middle.
   - c. Youngest.
   - d. Other.

8. You are:
   - a. Married.
   - b. Divorced.
   - c. Single.

9. Your highest level of formal education is:
   - a. Some high school.
   - b. High school diploma.
   - c. Bachelor's degree.
   - d. Master's degree.
   - e. Doctor's degree.

10. What is your primary motivation in starting a business?
    - a. To make money.
    - b. I don't like working for someone else.
    - c. To be famous.
    - d. As an outlet for excess energy.

11. Your relationship to the parent who provided most of the family's income was:
    - a. Strained.
    - b. Comfortable.
    - c. Competitive.
    - d. Nonexistent.

12. You find the answers to difficult questions by:
    - a. Working hard.
    - b. Working smart.
    - c. Both.

13. On whom do you rely for critical management advice?
    - a. Internal management teams.
    - b. External management professionals.
    - c. External financial professionals.
    - d. No one except myself.

14. If you were at the racetrack, which of these would you bet on?
    - a. The daily double—a chance to make a killing.
    - b. A 10-to-1 shot.
    - c. A 3-to-1 shot.
    - d. The 2-to-1 favorite.

15. The only ingredient that is both necessary and sufficient for starting a business is:
    a. Money.
    b. Customers.
    c. An idea or product.
    d. Motivation and hard work.

16. At a cocktail party, you:
    a. Are the life of the party.
    b. Never know what to say to people.
    c. Just fit into the crowd.
    d. You never go to cocktail parties.

17. You tend to "fall in love" too quickly with:
    a. New product ideas.
    b. New employees.
    c. New manufacturing ideas.
    d. New financial plans.
    e. All of the above.

18. Which of the following personality types is best suited to be your right-hand person?
    a. Bright and energetic.
    b. Bright and lazy.
    c. Dumb and energetic.

19. You accomplish tasks better because:
    a. You are always on time.
    b. You are super organized.
    c. You keep good records.

20. You hate to discuss:
    a. Problems involving employees.
    b. Signing expense accounts.
    c. New management practices.
    d. The future of the business.

21. Given a choice, you would prefer:
    a. Rolling dice with a 1-in-3 chance of winning.
    b. Working on a problem with a 1-in-3 chance of solving it in the time allocated.

22. If you could choose between the following competitive professions, your choice would be:
    a. Professional golf.
    b. Sales.
    c. Personnel counseling.
    d. Teaching.

23. If you had to choose between working with a partner who is a close friend and working with a stranger who is an expert in your field, you would choose:
    a. The close friend.
    b. The expert.
24. In business situations that demand action, clarifying who is in charge will help produce results.
    a. Agree.
    b. Agree, with reservations.
    c. Disagree.
25. In playing a competitive game, you are concerned with:
    a. How well you play.
    b. Winning or losing.
    c. Both of the above.
    d. None of the above.

Scoring

1. a–10 b–5 c–5 d–2 e–0	6. a–8 b–10 c–5 d–2	11. a–10 b–5 c–10 d–5	16. a–0 b–10 c–3 d–0
2. a–10 b–7 c–0	7. a–15 b–2 c–0 d–0	12. a–0 b–5 c–10	17. a–5 b–5 c–5 d–5 e–15
3. a–5 b–4 c–3 d–0	8. a–10 b–2 c–2	13. a–0 b–10 c–0 d–5	18. a–2 b–10 c–0
4. a–10 b–5 c–0	9. a–2 b–3 c–10 d–8 e–4	14. a–0 b–2 c–10 d–3	19. a–5 b–15 c–5
5. a–10 b–7 c–0	10. a–0 b–15 c–0 d–0	15. a–0 b–10 c–0 d–0	20. a–8 b–10 c–0 d–0

Scoring (*continued*)

21. a–0	23. a–0	25. a–8
b–15	b–10	b–10
		c–15
		d–0

22. a–3	24. a–10
b–10	b–2
c–0	c–0
d–0	

1. The independent way of life is not so much genetic as it is learned, and the first school for any entrepreneur is the home. So, it's only natural that a child who has grown up in a home where at least one parent is self-employed is more likely to try his hand at his own business than a child whose parents were in, say, the civil service. Our own research has shown this to be the case more than two-thirds of the time. Some good examples of this are Howard Hughes and New York real estate tycoon Donald Trump, both of whom parlayed modest family businesses into major fortunes.

2. This question is tricky because the independent-thinking entrepreneur will very often quit a job instead of waiting around to get fired. However, the dynamics of the situation are the same; the impasse results from the entrepreneur's brashness and his almost compulsive need to be right. Steven Jobs and Steven Wozniak went ahead with Apple Computer when their project was rejected by their respective employers, Atari and Hewlett-Packard. And when Thomas Watson was fired by National Cash Register in 1913, he joined up with the Computer-Tabulating-Recording Company and ran it until a month before his death in 1956. He also changed the company's name to IBM. The need to be right very often turns rejection into courage and courage into authority.

3. America is still the land of opportunity and a hotbed for entrepreneurship. The displaced people who arrive on our shores (and at our airports) every day, be they Cuban, Korean, or Vietnamese, can still turn hard work and enthusiasm into successful business enterprises. Fifteen years ago, Korean born entrepreneur K. Philip Hwang worked his way through college by sweeping the floors of a Lake Tahoe casino. Recently, Hwang took his company, TeleVideo, public, and his personal stock holdings are now valued at over $750 million. Though it is far from a necessary ingredient for entrepreneurship, the need to succeed is often greater among those whose backgrounds contain an extra struggle to fit into society.

4. I've heard it said that "Inside every corporate body, there's an entrepreneur struggling to escape." However, small business management is more than just a scaled

down version of big business management. The skills needed to run a big business are altogether different from those needed to orchestrate an entrepreneurial venture. While the professional manager is skilled at protecting resources, the entrepreneurial manager is skilled at creating them. An entrepreneur is at his best when he can still control all aspects of his company. That's why so many successful entrepreneurs have been kicked out of the top spot when their companies outgrew their talents. Of course, that isn't always a tragedy. For many, it offers the opportunity (and the capital) to start all over again.

5. The enterprising adult first appears as the enterprising child. Coin and stamp collecting, mowing lawns, shoveling snow, promoting dances and rock concerts are all common examples of early business ventures. The paper route of today could be the Federal Express of tomorrow.

6. The average age of entrepreneurs has been steadily shifting downward since the late fifties and early sixties when it was found to be between forty and forty-five. Our most recent research puts the highest concentration of entrepreneurs in their thirties, but people like Jobs and Wozniak of Apple Computer, Ed DeCastro and Herb Richman of Data General, and Fred Smith of Federal Express all got their businesses off the ground while still in their twenties. Although we look for this data to stabilize right around thirty, there are always exceptions that leave us wondering. Computer whiz Jonathon Rotenberg is just such an exception. He currently presides over the 8,500 member Boston Computer Society, is the publisher of the slick magazine *Computer Update,* and earns up to $1,500 a day as a consultant. Early on, Rotenberg's advice was solicited by the promoter of an upcoming public computer show. After conferring several times on the phone, the promoter suggested they meet for a drink to continue their discussions. "I can't," Rotenberg replied. When asked, "Why not?" Jonathan answered, "Because I'm only fifteen."

7. The answer to this question is always the same. Entrepreneurs are most commonly the oldest children in a family. With an average of 2.5 children per American family, the chances of being the first child are only 40 percent. However, entrepreneurs tend to be the oldest children more than 60 percent of the time.

In an interesting aside (and we're not quite sure what it means), a Mormon Church official has revealed that in cases of polygamous marriages, the first sons of the second or third marriage are generally more entrepreneurial than the first child of the first marriage.

8. Our research concluded that the vast majority of entrepreneurs are married. But then, most men in their thirties are married, so this alone is not a significant finding. However, follow-up studies have shown that most successful entrepreneurs have exceptionally supportive wives. (While our results did not provide conclusive results on female entrepreneurs, we suspect that their husbands would have to be doubly

supportive.) A supportive mate provides the love and stability necessary to balance the insecurity and stress of the job. A strained marriage, the pressures of a divorce, or a strained love life will simply add too much pressure to an already strained business life.

It's also interesting to note that bankers and venture capitalists look a lot more favorably on entrepreneurs who are married than on entrepreneurs living with their mates without the benefit of clergy. And this is more of a pragmatic attitude than it is a moralistic one. A venture capitalist remarked to us the other day that "If an entrepreneur isn't willing to make a commitment to the woman he loves, then I'll be damned if I'm going to make any financial commitment to him."

9. The question of formal education among entrepreneurs has always been controversial. Studies in the fifties and sixties showed that many entrepreneurs, like W. Clement Stone, had failed to finish high school, not to mention college. And Polaroid's founder, Edwin Land has long been held up as an example of an "entrepreneur in a hurry" because he dropped out of Harvard in his freshman year to get his business off the ground.

However, our data concludes that the most common educational level achieved by entrepreneurs is the bachelors degree, and the trend seems headed toward the MBA. Just the same, few entrepreneurs have the time or the patience to earn a doctorate. Notable exceptions include An Wang of Wang Laboratories, Robert Noyce and Gordon Moore of Intel, and Robert Collings of Data Terminal Systems.

10. Entrepreneurs don't like working for anyone but themselves. While money is always a consideration, there are easier ways to make money than by going it alone. More often than not, money is a by-product (albeit a welcome one) of an entrepreneur's motivation rather than the motivation itself.

11. These results really surprised us because past studies, including our own, have always emphasized the strained or competitive relationship between the entrepreneur and the income-producing parent (usually the father). The entrepreneur has traditionally been out to "pick up the pieces" for the family or to "show the old man," while at the same time, always seeking his grudging praise.

However, our latest study showed that a surprising percentage of the entrepreneurs we questioned had what they considered to be comfortable relationships with their income-producing parents. How do we explain this? To a large extent, we think it's directly related to the changing ages and educational backgrounds of the new entrepreneurs. The new entrepreneurs are children of the fifties and sixties, not the children of the Depression. In most cases they've been afforded the luxury of a college education, not forced to drop out of high school to help support the family. We think that the entrepreneur's innate independence has not come into such dramatic conflict with the father as it might have in the past. We still feel that a strained or competitive relationship best fits the entrepreneurial profile, though the nature of this relationship is no longer so black and white.

12. The difference between the hard worker and the smart worker is the difference between the hired hand and the boss. What's more, the entrepreneur usually enjoys what he's doing so much that he rarely notices how hard he's really working. I've always believed that a decision is an action taken by an executive when the information he has is so incomplete that the answer doesn't suggest itself. The entrepreneur's job is to make sure the answers always suggest themselves.

13. Entrepreneurs seldom rely on internal people for major policy decisions because employees very often have pet projects to protect or personal axes to grind. What's more, internal management people will seldom offer conflicting opinions on big decisions, and in the end the entrepreneur makes the decision on his own.

Outside financial sources are also infrequent sounding boards when it comes to big decisions because they simply lack the imagination that characterizes most entrepreneurs. The most noble ambition of most bankers and accountants is to maintain the status quo.

When it comes to critical decisions, entrepreneurs most often rely on outside management consultants and other entrepreneurs. In fact, our follow-up work has shown that outside management professionals have played a role in *every* successful business we've studied, which wasn't the case when it came to unsuccessful ventures.

14. Contrary to popular belief, entrepreneurs are not high risk takers. They tend to set realistic and achievable goals, and when they do take risks, they're usually calculated risks. They are very confident in their own skills and are much more willing to bet on their tennis or golf games than they are to buy lottery tickets or to bet on spectator sports. If an entrepreneur found himself in Atlantic City with just ten dollars in his pocket, chances are he'd spend it on telephone calls and not in slot machines.

15. All businesses begin with orders, and orders can only come from customers. You might think you're in business when you've developed a prototype or after you've raised capital, but bankers and venture capitalists only buy potential. It takes customers to buy products.

16. Like billionaire Daniel Ludwig, many entrepreneurs will adamantly state that they have *no* hobbies. But that doesn't mean that they have no social life. In fact, the entrepreneur is a very social person and, more often than not, a very charming person. (Remember, an entrepreneur is someone who gets things done, and getting things done often involves charming the right banker or supplier.) And while he will often only talk about things concerning himself or his business, his enthusiasm is such that anything he talks about sounds interesting.

17. One of the biggest weaknesses that entrepreneurs face is their tendency to "fall in love" too easily. They go wild over new employees, products, suppliers, machines,

methods, and financial plans. Anything new excites them. But these "love affairs" usually don't last long; many of them are over almost as suddenly as they begin. The problem is that during these affairs, entrepreneurs can quite easily alienate their staffs, become stubborn about listening to opposing views, and lose their objectivity.

18. The answer to this question is easy: "bright and energetic," right? Wrong. The natural inclination is to choose "bright and energetic" because that describes a personality like your own. But stop and think a minute. You're the boss. Would you be happy or, for that matter, efficient as someone else's right-hand man? Probably not. And you don't want to hire an entrepreneur to do a hired hand's job.

That's why the "bright and lazy" personality makes the best assistant. He's not out to prove himself so he won't be butting heads with the entrepreneur at every turn. And while he's relieved at not having to make critical decisions, he's a whiz when it comes to implementing them. Why? Because, unlike the entrepreneur, he's good at delegating responsibilities. Getting other people to do the work for him is his specialty!

19. Organization is the key to an entrepreneur's success. This is the fundamental principle on which all entrepreneurial ventures are based. Without it, no other principles matter. Organizational systems may differ, but you'll never find an entrepreneur who's without one. Some keep lists on their desks, always crossing things off from the top and adding to the bottom. Others use notecards, keeping a file in their jacket pockets. And still others will keep notes on scraps of paper, shuffling them from pocket to pocket in an elaborate filing and priority system. But it doesn't matter how you do it, just as long as it works.

20. The only thing an entrepreneur likes less than discussing employee problems is discussing petty cash slips and expense accounts. Solving problems is what an entrepreneur does best, but problems involving employees seldom require his intervention so discussing them is just an irritating distraction. Expense accounts are even worse. What an entrepreneur wants to know is how much his sales people are selling, not how much they're padding their expense accounts.

21. Entrepreneurs are participants, not observers; players, not fans. And to be an entrepreneur is to be an optimist, to believe that with the right amount of time and the right amount of money, you can do anything.

Of course, chance plays a part in anyone's career—being in the right place at the right time; but entrepreneurs have a tendency to make their own chances. I'm reminded of the story about the shoe manufacturer who sent his two sons to the Mediterranean to scout out new markets. One wired back: "No point in staying on. No one here wears shoes." The other son wired back: "Terrific opportunities. Thousands still without shoes." Who do you think eventually took over the business?

22. Sales gives instant feedback on your performance; it's the easiest job of all for measuring success. How does a personnel counselor or a teacher ever know if he's

winning or losing? Entrepreneurs need immediate feedback and are always capable of adjusting their strategies in order to win. Some entrepreneurs brag that they play by the rules when they're winning and change the rules when they're losing. Although we don't endorse it (look what happened to John DeLorean), when it works it's known as the win/win strategy.

23. While friends are important, solving problems is clearly more important. Often the best thing an entrepreneur can do for a friendship is to spare it the extra strain of a working relationship. By carefully dividing his work life and his social life, the entrepreneur insures that business decisions will always be in the best interest of his business.

24. Everyone knows that a camel is a horse that was designed by a committee, and unless it's clear that one person is in charge, decisions are bound to suffer from a committee mentality.

25. Vince Lombardi is famous for saying, "Winning isn't everything, it's the only thing," but a lesser known quote of his is closer to the entrepreneur's philosophy. Looking back at a season, Lombardi was heard to remark, "We didn't lose any games last season; we just ran out of time twice."

Entrepreneuring is a competitive game and an entrepreneur has to be prepared to run out of time, occasionally. Walt Disney, Henry Ford, and Milton Hershey all experienced bankruptcy before experiencing success. The right answer to this question is *c,* but the best answer is the game itself.

Your entrepreneurial profile

The CEM member profile is 234

225–275: Successful Entrepreneur
190–224: Entrepreneur
175–189: Latent Entrepreneur
160–174: Potential Entrepreneur
150–159: Borderline Entrepreneur
Below 149: Hired Hand

Annotated Bibliography

Annual Statement Studies, Robert Morris Associates, Philadelphia, annual. The "banker's bible" of financial date, by SIC Code.

Bangs, David H., Jr., *The Cash Flow Control Guide,* Upstart Publishing, Portsmouth, NH, 1987. Good synopsis of how to do cash flow planning.

Behrens, Robert H., *Commercial Loan Officer's Handbook,* Bankers Publishing Company, Boston, 1985. Read it and see how bankers are trained to look at you and your loan package.

Bird, Caroline, *Enterprising Women,* W. W. Norton & Company, Inc., New York, 1976. Information about American women in business.

Boroian, Donald D., and Boroian, Patrick J., *The Franchise Advantage,* National BestSeller Corporation, Schaumburg, IL, 1987. For when you are thinking of becoming a franchisor, written by experts who have helped many companies franchise their ideas.

Brestoff, Nelson E., *How to Borrow Money Below Prime,* Simon & Schuster, New York, 1985. Detailed information on how bankers price loans.

Dible, Donald M., *Up Your Own Organization,* The Entrepreneur Press, Mission Station Drawer 2759T, Santa Clara, CA 95051, 1971. List of forty lenders is good.

Directory of Directories, Gale Research, Detroit, Michigan, annual. Where to go to find associations in your target industry.

Drucker, Peter F., *Innovation and Entrepreneurship,* Harper & Row, New York, 1985. "The managerial guru" shares invaluable insights into how to best innovate and be entrepreneurial in all varieties of businesses, with emphasis on larger concerns.

Dubendorf, Donald R., and Storey, M. John, *The Insider Buyout,* Storey Communications, Inc., Pownal, VT 05261, 1985. Hard-to-get info—lots of anecdotes.

Encyclopedia of Associations, Gale Research, Detroit, Michigan, Annual. Listings of most of the major trade associations in the country for your deal flow.

Franchise Opportunities Handbook, U.S. Department of Commerce. List of franchises with descriptions, number, capital needed, training, assistance.

Fregly, Bert, *How to Be Self Employed,* ETC Publications, Palm Springs, CA 92262, 1977. Detailed guidebook.

Goldstein, Arnold S., *How to Save Your Business,* Enterprise Publishing, Inc., 725 Market St., Wilmington, DE 19801, 1983.

Goldstein, Arnold S., *Own Your Own: The No-Cash-Down Business Guide,* Prentice-Hall, New York, 1983. Good financing ideas.

Goldstein, Arnold S., *The Complete Guide to Buying and Selling a Business,* John Wiley & Sons (Mintor), New York, 1983. More of *Own Your Own.*

Guide to Business Development Programs in Indiana, A, Indiana Department of Commerce Directory—private sources. Most states have similar annual directories.

Guide to Business Financing Programs in Indiana, A, Indiana Department of Commerce Directory—governmental programs. Most states have similar annual directories.

Hansen, James M., *Guide to Buying or Selling a Business,* Prentice-Hall, Englewood Cliffs, NJ, 1975. Aimed toward would-be business brokers (especially real estate brokers). Good chapter on analyzing financials; good questions for evaluating management; rules of thumb for valuation of many businesses; many forms.

Hawkins, Paul, *Growing A Business,* Simon & Schuster, New York, 1987. General musings and philosophizing about owning your own business; many new, useful ideas.

Holland, Philip, *The Entrepreneur's Guide,* Penguin Books, New York, 1984. Good book of philosophy and useful techniques.

Horn, Thomas, *Business Valuation Manual,* Charter Oak Press, Lancaster, PA, 1985, 1987. Good basic information on valuation methods and which ones to avoid.

Ilich, John, *The Art and Skill of Successful Negotiations,* Prentice-Hall, Englewood Cliffs, NJ, 1973. Lots of good techniques—easily readable.

Kallen, Laurence H., *How to Get Rich Buying Bankrupt Companies,* Carol Communications—Lyle Stuart, New York, 1989. Good discussion of the practicalities of buying companies (some of which may still be in business) out of bankruptcy, at bargain prices.

Kiam, Victor, *Going for It!,* William Morrow and Co., New York, 1986. A must-read!

Kirkpatrick, Frank, *How to Buy a Country Business,* Contemporary Books, Inc., Chicago, 1981. Good ideas and practical advice. Innovative valuation formula.

Klauser, Henrietta Anne, *Writing on Both Sides of the Brain,* Harper & Row, New York, 1987. Good ideas adaptable to help with business plans and planning in general.

Kursh, Harry, *The Franchise Boom,* Prentice-Hall, Englewood Cliffs, NJ, 1968. Good ideas and attitude.

Lowry, Albert J., *How to Become Financially Successful By Owning Your Own Business,* Simon & Schuster, New York, 1981. Good overall guide.

McKeever, Mike P., *Start Up Money: How to Finance Your New Small Business,* Nolo Press, 950 Parker St., Berkeley, CA, 94710, 1984. Good list of financing sources—practical for small businesses.

Mancuso, Joseph R., *How to Get a Business Loan, Without Signing Your Life Away,* Prentice Hall Press, New York, 1990. Good in-depth practical techniques.

Mancuso, Joseph R., *How to Prepare and Present a Business Plan,* Prentice-Hall, New York, 1983. Just what the title says, plus nine useful appendixes, including five sample real-life business plans.

Mancuso, Joseph R., *How to Start, Finance, and Manage Your Own Small Business,* Prentice-Hall, New York, 1978, revised 1984. Research about who are entrepreneurs; sample business plans; bibliography. The classic, a must-have.

Mancuso, Joseph R., *How to Write a Winning Business Plan,* Prentice-Hall, New York, 1985. More details on romancing the money people and several useful checklists.

Mancuso, Joseph R., *Mancuso's Small Business Resource Guide,* Prentice Hall Press, New York, 1988. Excellent place to look for hard-to-find information on every topic of importance to small business.

Mancuso, Joseph R., *The Small Business Survival Guide,* Prentice-Hall, Englewood Cliffs, NJ, 1980. Sourcebook and bibliography of independent business information, directory of SBICs.

Merrill Lynch, "How To Read A Financial Report," Pamphlet. Free at any Merrill Lynch office. Useful in financial analysis.

National Bankruptcy Reporter, The, Andrews Publications, Box 200, Edgemont, PA 19028. Newsletter. Information on large bankruptcies.

Nierenberg, Gerard I., *The Art of Negotiating,* Hawthorn Books, New York, 1968. Good list of strategies; proponent of win-win negotiating.

1986 Directory of Franchising Organizations, Pilot Industries, Inc., 103 Cooper St., Babylon, NY 11702, 1986. Categorized list of franchisors, showing investment required.

Owen, Robert R., Garner, Daniel R., and Bunder, Dennis S., *The Arthur Young Guide to Financing for Growth,* John Wiley & Sons, New York, 1986. Good catalog of available sources and requirements.

Peterson, Carl D., *How to Leave Your Job and Buy a Business of Your Own,* McGraw-Hill, New York, 1988. A good basic text with some useful checklists.

Polk's Bank Directory, R. L. Polk and Co., Nashville, TN, semi-annual.

Silver, A. David, *Up Front Financing: The Entrepreneur's Guide,* John Wiley & Sons, New York, 1982. Good description of hypothetical deals for LBOs; lots of questions and answers.

Sparks, Kenneth W., *Successful Business Borrowing,* Walker & Company, New York, 1986. Moderately good regarding techniques.

Stegall, D. P., Steinmetz, L. L., and Kline, J. B., *Managing the Small Business,* Richard D. Irvin, Inc., Homewood, IL, 1976. Good chapter on reasons behind buying a business.

Stevens, Mark, *How to Borrow a Million Dollars,* Macmillan, New York, 1982. Lots of good ideas presented in an interesting way, lists of sources, good psychology.

Thomas Register of American Manufacturers, Thomas Publishing Co., New York, annual. Useful place to check out targets or start a deal flow.

Troy, Leo, Ph.D., *Almanac of Business and Industrial Financial Ratios,* Prentice-Hall, Inc., Englewood Cliffs, NJ, revised periodically. Tax return information about businesses, both profitable and not. Useful for comparing to your target.

Who Owns Whom: The Directory of Corporate Affiliations, National Register Publishing Co., Inc., annual. Useful in checking subsidiaries to find those in your target area.

Yate, Martin John, *Hiring the Best,* Bob Adams, Inc., Boston, 1988. Excellent questions and complete interviews to help you find and evaluate potential employees.

Index

About the Authors

Joseph R. Mancuso is the nationally acclaimed author of such bestselling business books as *How to Start, Finance and Manage Your Own Small Business, Mancuso's Small Business Resource Guide,* and *How to Get a Business Loan, Without Signing Your Life Away.* An accomplished entrepreneur who has launched eight successful businesses, Dr. Mancuso is the founder of the New York City-based Center for Entrepreneurial Management—an original source of high-quality information for entrepreneurial managers and the professionals who advise them. Dr. Mancuso's extensive academic credentials include a B.S.E.E. from Worcester Polytechnic Institute, and an M.B.A. from Harvard Business School, and a doctorate in education from Boston University.

Douglas D. Germann, Sr., is an attorney/CPA in South Bend-Mishawaka, Indiana. He has helped dozens of clients through business purchases and sales. A speaker who conducts workshops nationally on entrepreneurial subjects, Doug is the founder of Acquisition Resources, Inc., a firm which helps companies and individuals develop deal flows, investigate targets, find financing, and successfully acquire operating businesses. Mr. Germann's academic credentials include a B.S. in Business Administration and a J.D., both from Valparaiso University. Doug is licensed as an attorney in Indiana and Michigan, and holds a CPA certificate in both Indiana and Illinois.